ISSUES IN POLICE AND CRIMINAL PSYCHOLOGY

Sponsored by The Society of Police and Criminal Psychology

William Taylor
University of Southern Mississippi
and
Michael Braswell
East Tennessee State University

University Press of America™

Copyright © 1978 by

University Press of America, Inc.™

4710 Auth Place, S.E., Washington, D.C. 20023

ISBN: 0-8191-0624-0

Library of Congress Catalog Card Number: 78-61915

ACKNOWLEDGEMENT

The Society of Police & Criminal Psychology would like to thank the following journals for allowing selected articles to be reprinted in this book: <u>L.A.E. Journal,</u> (1) "Planning and the Administration of Justice: by Foster & Schneider and (2) "Behavior Modification & Corrections: An Analysis" by Alonzo & Braswell. <u>Trial Magazine,</u> (1) "Making Time Fit the Crime" by Sen. Edward Kennedy and (2) "The Future of Prisons" by Norman Carlson. <u>Journal ofHumanics,</u> "Public Assistance Fraud: An Analysis" by Vernon Wherry, "Disposition of Persons Utilizing the Insanity Plea in a Rural State" by Pasewark & Lanthorn, "Perspective on Police Corruption: Research & Exposure" by Thomas Barker, and "The Americanization of Parens Patrie: A Right to Treatment For Juvenile Offenders?" by Taylor, Slay, and Carimi.

TABLE OF CONTENTS

ABOUT THE AUTHORS

Thomas Alonzo, M.S., Mississippi Department of Youth Services.

Thomas Barker, Ph.D., Dean, College of Criminal Justice, Jacksonville State University.

Michael Braswell, Ph.D., Department of Criminal Justice, East Tennessee State University.

William Broome, M.S., Department of Criminal Justice, Mississippi Gulf Coast Junior College.

Nicholas Carimi, J.D., Department of Criminal Justice, East Tennessee State University.

Norman Carlson, Director, United States Bureau of Prisons.

Todd Clear, Ph.D., Department of Corrections and Criminal Justice, Ball State University.

Robert Culbertson, Ph.D., Department of Criminal Justice Sciences, Illinois State University.

Francis Devine, Ph.D., Department of Criminal Justice, University of Southern Mississippi.

John Dussich, Ph.D., Department of Criminal Justice, University of Southern Mississippi.

Charles Eckenrode, Ph.D., Department of Sociology, University of Georgia.

Don Ellis, Ed.D., Director of Testing, City of Fort Worth.

Kenneth Evans, M.Ed., Secondary School Administrator, Mississippi.

Richard Foster, Ph.D., Department of Criminal Justice, Idaho State University.

Laurence French, Ph.D., Department of Criminal Justice, University of Nebraska at Omaha.

Robert Gaunt, Ph.D., Educational Administrator, Mississippi.

Arthur Gavin, Inmate Services Department, Georgia Diagnostic and Classification Center.

Bill Kennedy, Deputy Chief, Fort Worth Police Department.

Edward Kennedy, Senior United States Senator from the State of Massachusetts.

Wayne Lanthorn, Ph.D., Holston Valley Hospital Mental Health Center.

Sloan Letman, J.D., Criminal Justice Program, Loyola University of Chicago.

Glenn Littlepage, Ph.D., Department of Psychology, Middle Tennessee State University.

Sam McKinstry, Ph.D., Department of Political Science, East Tennessee State University.

John Milligan, Ph.D., Department of Criminal Justice, University of Alabama at Birmingham.

Richard Pasewark, Ph.D., Department of Psychology, University of Wyoming.

James Pipher, Ph.D., Department of Psychology, University of Nebraska at Lincoln.

Janet Porter, Ph.D., Department of Criminal Justice, University of Nebraska at Omaha.

Clayton Rivers, Ph.D., Department of Psychology, University of Nebraska at Lincoln.

Ronald Schneider, Ph.D., Department of Criminal Justice, Idaho State University.

John Schnelle, Ph.D., Department of Psychology, Middle Tennessee State University.

Lawrence Schoenfeld, Ph.D., Department of Psychiatry, University of Texas Health Science Center.

Lewis Slay, M.S., United States Probation Officer, Mississippi.

S. A. Somodevilla, Ph.D., Psychological Services Unit, Dallas Police Department.

James Turner, Ph.D., Mental Hygiene Consultation Service, Fort Stewart/Hunter Army Airfield.

Eugene Waters, Ed.S., Department of Sociology and Criminal Justice, Gordon Junior College.

Vermon Wherry, M.S., Department of Criminal Justice, East Tennessee State University.

FOREWORD

Today's Criminal Justice System is in an era of change. One rarely attends a professional convention or reads a professional or scholarly journal or newsletter without finding some discussion of the future of the Criminal Justice System and its practitioners. It has become commonplace to question the foundations, philosophy and relevance of present day methods and practices of defining and dealing with crime and criminals. We have become accustomed to the debates which surround the current practices of organizing police departments, selecting police officers, and dealing with the stress that individual police officers encounter during their occupational duties. But where are the textbooks which deal with these topics? Unfortunately, we have few textbooks which deal with these issues. Therefore, the typical Criminal Justice educator finds himself or herself faced with a difficult decision when the time comes to select textbooks and recommend readings which are relevant, timely, and also informative and interesting to our students. To be exact, it is often a monumental task to pull together source materials which deal with contemporary problems in the Criminal Justice System. This book, edited by two distinguished Criminal Justice educators and sponsored by the Society of Police and Criminal Psychology- accomplishes many of these tasks in one volume.

The reader of this text will find some of the most contemporary theoretical and empirical literature in the field written by distinguished scholars, authors, and Criminal Justice practitioners. In addition, the issue oriented theme of this work contributes to its value. The topics selected for inclusion in the text represent a combination of perennial problems and new issues which must be dealt with by all who consider themselves students of the Criminal Justice System. In fact, one will find discussions of issues which rarely appear in other works, e.g., the Federal "Speedy Trial Act of 1974", public assistance fraud, biofeedback training to alleviate stress in police officers, etc. Those issues are absent from most textbooks not because they are not worthy of discussion. They are absent because few materials have been published on many of these issues and few editors have taken the time and effort to search out the extant publications. Consequently, the Criminal Justice instructor should find this work to be a valuable addition to his or her list of source materials. Furthermore; even though, *Issues in Police and Criminal Psychology* is primarily designed for classroom use, the book has much to offer the Criminal Justice practitioner who must daily face the issues discussed in this text.

Thomas Barker, Ph.D.
Dean, College of Criminal Justice
Jacksonville State University
Jacksonville, Alabama

PART I: CRIME & THE ADMINISTRATION OF JUSTICE

JUSTICE IN AMERICA
Sam W. McKinstry

INTRODUCTION

Justice in America" is a concept which produces almost as many types of responses as there are members within our society, for each person has his or her own conceptualization of what "justice" entails. Thus, it is a practical impossibility to clearly identify a single conceptualization as the standard definition. For the scholar involved in the study of justice, it becomes necessary to classify the various conceptualizations into general categories, which really amounts to a sorting process not unlike that of separating grain from chaff. In this instance, it becomes a matter of identifying conceptualizations in terms of ideal and reality. Scholars interested in the relationship between law and society often refer to this as the "law on the books" versus the "law in action".

Among the more common notions which can be labeled as "ideal-type" are: "Equal Justice Under Law", "Majority Rule, Minority Rights", "Blind Justice", "Due Process of Law" and Equal Protection of the Laws". These are concepts which permeate the entire system of justice in the United States -- the very core of its *raison d'etre* in public estimation.

At the same time, for the individual who has been "seasoned" -- the world of reality raises its ugly head and exposes the shortcomings of the ideals which all Americans have been taught to revere. In this vein, we find such things as delay, plea bargaining, excessive bail, discretion and economics all reducing the core concepts to little more than verbal panaceas for a continuing and ever-increasing problematical area.

Currently, the population of the United States hovers at a figure well over 250 million people and comprises a society which can be labeled as litigation-minded.[1] Yet, in spite of the litigation, we still face innumerable problems within the basic system itself, largely a result of the fact that within both the Federal and State judicial systems, we have not progressed far beyond the point which served as the cornerstone of Dean Roscoe Pound's 1906 speech to the American Bar Association, in which he admonished them for " . . . tinkering around where comprehensive reform is needed. . . ."[2] Much of this problem, of course, centers around the fact that federalism has produced a judicial system which is dualistic in nature and, because of the duality of courts -- Federal and State -- we have not only fifty-one separate systems of justice, but indeed within the state systems, there are variants as one moves within the various levels of each. While in many ways, the basic operations are similar, there are still marked differences, in that none of them operates with exact and precise duplication of its counterpart both within the same system or within adjoining state systems. Add to these variances the federal system and the degree of difference becomes compounded.[3]

Thus, while Americans have often seen the courts as the last bastion of defense against invasion of their cherished rights and liberties, especially when they are unable to obtain redress from either the Executive or Legislative branches, they are also aware of the kinds of concepts which were developed by Former Attorney General Ramsey Clark in his description of the criminal justice system as a "failing system."[4] Mr. Clark identified the problem areas as (a) low rates of conviction, (b) delay in bringing individuals charged with having committed offenses labeled "illegal" by society to trial and (c) extremely low levels of successful rehabilitation of those individuals who have been convicted and sentenced to serve time in our penal institutions.

Numerous social scientists have tried to identify the nature of the problems and how they might be diminished.[5] However, almost without exception, they, too, reach the same general conclusions which have already been identified as the roots of discontent and general disdain for the justice system currently expressed by many Americans, particularly those who have been exposed to the operations of the system and have come away feeling as if they have been "on a shake-down cruise."

ANALYSIS OF THE PROBLEMS

Justice has been identified by scholars as falling within two basic but inescapable categories -- "justice for the rich" and "justice for the poor". Translating this into the area of practical application, the individual with economic resources at his disposal will find that the kind of legal representation he has before the courts will be quite different from the individual who is forced to depend upon the public defender or court-appointed attorney. Likewise, economic resources or at least the ability to tap them will also decide the difference between the accused languishing in jail before his case is called for trial or being released on bail or on his own recognizance. While it is true that the United States Supreme Court (in such cases as Gideon v. Wainwright, 372 U.S. 335, (1963); Miranda v. Arizona, 384 U.S. 436, (1966) and Stack v. Boyle, 342 U.S. 1, (1951) has established the right of an indigent defendant to court-appointed counsel in both capital and non-capital cases, upheld the basic rights of the accused during the period of interrogation and determined the proper manner in which bail is to be set, it remains a basic fact that it is one thing for the United States Supreme Court -- or any court, for that matter -- to make a ruling and quite another for it to be applied. For, it must be remembered that the Supreme Court, like all other courts in the American Judicial System, has no power at its disposal to enforce its own decisions.[6]

What does this mean for the individual involved in the justice system? Initially, he is placed in the position whereby he must trust that the local agents involved in the entire process -- police, prosecutor and judge -- have taken the rulings of the U.S. Supreme Court at face value and are willing to operate according to these basic principles. But, what if these officials within the hierarchical structure have not? Then, he faces the possibility of having to appeal his case through the system, hoping that the Supreme Court, in its great widsom and understanding, will agree to grant his petition for certiorari.[7] And, concomitant to the fact that this procedure is often painfully slow, it is also painfully expensive.

Closely akin to the matter of economics is that of defendants' ethnic backgrounds. Numerous studies[8] show that the ethnic background of the individual has a critical impact upon the manner in which he is initially perceived (a) by the law enforcement officers, (b) by the judge following the trial and during the sentencing procedure, (c) during his period of incarceration and (d) once he is placed back in society following his release from a penal institution. Many of the problems which are encountered by ethnic minorities, as they confront the processes of the administration of justice, are directly related to their economic condition. In the large metropolitan areas, these social groups are often found in the older, run-down ghetto areas. While they are no more frequent in committing many of the types of actions labeled criminal than individuals from higher economic backgrounds, it remains a fact that their increased visibility accounts for more of them being apprehended than their counterparts in the other sectors of society. And, once apprehended, they more often than not must forego the possibility of hiring an expensive attorney to represent them and rely upon either court-appointed counsel or a public defender. This is one more example of the disparities created by the basic law of economics.

The second problem of significant magnitude facing the administration of justice in America today is that of delay. Part of this problem is brought about by the fact that we have a significant increase in the basic case load in

our courts, but there are other factors which also contribute to the problem.
Among these additional contributing factors, failure to be prepared on the
part of either the prosecution or defense accounts for many of the delays.
The impact of delay upon the defendant centers in several areas. First, each
and every time his case is postponed, it means that the cost factor has again
multiplied, since he must continue to pay his attorney for the time it requires him to handle the case -- even if this means merely making an appearance
in Court to find that the other side is not ready. Second, with the lapse of
time there is the ever-present problem of evidence and witnesses becoming
stale. This results in the defendant's case becoming weaker over time. However, this can also have the opposite effect, in that it can serve to limit the
possibility of the prosecution obtaining a conviction. The immediate impact of
this latter situation is to cast aspersions upon the system's effectiveness in
bringing those individuals guilty of having committed offenses against society
to justice. And, in light of the constitutional prescription that each and
every person accused of having committed a criminal offense is entitled to a
speedy trial, the existence of delay within the system serves to tarnish the
patina of this ideal.

Thirdly, the matter of plea bargaining creates the possibility that justice is a concept which is composed of significant variance between the ideal
and reality. Many times, the defendant is encouraged by his attorney to plead
guilty to a lesser charge, after the "deal" has been struck between the prosecution and defense attorney in the absence of the defendant. What chance does
the defendant have in this type of situation? Also, there are many people who
have developed the notion that use of the plea bargain is simply a means whereby prosecutors, especially if their case is somewhat less than strong, will
ask an accused to plead guilty to a lesser offense in order to assure at least
some type of conviction. As is seen, the use of the plea bargain is one of
the various aspects of discretionary action open to the prosecutor as he plies
his trade. And, this use of discretionary power by the prosecutor places him
in a position whereby he can ". . . make decisions of crucial importance for
arrested individuals. . . . ."[9]

However, discretion is not something which is only possessed by the prosecutor. Judges and police also have a great deal of discretionary power a-
vailable to them, and its use often contributes to the development of negative
attitudes on the part of the general public. How many times have you heard
someone suggest that an individual should execute a warrant against another
person for some action which he has committed, only to hear the reply that

"It wouldn't do any good." This is a phrase often repeated throughout American society and one which again often relates to the question of economics. In addition, we have the use of discretion on the part of the police -- why did they not arrest that individual for the manner in which he was driving his car? Why do not the police crack down on certain kinds of offenses? Why is not the leash law enforced? Why do not the police patrol certain streets, where it is known that traffic violations occur with regularity? These are but some of the many instances in which discretion and its effects are openly visible to members of society. We are taught that justice is blind, that there is equal justice under law. Perhaps so, but when the law in action is compared to the law on the books, there is a great deal of visible difference between the two.

CONCLUSIONS

One of the immediate questions which arises when attempting to develop a set of conclusions to the problems identified is, "Where do we go from here?" Unfortunately, the answer to this question is almost as elusive as the answer to the question "What is justice?"

There have been several meaningful steps taken in the Federal and several of the state systems. And, within other state systems, there are genuine considerations currently being given to the whole problem of the administration of justice.

One of the largest and most obvious areas where action has been considered and also taken lies in the area of court reform. This area is seen as critical, since it is here that the outputs of the system are received by the consumers.[10] Unfortunately, however, the role of politics has often succeeded in hamstringing many of the efforts at genuine reform, requiring compromise on various issues and thus prolonging the final outcome. Among the suggested and sometimes implemented reforms have been such things as the appointment of judges rather than direct partisan election; the implementation of the Missouri Plan of Judicial Selection or some variant thereof; court reorganization, so as to streamline the system itself; the development of the position of court administrator, so as to improve the entire system of records-keeping and general court business; the development of the small claims court, to relieve the other courts of part of their overload; placing controls on the bail bondsman; requiring more extensive educational training for police; the development of new concepts related to the sentencing process, thereby making the sentence more closely fit the crime; and the passage of the Speedy Crime Act of 1974, in order to try to eliminate some of the problems related to delay. Yet, despite all of these attempts to improve the system, there remains that one single element which is of such overarching concern to the social scientist -- people. For it is people who make the system work and it is people against whom the system does work. As long as we are dealing with people and not with programmed computers, it appears plausible to assume that at least some level of general discontent will remain. However, the goal remains one of minimizing the discontent and maximizing the overall effectiveness of the system. In the words of Chief Justice Warren E. Burger,

> . . . Perhaps what we need now are some imaginative Wright Brothers of the law to invent, and Henry Fords of the law to perfect new machinery for resolving disputes. . . .11

REFERENCES

1. See Whitney North Seymour, Jr., *Why Justice Fails* (New York, N.Y.: William Morrow & Company, 1973), pp. 2-6, where the author discusses the reasons why increased numbers of Americans have turned to the courts to solve social issues.

2. Roscoe Pound, "The Causes of Popular Dissatisfaction with the Administration of Justice." *American Bar Association Reports,* 29 (1906) 395.

3. See George F. Cole, "Politics and the Administration of Justice" in George F. Cole, ed. *Criminal Justice: Law and Politics* (2nd Ed.; Belmont, California: Duxbury Press, a Division of Wadsworth Publishing Company, Inc., 1976), pp. 2-3, for a general discussion of this problem.

4. Ramsey Clark, *Crime in America* (New York, N.Y.: Simon and Schuster, 1970), pp. 117-131.

5. Oliver Williams and Richard J. Richardson, "The Impact of Criminal Justice Policy on Blacks in Trial Courts of a Southern State" in George F. Cole, ed. *Criminal Justice: Law and Politics* (2nd Ed.; Belmont, Calif.: Duxbury Press, a Division of Wadsworth Publishing Company, Inc., 1976), pp. 68-84; Herbert Jacob, *Debtors In Court: The Consumption of Government Services* (Chicago, Illinois.: Rand McNally & Company, 1969); _____, *Urban Justice: Law and Order in American Cities* (Englewood Cliffs, N.J.: Prentice-Hall, Inc., 1973); _____, *Justice in America* (Boston, Mass.: Little, Brown & Company, 1965); Michael Meltsner, *Cruel and Unusual: The Supreme Court and Capital Punishment* (New York, N.Y.: William Morrow & Company, Inc., 1974); Wayne Thomas, Jr., *Bail Reform in America* (Berkeley, Los Angeles and London: University of California Press, 1976); Lloyd L. Weinreb, *Denial of Justice: Criminal Process in the United States* (New York, N.Y.: The Free Press, A Division of Macmillan Publishing Company, Inc., 1977); James Eisenstein, *Politics and the Legal Process* (New York, Evanston, San Francisco and London: Harper & Row, Publishers, 1973); Whitney North Seymour, Jr., op. cit., to name but a few.

6. See Jay A. Sigler, *An Introduction ot the Legal System* (Homewood, Ill.: The Dorsey Press, 1968), pp. 216-223, for detailed coverage of this problem.

7. In this area, there is no guarantee that the Supreme Court will hear the case, since the Judiciary Act of 1925 ahd the practical impact of allowing the Court to serve as the "mistress of its own destiny," whereby the Court can limit its attention to those cases deemed critical by the members of the Court. See: Sheldon Goldman and Thomas P. Jahnige, *The Federal Courts as a Political System* (2nd Ed.; New York, N.Y.: Harper & Row, Publishers, 1976), pp. 130-136, for treatment of the gatekeeping function of the Court *via* certiorari.

8. Clement E. Vose, *Caucasions Only: The Supreme Court, The NAACP, and the Restrictive Covenant Cases* (Berkeley, Los Angeles and London: University of California Press, 1959); Jack Greenberg, *Race Relations and American Law* (New York and London: Columbia University Press, 1959); Oliver Williams and Richard J. Richardson, op. cit.; Herbert Jacob, "Politics and Criminal Prosecution in New Orleans." *Tulane Studies in Political Science,* 8 (1963), pp. 77-98; Joseph C. Howard, "Racial Discrimination in Sentencing." *Judicature,* 59 (October, 1975), pp. 121-125; Alan F. Arcuri, "Judges as Prisoners See Them." *Judicature,* 59 (August-September, 1975), pp. 72-77; Jerome H. Skolnick, *Justice Without Trial: Law Enforcement in Democratic Society* (New York, London and Sydney: John Wiley & Sons, Inc., 1967), pp. 49-50, 80-86; Kenneth N. Vines, "Federal District Judges and Race Relations Cases in the South." *Journal of Politics,* 26 (1964), pp. 337-357; Nathan Goldman, *The Differential Selection of Juvenile Offenders for Court Appearance* (New York, N.Y.: National Research and Information Center of the National Council on Crime and Delinquency, 1963); Herbert Jacob, *Urban Justice: Law and Order in American Cities,* op. cit.; Jay A. Sigler, *American Rights Policies* (Homewood, Illinois: The Dorsey Press, 1975), pp. 154-169, 240-241; Lynn M. Mather, "Some Determinants of the Method of Case Disposition: Decision-Making by Public Defenders in Los Angeles." *Law and Society Review,* 8 (Winter, 1974), pp. 187-216; Fred J. Hiestand, "The Politics of Poverty Law" in Bruce Wasserstein and Mark J. Green, eds. *With Justice for Some: An Indictment of the Law by Young Advocates* (Boston, Mass.: Beacon Press, 1970), pp. 160-189.

9. Eisenstein, op. cit., p. 102.

10. *Consumers* refers to plaintiffs and defendants in civil cases; defendants and prosecution in criminal cases.

11. Warren E. Burger, "Agenda for 2000 A.D. -- Need for Systematic Anticipation." Keynote Address at the National Conference on the Causes of Popular Dissatisfaction with the Administration of Justice, St. Paul, Minnesota, April 7, 1976, p. 3.

PLANNING AND THE ADMINISTRATION OF JUSTICE
Richard Foster and Ronald Schneider

It now seems generally accepted that the existence of a well defined system of criminal justice is a myth.[1]

> A system implies some unity of purpose and organized inter-
> relationship among component parts. In the typical American
> city and state, and under federal jurisdiction as well, no such
> relationship exists.[2]

Reasons for this state of affairs are many and varied. Clearly, the extreme
geographic fragmentation of agencies charged with the administration of justice is a major contributing factor. While this decentralization might appear to indicate many discrete systems, such is not the case. Different levels
of government share responsibility for different components of the system.

> States and counties remain dominant in operation of correctional
> institutions, counties and municipalities have prime responsibility
> for police activities, and states and counties shoulder the major
> lead in operation of courts and prosecution systems.[3]

Further, there is a functional fragmentation of the system's components.
Law enforcement, the judicial process, and corrections are usually autonomous
bureaucracies operating at best independently and at worst actively against
each other. Given this myriad of bureaucracies marked by geographic and functional fragmentation, it is not surprising to find little concern among the
agencies involved for the problems such independence creates. Owing, at least
in part, to the existence of this "non-system", crime has not been controlled[4]
and the complex of agencies organized to handle crime are in serious danger of
collapse. Due to this critical state of affairs it is essential that attempts
at correction be made. The purpose of this investigation is to address the
problem from a planning viewpoint and to suggest possible solutions.

THE ROLE OF PLANNING

In an attempt to correct some of the problems of fragmentation at the
national level, systematic analysis and long range planning were introduced in
the United States Department of Defense in 1961. Four years later, as a result
of the perceived success of the program, these interrelated concepts, generally
called Planning-Programming-Budgeting-Systems (PPBS) were instituted throughout

the federal bureaucracy.[6]

The general concept behind PPBS is that better budgetary decisions can be made by focusing on outputs such as governmental goals, objectives, and end products rather than on inputs such as equipment and personnel.[7] The initial idea was a reasonably simple one. First, it called for a careful identification and analysis of goals and objectives in all major areas of activity. It then required that the most efficient means of reaching those goals be instituted. Thus, PPBS was considered to be little more than a means to help rationalize decision-making.

The road between theory and implementation, however, has been a rocky and almost impassable one. Aaron Wilkavsky has remarked that PPBS " . . . failed everywhere and all times."[8] He noted further that due to the difficulty of using PPBS as a budgetary technique it has been implemented in form but not in substance.[9] Since PPBS did not accomplish what its proponents had predicted, many observers have concluded that comprehensive planning is an unworkable concept. It is our contention that this is a misreading of the evidence. We believe, with Wildavsky, that the failure of PPBS can be traced to an overemphasis on the budgeting aspect of the reform. When viewed in isolation the planning component achieved many notable successes. Thus, since the planning and budgeting functions are not inseparably linked we feel there are many valuable lessons for the criminal justice network which can be learned and many mistakes which can be avoided by an examination of the planning experience at the national level. In short, rather than budgeting technique, we are concerned with planning problem as it relates to bureaucratic fragmentation and stalemate. The question, then, is not how to budget or reduce bureaucratic power, but how the criminal justice agencies can better define their goals and take the steps necessary to meet them. That is, the emphasis should be on the planning process.

GOAL DEFINITION

It is essential for successful planning that there be a clear statement of program objectives. This, of course, can be quite difficult. Although experience has shown goal formulation to be an essential part of the political milieu, planners continue to act as if they believe policy would be more successful if it could be removed from the uncertainties of the political process. It cannot, however, and if even the most general goals are to be formulated, political feasibility must be made an integral part of the planning process.

An instructive lesson for criminal justice planners can be illustrated by a comparison between the attempts at goal definition in the Defense Department

and various civilian bureaucracies. When Robert McNamara was appointed to
head the Defense Department, it resembled a collection of independent, autonomous fiefdoms.

> Each service tended to exercise its own priorities, favoring
> its own unique missions to the detriment of joint missions,
> . . . and protecting the over-all size of its own forces even
> at the cost of readiness.[10]

When McNamara assumed office the situation changed. He forced the Department to define its goal as the defense of the nation and once this was accomplished the major question remaining was, simply, what service or combination of services could accomplish a particular mission most effectively.

This clear statement of goals, however, became a problem of epic propor-
tions in the domestic bureaucracies. While the Pentagon's top-priority goal,
national security, is relatively easy to identify, most civilian agencies
have multiple and conflicting goals. For example, while the goal of welfare
may be to end poverty, work incentives are also considered very important. We
could end poverty simply by giving the poor enough money to live comfortably.
But what would this do to the incentive to work? Hunger is undoubtedly an
effective work incentive and we could maximize this idea by lowering welfare
payments. But how would this affect the commitment to reduce poverty? Which
one of these objectives is more important and how much more important is one
than the other?

This notion of clearly stated goals presents other political problems as
well. Most governmental agencies are watched quite closely by a Congress composed of individuals possessing widely differing values. Forcing agreement on
clearly stated goals before programs are instituted may well lead to stalemate
since agreement on specific objectives may be impossible. Charles Schultze,
former director of the Bureau of the Budget, provides an example of what might
occur if agreed upon goals were required before substantive policy decisions
could be made.

> The Elementary and Secondary Education Act of 1965 broke new
> ground in terms of federal aid to education. It was enacted
> precisely because it was constructed to attract the support of
> three groups, each with quite different ends in view. . . . If
> there had been any attempt to secure advance agreement on a set
> of long-run objectives, important elements of support for the
> bill would have been lost, and its defeat assured.[11]

The problem for criminal justice agencies as to goal definition would appear to be more complex than was the case with the Department of Defense but

somewhat less involved than in many domestic bureaucracies. Unlike the Defense Department there is little consensus among justice system administrators concerning system-wide goals. As Robert P. Rhodes has noted

> . . . disjointed planning and evaluation efforts in criminal
> justice today reflect not merely uncertainty as to solutions,
> but powerful disconsensus as to the nature of our criminal
> justice problems.12

However, while the goals of crime prevention, apprehension of criminals, and rehabilitation of law violators may be difficult to reconcile, they would not seem to strike at such basic values as the work ethic when discussing poverty programs, or birth control when attempting to formulate programs for population stabilization. It would appear that if, for example, solid evidence could show a substantial reduction in crime was directly linked to programs aimed at crime prevention or rehabilitation, the opposition to these types of enterprises would be reduced significantly. This is not to imply that grave difficulties do not exist in the definition of goals for the criminal justice network. It is only to suggest that these problems appear to be no more serious than those confronting other agencies.

Goal definition is undertaken primarily to help choose a policy and an attendant course of action. The task of the decision-maker is to decide what these goals and objectives are (or should be) in order to measure the extent to which these may be attained by various courses of action. This, of course, is not to suggest that departments with widely varying perspectives, such as the police on the one hand and rehabilitation services on the other, can or should be forced to reach total agreement on specific goals. Dogmatic insistence on clearly stated system-wide objectives may well be dysfunctional, causing even greater antagonisms between the various departments. *Agencies should, however, be encouraged to step back and reflect on their real objectives and how these can best interface with those of complementary departments within the criminal justice network.*

THE ALTERNATIVES

Very simply, alternatives are the various means by which the previously formulated objectives can best attained. Alternatives may be policies, strategies or specific actions. Alternatives, in addition, need not be obvious substitutes for each other or perform the same specific function. Clearly then, education, anti-poverty measures, police protection, probation services, and slum clearance may be alternatives in attempts to combat juvenile delinquency.[13]

The search for alternatives entails determining what is presently being done and what is being accomplished, defining alternatives for the future, and predicting what each would do and what each would cost. As Alice Rivlin has noted

> . . . The problem facing decision makers is the classic economic problem of allocating scarce resources among competing ends. What would do the most good?[14]

While this may appear obvious it is often a staggering analytical undertaking. The literature chronicling the federal bureaucracy's attempts to formulate alternatives has shown that most agencies know very little about the impact of their programs and, as a result, have little basis on which to evaluate new proposals.[15]

The similarities between the federal bureaucracy and the justice network are striking. As in the federal agencies there is a lack of solid data. We know very little about who commits crime and how many offenders there are. As Nelson and Richardson have reported

> . . . until we have more adequate measures of the amounts and kinds of criminal behavior, we will not be sufficiently well informed to act effectively in their prevention and treatment.[17]

There are many differences, however, between the justice system and the federal bureaucracy and an analysis of these differences would suggest that many of the problems encountered at the national level could be more easily overcome within the justice agencies. One of the major factors is the basic fact that the introduction of planning is taking place over ten years after it occurred within the federal system and is generally viewed with less skepticism than a decade ago. Agency heads

> . . . no longer need to be reassured that they are not about to be put out of business by a computer . . . Civil servants realize that systems analysts do not have pointy heads, . . . they can be helpful and sometimes even right.[18]

Criminal justice agencies have another large advantage over the civilian departments of the federal government regarding the effective utilization of planning. This concerns interest group involvement in decisions as to which of the available alternatives to adopt. Many governmental programs produce goods and services valued highly by various segments of the electorate. That is, many programs have a direct impact on income distribution.[19] And it is no accident the programs adopted generally work to the advantage of those possessing

the greatest political influence. Thus, attempts to alter existing policies
will generate opposition from those very individuals who can bring the greatest
political pressures to bear. The successful experiment in the Department of
Defense offers persuasive evidence that the implementation of the most effective
alternatives can more easily be accomplished in agencies whose programs do
not have a fundamental impact on income distribution. This does not mean, of
course, that a dichotomy can be drawn between those departments whose programs
do and do not affect the distribution of income. As Charles Schultze has
correctly noted, any program has some effect.[20] However, decisions involving
resource allocation in agencies such as the DOD create more of an incidental
impact. To use Schultze's example,

> . . . The purchase of fighter aircraft will result in a different
> distribution of income by income group and by geographical area
> than a decision to produce M-16 rifles because the skill compo-
> sition of the work force and location of plants is not the same
> in the two industries.[21]

But the impact on income distribution here affects only a relatively small
portion of the electorate rather than a whole category of interests such as a
decision to reduce farm subsidy payments would do.[22] Therefore, there is less
external pressure on Congress to enact particular programs. Allocative decisions can more easily be based on guidelines generated within the department
rather than on the preferences of external groups who stand to benefit directly
by the adoption of one program over another.

The justice network here would appear to be in an even more advantageous
position than the Defense Department. While decisions as to the most efficient
means of crime reduction are infused with other values, the programs would
seem to have even less of an effect on income distribution than those of the
DOD. Because of this rather minimal impact, influential portions of the electorate should have less interest and, thus exert less pressure on elected
officials. The California experience with their probation subsidy experiment
would appear to support this contention. Although a massive redistribution of
funds was involved and implementation of the program was preceded by conflicts
among the agencies involved, interference from groups outside the system was
almost entirely absent. This, of course, is not meant to imply that the
justice network can (or should) operate entirely free of pressure from the public sector. If, for example, plans were adopted to increase the number of detention facilities near population centers subsequent to studies indicating
reduced recidivism rates among those incarcerated in these types of institutions,
there most likely would be great public pressure to "keep the criminals out of

the community". However, it seems probable that the pressures would be of
less intensity than those applied if a proposed policy had a direct and fundamental impact on the income of an influential portion of the electorate.

The experience at the national level also contains some valuable lessons
for the justice network as to the limitations of planning and analysis. Due
to the federal experience those in the justice field should have a greater
appreciation of the fact that choices among various programs are often infused
with values and may be extraordinarily difficult. For example, if it were found
that apprehension deters the commission of future crimes by a certain type of
criminal to a greater extent than for other kinds of offenders, efficiency
would dictate concentrating police resources where these types of crimes are
most likely to occur. However, this procedure would leave different groups
or individuals with different probabilities of being victimized.[23] The question
would then arise concerning the right of all members of the population to have
an equal chance of victimization. If this is found to be important, police
might have to be used in areas where apprehension has little effect on the
probability of future commission of crimes.[24]

While planning and all it implies raises such questions as these it provides few answers. This is not to say that planning is dysfunctional. It is
only meant to point out that it does not have all the answers and should not
be viewed as a panacea for the ills of the justice system. This more realistic
view gained from the federal experience should help the criminal justice network in avoiding some of the problems encountered in attempting to institute
systematic planning in Washington.

EVALUATION

It is extremely important that programs be designed in a manner such that
evaluation is possible. Evaluation is necessary for the simple reason that it
is the only means available for determining the utility or the benefits of a
particular program. Unfortunately, as the federal experience has shown, there
is often very little basis for judging whether a specific program is working
as planned, and, concomitantly, how well the clientele is being served. For
example, a decline in the infant mortality rate may be due to prenatal care
programs, or better nutrition, or higher income, or a lower birth rate, or a
combination of all these factors.[25] Disentangling the impact of a program
from all other variables which might affect variations in outcome is often an
enormous undertaking. Nevertheless, for effective planning within the criminal
justice network it is imperative to design techniques which will measure ef-

fectively the impact of alternative programs. *Consideration of goals, discussion of alternatives, and concern with costs must take place concomitant with an awareness of evaluation imperatives.* This is not to imply that goals and alternatives should be selected solely on the basis of ease of evaluation. Rather it is to say that evaluation techniques must be given serious consideration and become an integral part of the process of goal and alternative selection.

CONCLUSION

Planning for criminal justice must be a continuing activity. Planning is a process, not an event. The consideration of goals, alternatives, and evaluative measures does not take place in neat, clearly defined and separate time frames. They must all go forward together.

As mentioned previously, we believe that PPBS failed due largely to its overemphasis on the budgeting aspect of the program. However, the impact of the attempts to implement PPBS during its short tenure in Washington has been substantial and in many regards beneficial. It did not revolutionize decision-making but it did force decision-makers to begin asking the right questions. It showed the futility of formulating poverty programs without knowing who is poor and why they are poor. It pointed out the senselessness of requiring more education for teachers and fewer pupils per classroom without knowing whether either had any effect on learning. It showed officials how little they knew and how far they had to travel to accumulate this information. While it provided no easy answers, it forced agency heads to confront the important questions.

The weight of the evidence in the preceding analysis would indicate that the criminal justice network faces obstacles of a less serious nature than did many federal bureaucracies in their attempts to utilize planning and systematic analysis. Thus, the positive lessons learned at the federal level should have an even greater impact within the justice agencies. Rather than endless debates concerning the relative effectiveness of one program over another, the dictates of the planning process should force justice agency administrators to investigate their assumptions objectively. The logic inherent in the planning process should also point out the absurdity of maintaining police, courts, and corrections as completely autonomous units and result in at least some subordination of agency objectives in favor of a heightened appreciation for the needs of the entire system.

Thus, at the very minimum, the use of systematic planning in the criminal justice field should, as it did in Washington, force decision-makers to begin asking the right questions and challenging traditional assumptions. And, if the justice network possesses the advantages over the federal agencies which it appears to, the planning process should make an even greater contribution towards the rationalization of decision-making.

REFERENCES

1. For a review of some of the works which have come to this conclusion, see Alvin W. Cohn, "Training in the Criminal Justice Nonsystem", *Federal Probation,* 38 (June, 1974), p. 33.

2. Daniel Freed, "The Nonsystem of Criminal Justice", Task Force on Law and Law Enforcement, *Law and Order Reconsidered* (New York: Bantam Books, 1970), p. 264.

3. Daniel Skoler, "Comprehensive Criminal Justice Planning", *Crime and Delinquency,* 14 (July, 1968), p. 201.

4. Cohn, 1974.

5. A.W. McEachern, et al., "Criminal Justice System Stimulation Study", Public Systems Research Institute, (June, 1970), p. 2, mimeo.

6. Virginia Held, "PPBS Comes to Washington", *The Public Interest* (Summer, 1966), p. 102.

7. Aaron Wildavsky, *The Politics of the Budgetary Process* (Boston: Little Brown, and Company, 1974, Second edition), pp. 181-182.

8. Wildavsky, p. 205.

9. Wildavsky, p. 197.

10. Charles Hitch, *Decision-Making for Defense* (Berkeley and Los Angeles: University of California Press, 1965), p. 24.

11. Charles Schultze, *The Politics and Economics of Public Spending* (Washington, D.C.: The Brookings Institution, 1968), p. 24.

12. Robert P. Rhodes, "Political Theory, Policy Analysis, and the Insoluble Problems of Criminal Justice", *Policy Studies Journal* 3 (Autumn, 1974), p. 83.

13. Henry Rowen, "Objectives, Alternatives, Costs, and Effectiveness", in *Program Budgeting and Benefit-Cost Analysis: Cases, Test, and Readings,* ed. by Harley H. Hinrechs and Graeme M. Taylor (Pacific Palisades, California: Goodyear Publishing Co., 1969), p. 85.

14. Alice Rivlin, *Systematic Thinking for Social Action* (Washington, D.C.: The Brookings Institution, 1971), p. 46.

15. For example, see Arthur Levin, *The Satisficers* (New York: McCall Publishing Company, 1970).

16. Alice Rivlin, "The Planning, Programming, and Budgeting System in the Department of Health, Education, and Welfare", in *Public Expenditures and Policy Analysis*, ed. by Robert Haveman and Julius Margolis (Chicago: Markham Publishing Company, 1970), p. 509.

17. E.K. Nelson, Jr. and Fred Richardson, "Perennial Problems in Criminological Research", *Crime and Delinquency*, 17 (January, 1971), p. 25.

18. Rivlin, *Systematic Thinking for Social Action*, p. 4.

19. Schultze, p. 84.

20. Schultze, p. 84.

21. Schultze, p. 84.

22. Mason Gaffney, "The Benefits of Farm Programs", *American Journal of Economics and Sociology*, 26 (July, 1967), pp. 237-250.

23. Lester Thurow, "Equity versus Efficiency in Law Enforcement", *Public Policy*, 18 (Summer, 1970), p. 452.

24. Thurow, p. 455.

25. Rivlin, The Planning, Programming and Budgeting System . . ., p. 507.

DETERMINATE v. INDETERMINATE SENTENCING:
SOME MYTHS IN THE CONTROVERSY

Todd R. Clear and Robert G. Culbertson

Perhaps no area of criminal justice decision-making is receiving more attention today than the sentencing decision. The impetus for reform is strong, and, based on a belief that treatment in corrections has "failed", results in a new set of assumptions and expectations for sentencing offenders. In the following discussion, an effort has been made to analyze the failure of the traditional treatment model, and the complex issues which contributed to that failure. Then, consideration is given to the major arguments in the debate on sentencing reform. Assumptions undergirding approaches to sentencing reform are clarified and a summary of the evidence supporting these assumptions is presented. Finally, a comprehensive reintegration model is proposed which can be utilized as a guide in the development of programming in corrections.

The demise of the treatment model for rehabilitation was inevitable. Conceived in a process pervaded by "groupthink," the treatment model was, and is, naive.* (See Notes) However, critics who contend that it is now time to replace the treatment model with a more punishment-oriented model seem also to be possessed by the same groupthink and naivete. It is easy to develop criticism to demonstrate the failure of a concept or program, but the task of providing an appropriate alternative is extremely complex. Critics of the treatment model fail to realize the complexity of the problem. Their arguments for more punitive models are philosophically attractive, but have policy implications which are potentially disastrous. The treatment model and its parent, the indeterminate sentence, have failed in many respects; however, if we do not carefully analyze the reasons for that failure, we will find ourselves snared by the same set of complex issues which were ignored in the 1950's as "treatment" emerged as the dominant theme in corrections.

The failure of the treatment model has been discussed elsewhere in considerable detail.[1,2,3,4] The major issues can be summarized here:

First, there is little basic agreement in our society regarding the function and purpose of the criminal law. The criminal law, according to Packer,[5] is caught between two fires. There are those who support the retributive position and content it is right and proper for the law to revenge wrongful acts. Punishment should be designed to reflect the seriousness of the offending conduct rather than to prevent its reoccurence. At the same time, there are those who support the utilitarian position and contend that the primary purpose of the criminal law is to prevent anti-social behavior. Punishment, according to the utilitarian position, must emphasize modification of future behavior of the criminal. The opposing emphases on immediate vs. futuristic concerns of the two positions presents dilemmas for correctional administrators. With an absence of goal concensus at the system level, it is difficult for the corrections process to function rationally.

Second, there is some evidence that crime and the criminal are functional in a society. Mead[6] and Durkheim[7] contend that crime and the criminal increase the level of social solidarity. This seemingly contradictory process, according to Mead's "psychology of punitive justice", occurs when the criminal, by stimulating negative attitudes and hostile feelings in the community, actually brings the community closer together. It is Mead's position that:

> ". . . the attitude of hostility toward the lawbreaker has the unique advantage of uniting all members of the community in the emotional solidarity of aggression toward the lawbreaker. Hostility toward the lawbreaker inevitably brings with it the attitudes of retribution, repression and exclusion. These provide no principle for the eradication of crime, for returning the delinquent to normal social relations, nor for stating the transgressed rights of institutions in terms of their positive social functions."[8]

The advocates of the treatment model, working and writing in an atmosphere of groupthink, failed to comprehend the possibility that their efforts were not supported by the larger society. The treatment agents, well intentioned, failed to grasp the basic fact that punitive and hostile attitudes in a society can be functional. In some instances treatment agents have even failed to listen to their own clients. For example, inmate Griswold, writing in *An Eye For An Eye* contends,

> With the absolute certainty of offending many people, I have to say that the American people want, desire, lust for and need crime and criminality. They need, albeit on a subconscious level, an easily identifiable group whom they can look down upon, feel superior to, castigate, segregate and inflict emotional, psychological, and physical punishment upon. The public needs its criminally deviant individuals so that through an act of catharsis they can expunge their own guilt feelings, and every once in a while call up from the darker side of their souls all the repressed hate and fury that dwells within.[9]

Third, crime themes are pervasive in our society. Edwin Schur's classic work carefully documents the extent to which crime is deeply rooted in our legal, political, social, economic and military institutions.[10] Schur has identified the demand for illegal services provided by organized crime, and several levels of "respectable" crime. Embezzlement, tax evasion and a host of white collar crimes are viewed by many as nothing more than skillful manipulation in an achievement oriented society. In a journalistic effort, Bacon provides current supporting data for Schur's position.[11] Bacon sees the new American way of life as "ripping off." His convincing and detailed account indicates the extent of various types of crime and economic exploitation in our society. The result, according to Bacon, is a high level of tolerance for criminal behavior which enhances cynicism. Cynicism in turn stimulates persons to cut corners and commit crime. The internalization of cynicism functions to effectively neutralize responsibility and accountability as the offender perceives, and correctly, the high tolerance for criminal behavior in our society.

Treatment agents, often functioning in the vacuums of their clinical settings failed to ask a critical question: rehabilitation for what? The possibility exists that treatment agents have asked their clients to internalize a set of values quite different than those held in the communities in which the "ex-offender" might live.

Fourth, treatment agents ignored the ecology of the behavior setting in which they applied their strategies. The remote fortress we call a prison or penitentiary was never intended for rehabilitation. These monuments of steel and concrete clearly identify the function of the criminal law. That function is the removal of persons from society who have been convicted of committing a crime, with subsequent placement in a setting where they will feel pain and suffering for what they have done. We are often reminded that persons are incarcerated *as* punishment and not *for* punishment. Unfortunately, our methods of incarceration reflect the latter position.

The totalitarian environment that is pervasive in most prisons has functioned as a major barrier to treatment. The prison administrator is judged by his ability to maintain order and to prevent escapes. To say that prisons are custody-oriented is not enough. The prison, as a punishment mechanism in our society, is committed to the degradation of the persons incarcerated. Persons who are housed in cages come to act like animals, not "patients" or clients, and the treatment community, for the most part, has not considered the overbearing impact of the prison setting. There is little which can be done about the many bastilles which were built before the turn of the century.

Fifth, corrections, operating "between two fires" lacks an overall theoretical framework. The contributions of social scientists to public policy in corrections in many instances has been negative. Unfortunately the recom-

mendations from social scientists have been more influenced by personal ideological convictions that by an understanding of facts. Social scientists have,
on occasion, peddled ideological convictions under the guise of expert knowledge. An example can be found in the early work of Sheldon and Eleanor Gluek.[11]
In the 1950's, the Glueks developed a number of delinquency predictors, including such variables as parental affection and discipline. Follow-up work
has shown that family dynamics are indeed a highly predictive indicator of
delinquency. But no one knows then, or knows now, how a government can restore
affection and consistent discipline within the family. This inability did not
in any way inhibit the social scientists from offering themselves as experts
in the area of public policy. In other words, one kind of expertise - in this
case, knowledge about certain predictive factors relating to delinquency - does
not necessarily translate as another kind of expertise - knowledge relating to
public policy. To the extent that social scientists have failed to distinguish
between what they know as scholars from what they believe as citizens, social
scientists confused the correctional process, with the result that treatment
strategies were often based on ideological convictions not supported by data.

Sixth, treatment programs have been guided by the medical model, an in-
trinsic feature of the indeterminate sentence. The emergence of the medical
model reflects the power dimensions in the area of human service. In the treatment community, the psychiatrist is undoubtedly the most prestigious treatment
agent. The power to define inevitably results in the power to treat. When the
psychiatric profession succeeded in defining the criminal as "sick", this group
was able to establish and control the treatment process. The fact that the
definition of "sick" was imposed without sound data is not relevant at this
point except to note that the definition has proven to be, for the most part,
erroneous. Inappropriate definitions resulted in inappropriate labelling,
which resulted in faulty treatment models. Failure was inevitable.

Despite the fact that they are not the same thing, the medical model and
the indeterminate sentence have become inseparable concepts in the public mind.
Because the medical model was doomed to failure from the outset, it is now assumed that the indeterminate sentence should share the same fate. In the following section, we will examine the issue of sentencing and the controversy
surrounding the indeterminate and determinate sentence.

Determinate v. Indeterminate Sentencing: Pros and Cons

Hearing correctional reformers discuss the issue of sentencing reminds one
of seven blind men arguing over the description of an elephant. Descriptions

of sentencing problems vary in accord with the number of participants. We are deluged by information from sentencing reformers who argue for diverse changes. This confusion is enhanced because the participants in the debate have widely differing and often mutually exclusive perceptions of the problems which have become a part of contemporary sentencing systems. These perceptions, as noted earlier, are often based on divergent assumptions about punishment and the role of the penal sanction in the criminal justice system.

Two problem areas can be identified in which there appears to be some level of agreement. The first problem area is sentencing disparity, defined simply as the application of unjustifiably different penalties to similar offenders convicted of the same offense. For example, it is not uncommon to find considerable sentencing disparity when one compares sentences for inmates who come from urban centers to sentences for inmates who come from rural areas. A second problem area is the inappropriate sentence, defined as a sentence which may be too severe or too lenient given the nature of the offense. Long prison terms for the possession of marijuana are one example. Another example is short prison terms, and more frequently fines, in cases of massive pollution affecting the lives of thousands of persons. In both situations, the sentence is appropriate when one considers the level of social injury.

In the United States, sentencing systems have resulted, with lesser or greater frequency, in both inappropriate and disparate sentences. This fact has been well established and is therefore not an issue in this discussion.[12] Rather, the problem is whether inappropriate and disparate sentences are an inevitable result of any democratic punishment system. At issue is the relative effectiveness of different approaches to the problem of reducing or eliminating inappropriate and disparate sentences.

In the study of sentencing reform, it is important to note that sentencing is not a single decision made by any one person or any one agency. Rather, sentencing is a series of decisions made by a number of criminal justice decision makers, all of which influence the final sentencing decision. Police, for example, influence sentencing by the decision whether or not to arrest,[13] and by determining the initial charge at the time of arrest. They also influence the sentencing decision by their evidence gathering activities in that they determine, for the most part, the kinds of evidence which will be used at the time of trial.[14] The prosecutor exerts extensive power over the sentencing process through determining the official charge[15] and making recommendations to the court.[16] Prosecutors also control the plea bargaining pro-

cess which often results in charge reduction in exchange for a plea of guilty.[17]
In reducing the charge, to a large extent the prosecutor determines the sentence. Judges preside over the sentencing hearing[18] and select a sentence from legislatively provided optional punishments.[19] In states which have a wide range of years between the minimum and maximum sentence, judges have enormous power. Finally, corrections officials, through the parole board,[20] or with the provision of good time play the final role in determining the actual amount of time to be served.[21]

Thus, the basic issue in sentencing reform can be stated as a question: Who should decide the nature and extent of punishment? Theoretically, there are a number of answers to this question. Sentencing statutes could be designed which vary from providing legislatively established mandatory (fixed) penalities for each offense, to creating totally indeterminate sentences whereby corrections officials decide when, if ever, persons are to be released from prison.

Because of the "multiple discretion" in current sentences, the debate over sentencing reform has focused on one issue - whether the penalty should be fixed by the judge at the time of sentencing (determinate sentencing), or whether the judge should only set a range with a mimimum and maximum leaving the final release date to corrections officials (partially indeterminate sentencing).[22]

Symbolically, the debate over sentencing can be characterized as a series of competing assertions about the realities of punishment and sentencing reform. Each competing assertion rests on both evidence and ideology and can be presented in the form of sets of opposing statements on sentencing reform. In Table I, ten pairs of opposing statements are presented. The statements represent common areas of disagreement in the sentencing debate and have been grouped in three areas of concern: 1) effectiveness - the ability of the sentencing model to produce a useful result; 2) humaneness - the degree to which the model advances or expresses concern for the dignity and rights of the offender; and 3) justice - the degree to which the model provides external and internal equity in the distribution of penalties. Each of the three areas will be discussed in the following section with a presentation of the contentions made by the current reformers who advocate determinate sentencing, followed by the responses of the traditionalists who advocate partially indeterminate sentencing. (See Table I.)

Effectiveness - Reformist Contentions

The argument against indeterminate sentencing generally begins with the allegation that its assumptions are grounded in techniques which have been proven to be ineffective, an allegation that is supported by a number of research findings and evaluation projects.[23,24,25,26] The impressive array of negative results have lead critics of indeterminate sentencing to conclude that " . . . rehabilitation within the correctional system is a myth."[27]

Once it has been established that rehabilitation is a sham, the reformers wonder what possible justification there can be for parole release decisions based on rehabilitation. Parole decisions based on superficial rehabilitative concerns, such as program participation, reflect tenuous and questionable predictions of future behavior by the offender. Our ability to predict violent human behavior is very limited. At the same time, the stakes are very high--human freedom v. potential for violent behavior--and the tendency is for parole boards to make conservative decisions called "overprediction". As a result, many non-dangerous offenders are kept in prison because parole boards are unsure about the suitability of their release.

The failure of rehabilitation programs in prisons and the difficult problems involved in predicting future behavior have resulted in parole decisions which are inaccurate and ineffective in terms of crime reduction. Unfortunately, the maintenance of parole release in a system pervaded by failure functions to insure that parole decisions are either essentially arbitrary,[28] or that decisions become extensions of the prison disciplinary system. In the latter instance, disruptive inmates can be punished by parole denial.[29]

The only solution to these dilemmas, the reformers argue, is to completely remove the influence of treatment programs as a determining factor in the amount of time to be served by the inmates. Accordingly, release from prison should be based only on the seriousness of the offense with time reduction for good behavior. Participation in prison run treatment programs should be totally voluntary and unrelated to the release date. Making the programs voluntary, it is argued, recognizes the fact that people cannot be coerced into change that has any lasting significance.[30]

The reformers further contend that once the facade of treatment is removed, the more reasonable and defensible deterrent purposes of punishment can be emphasized.[31] Unwittingly, the reformers argue, the defenders of treatment have systematically taken the "teeth" out of the criminal law. This has been done by reducing the certainty of punishment though extensive use of probation, and providing an indeterminate sentencing system which provides punishment of uncertain length. If all convicted offenders were given a precise and certain punishment, the deterrent effect of the law, embodied in its credibility as a warning to potential offenders, would be strengthened.

Effectiveness - Traditionalist Response

The defenders of partially indeterminate sentencing generally agree that while the results of treatment programs have not been particularly positive, available research does not sustain the conclusion that "nothing works". On the contrary, there is substantial evidence which indicates that, for certain types of offenders, specific kinds of treatment are effective.[32,33,34]

The problem reflects generally simplistic treatment approaches. Treatment strategies have often assumed that a single program, such as group counseling, could be applied to all offenders incarcerated and would significantly reduce future criminal behavior. That this is not the case should come as no surprise. No treatment is appropriate for all offenders. In fact, evidence indicates that inappropriate treatment actually reduces post institutionalization success rates.[35] The fact that shotgun-type treatment programs have no significant effect reflects the probability that positive results for some offenders, who may have needed the treatment, have been negated by the contrary results for those whose chances for success were reduced through application of an inappropriate treatment program.

The available research does not support the conclusion of the reformers that treatment should be abolished. Rather, the evidence indicates a need for further experimentation, additional research focusing on the relationship between treatment strategy and type of offender, and most importantly, an increase in the reliance on differential treatment methods. The result should be the creation of more sophisticated and realistic program models which reflect the needs of individual inmates while rejecting the "counseling-for-everybody" approach which currently pervades corrections systems.

As for voluntary programming participation, the traditionalists argue that this is contrary to learning experiences in our society. The arguments for volunteerism are clearly facetious and ignore the competitive reality of everyday life: Teachers give grades to force students to change their study behavior; industry provides bonuses to change worker behavior; and, the criminal law is an attempt to coercively change behavior. The issue is not whether behavior change can or cannot be coerced. The problem is to achieve behavior change effectively with as little coercion as possible, recognizing the need for programming to be responsive to inmate needs. Besides it is pure mythology to assume that coercion is ended by making prison programs voluntary. The very existence of the prison, as a total institution, reflects a society at its most coercive. Historically, the problem has been the requirement that inmates participate in shoddy treatment programs in order to be considered for parole. There is a distinct need, indeed a social requirement, to provide a variety of specialized programs which will attract inmate participation and thereby diminish coercion as an issue.

Defenders of treatment programming argue that a de-emphasis in this area will enhance the punitive and degrading aspects of prisons. As long as rehabilitation remains an important goal for the correctional process, there is a rationale for finding training, education and treatment programs in prisons. If the emphasis of the prison is to be punishment there is a very real possibility that prisons and prison programs will receive little support from legislatures and become more desolate, brutal human cages.[36] Historically, legislatures have ignored the needs of corrections. An emphasis on punishment to the exclusion of treatment will support the current legislative policy of neglect.

When one examines the potentials for increased degradation, the reformer's claim that fixed sentencing will increase the deterrent effect of the criminal, law becomes questionable. When sentencing schemes contain mandatory prison sentences it is probable that prison populations will be increased.[37] In other instances sentencing time has been increased beyond the current parole eligibility date for the offense further increasing the prison population. Increased population density paralleled with minimal programming will, undoubtedly, enhance the very problems we now complain so much about--idleness, subculture values, and violence.

The belief that increased use of incarceration will enhance deterrence because of increased certainty of punishment confuses the issues. The reformers, the traditionalists argue, think in a vacuum of idealism and fail to accept the basic premise that the criminal justice system is not working. Increased incarceration will not incapacitate those who commit offenses which are not reported, or those offenders whose reported offenses do not result in arrest or conviction. Nor does increased incarceration deal with the concept of multiple discretion identified earlier. The reformers contend that if we manipulate the sentencing system, certainty can be increased. The increment in certainty is unknown and is miniscule at best. At worst, the determinate sentencing model is an expensive sham on the public which will result in increased costs,[38] forced plea bargaining to avoid mandatory penalties which are excessive,[39] and will not provide any meaningful incapacitation protection.[40]

Humaneness - Reformist Contentions

Regardless of the effectiveness of treatment, reformers believe that reliance on program participation as a criterion for release should be abolished.
Such a criterion is abusive, according to the reformers, because of the power
the parole decision places in the hands of authorities. Inmates feel helpless
in the present situation. Program participation becomes mandatory if one
wants to be seriously considered for parole. Furthermore, there is clear
evidence that some treatment programs have been inhumane and others have been
unnecessarily intrusive in nature. The use of tranquilizers, for example, reflects institutional needs to maintain control far more than concern for
treatment for inmates. Constitutional violations become obvious.

Inmates have been encouraged to participate in medical research and experimentation to demonstrate their institutional adjustment and readiness for
parole. Phase one drug testing for drug manufacturers ceases to be voluntary
when participation is linked to a good time and early release. The parole
system has been made into " . . . a potent psychological instrument for inmate
manipulation and control."[41] The treatment ideology supports virtually any
intrusion into the lives of prisoners because it can be " . . . rationalized in
terms of public protection. . ."[42]

The parole hearing itself is abusive. Described in official prison literature as a time for evaluating the adjustment of the inmate and determining
parole readiness, the typical parole hearing is conducted in a manner that
suggests a practiced disregard for careful consideration and deliberation of
the respective inmate's case. It is not unusual for hearings with the inmate
to average five minutes, with board members' deliberations and decision taking
a few additional minutes in closed session. Frequently, the inmate must wait
weeks before he is notified of the decision and generally no reason is given
for denial.[43] Considering the arbitrary nature of the power, it comes as no
surprise that the parole decision is a source of intense bitterness and frustration. Parole, as it presently functions in some states, may actually diminish the effects of treatment programming.

The most devastating impact of treatment programs has been to make a
"game" out of decisions relating to punishment. Rather than to establish a
punishment based on the seriousness of the offender's crime, the punishment
depends on the prisoner "getting a program", "showing growth", and in other
obscure ways proving to prison and parole authorities that he has seen the error of his ways. The appearance of change becomes more significant than actual
change.

By fixing the amount of punishment at the time of sentencing, the facade of rehabilitation, sham programs and arbitrary use of power can be minimized. The sentence will be dependent on the offense, not on the ability of the inmate to "con" a system which rewards short term transitory change.

Humaneness - Traditionalist Response

Again, the criticisms of the reformers can be substantiated and supporters of the rehabilitative ideal are forced to recognize the abuses of the treatment model. Treatment, the traditionalists argue, need not be abusive. It is important to note that treatment methods vary considerably. Some are admittedly physically and emotionally intrusive and limitations can be placed on a number of programs limiting these negative characteristics.[44,45,46] Chemo-therapy, body alterations such as pre-frontal lobotomies, sterilization and a considerable amount of medical experimentation should be excluded from the prison setting and its coercive atmosphere. On the other hand, less intrusive programs such as religious counseling, individual and group therapy should be available on a voluntary basis. Finally, programs which include job training and education are so minimally intrusive that required participation in one of a number of programs is not unreasonable intrusive.[47]

It is not unreasonable to expect the offender to use the time spent in prison in a meaningful way and to select programming which will result in self-improvement. Traditionalists recognize that the coercive power of the state is only justified when the state has a compelling interest. In this instance, the compelling interest is the maintenance of humane institutions. One virtue of the treatment model which has generally been ignored is that the model placed responsibility on the state to make prisons suitable environments in which offenders would have an opportunity to improve their prospects for success upon release. That the state has never fully accepted this responsibility does not negate the obligation.

If the state's responsibility in the area of programming and rehabilitation is terminated, and if the prison comes to be viewed only as an instrument of punishment as some propose in determinate sentencing schemes, then we can expect implementation of the "principle of least eligibility". The principle of least eligibility argues that prisoners should not be better provided for than the "least" member of free society. The future, under many of the proposed schemes, is one of a desolate, aimless existence for forgotten citizens.[48]

It is also quite unlikely that determinate sentencing will end inmate bitterness and manipulation of time to be served. If parole is abolished, prison authorities will require some means of power to insure prison discipline. In the case of determinate sentencing, the control mechanism will be the allocation of "good time". Regardless of the mechanism, control will not be achieved without manipulation. Control mechanisms are certain to engender the same inmate hostility that is now associated with parole release and for the same reasons; manipulation of the time to be served.

The argument that determinate sentencing will not result in increased prison populations is a myth. Legislators frequently engage in denunciations of a variety of behaviors while responding to the expectation that they "do something" about crime. This has resulted in substantially longer prison terms under determinate sentencing statutes when compared to time served under the partially indeterminate statutes.[49]

Justice - Reformist Contentions

The movement is especially interesting because of the different symbolic meanings of justice which are espoused. At the symbolic level, it is clear that the criminal law should be returned to the foundation of retribution. Simply, punishment should reflect the seriousness of the offense. Any other factors which might be included will only function to reduce the quality of justice. The indeterminate sentencing philosophy is wrought with flaws, most of which reflect a policy which determines punishment on the basis of some future hypothetical acts the criminal "might" commit.[50] Indeterminate sentencing responds to the offender's current status instead of his past conduct. Finally, the emphasis on treatment reduces the pedagogical impact of the law by de-emphasizing the "moral condemnation" of retributive punishment.[51]

In application, the indeterminate sentence is unjust because unregulated discretion has created the potential for widespread sentence disparity. Under the current model, " . . . far too many criminals receive sentences that are simply not severe enough. At the same time, far too many criminals receive sentences that are too severe . . ."[52] If justice is to be achieved, the range in sentences given to similarly situated offenders must be reduced. The primary means for accomplishing this task is to legislate mandatory sentences for accomplishing this task is to legislate mandatory sentences for specific offenses.

Judicial determination of the sentence is intended to reduce sentencing disparity, however, this approach is recommended as a policy matter because some contend that the determination of punishment properly resides with the judiciary. Correctional administrators, through the partially indeterminate sentence and parole, will subvert the intended purpose of punishment, therefore,

they should have limited authority. Judicial determination will function to
enhance the attention which should be given to the offense and lessen the emphasis on the offender thereby establishing a greater amount of equity in the
sentencing process. Punishing the offense rather than the offender rein-
forces important values in our culture. First, it treats the citizen, even the
criminal, as a whole person responsible for exercising a free will. Punishing
the act, rather than the person, rejects the state's ability to regulate the
individual's private or public thoughts, emotions or beliefs. The penal system
becomes one of expiation; the citizen who violates the law is punished and,
once having paid the penalty for the act, is returned to society a full and
equal citizen.[53]

Justice - The Traditionalist Response

    The defenders of the partially indeterminate sentence argue that the idea
of "justice" must be understood within the context of the bureaucratic structure
of the criminal justice system. Understanding the concept of justice in this
sense underscores the need for sentencing discretion in the corrections system.

    In the real world, sentencing will never approach the determinate model.
Prosecutors and law enforcement agencies, as previously indicated, play an
intensive role in deciding the sentence through their decision-making capaci-
ties. Prison disciplinary mechanisms function to influence the length of
time-served. The common practice of awarding "good time" for good behavior
vests considerable discretion in the corrections system.[54] The issue of
whether sentencing power should reside solely in the judiciary is irrelevant;
this will never occur in the various levels of discretion which already exist
in several components of the American criminal justice system as presently
constituted. The most salient issue is how to equitably distribute sentencing
discretion among the various criminal justice decision makers.[55]

    The resolution of this issue requires an understanding of the causes of
sentencing disparity. Sentencing disparity can occur through the parole release decision. However, there are a number of other sources of disparity
which have historical roots. Rural-urban differences in the sentencing process
have been documented in a number of studies. Unique judicial and prosecutorial
biases have also been demonstrated in focusing on various jurisdictions. The
irony is that the parole system, which has received the most severe criticism,
has functioned to adjust for a number of disparities. The abolition of parole
may in fact enhance the permanence of historical and traditional disparities
which are entrenched in the present system. Moreover, the theoretical con-
straints that determinate sentencing allegedly places on judicial power have in

fact been eliminated in a number of proposals now being debated. Some determinate sentencing models provide a greater variation in sentencing than the
partially indeterminate models they are designed to replace.[56]

Because of these problems, the traditionalists profoundly question the
extent to which the determinate sentence will "affirm" individual dignity and
responsibility. In the move toward determinate sentencing, the traditionalists
see a movement that will create stagnant institutions, over-populated with
disillusioned prisoners serving longer sentences, without useful programs to
prepare the offender for eventual release. Moreover, the law will continue
to differentially over-select from the lower income groups in our society regardless of the sentencing mode. It is therefore difficult to see such a
system "affirming" any positive values.

A Reintegration Mode

The problems with indeterminate sentencing may not be inherent to the
method so much as they are an artifact of pairing indeterminacy with the
"medical model" of rehabilitation, one which should be replaced with a comprehensive "reintegration model". As the distinguished criminologist, John
Conrad has noted, "We Should Never Have Promised a Hospital".[57] The concepts
and definitions sold to us by psychiatrists, social workers and their en-
tourages resulted in criminality being defined as a disease, and the criminal
defined as "sick".

> The general model for classification (and treatment) is a
> variation on the caseworker plan adopted from the social
> worker profession, which assumes that the offender is 'sick'
> and therefore requires 'help' from the treatment team whether
> he wants it or not.[58]

The medical model utilized in medical settings assumes a patient (P), plus
diagnosis (D), plus a hospital treatment program (HTP) will result in success -
good health (S) or failure - death (F), or a level of health somewhere between
S and F. The level of health reflects the extent to which the patient (P) responds positively to the hospital treatment program (HTP). The similarities
between the medical model and the treatment for corrections are obvious as indicated in the following comparison:

MEDICAL MODEL $P+D+HTP=S/F$

TREATMENT MODEL $O+D+OTP=S/F$

Corrections treatment programs, under the direction of psychiatrists and
social workers assumed, as in the case of the medical model, that an offender

(0) plus diagnosis (D), plus an offender treatment program (OTP) would result in successful law abiding behavior (S), or failure - recidivism (F). The simplistic nature of the medical model made it attractive to corrections officials. The reassurances provided by psychiatrists and social workers, supported by their dominance in human science delivery systems, reinforced the basic notion that criminal behavior could be treated by focusing the therapeutic effort on the inmate. This required, of course, that the offender be placed in the hands of the treatment agents for an indeterminate period of time. The treatment agents determined "how sick" the offender was, and the length of time the offender would be exposed to treatment was also determined by the treatment agents after assessing the offender's response to the treatment program. The extent to which treatment agents were able to impose the medical model on corrections reflected more the powerless position of the inmate client system than the success of the mode. Social workers ignored two basic tenets of their profession. First, the individual must perceive he has a problem and be motivated to seek help. Second, goals in the casework process must be established by the client. The issues of voluntarism and self-determination were ignored and a "Catch 22" situation was created:

> That is, we know you're sick. If you deny that you're sick,
> you're really sick. But if you acknowledge that you're sick,
> then you must really must be sick or you wouldn't admit it.[59]

The utilization of the medical model in corrections has been an unmitigated failure. The basic assumption that criminals are "sick" has generally been rejected. In addition to the fact that the label was imposed without substantive research, the longitudinal studies now available indicate application of the model has been a failure. Simply, inappropriate diagnoses of the offender at the entry level resulted in inappropriate treatment strategies during the treatment process. The problem is compounded by the fact that the diagnostic phase in corrections has generally been quite superficial. In the area of human services, it would be difficult to find a system that knows less about its clientele. Unfortunately, the lack of knowledge about the offenders did not hinder the treatment agents operating on the assumptions set forth in the medical model. The criminal was "sick" and needed to be "cured".

In a comprehensive reintegration model, on the other hand, the major assumption is that criminal behavior results from the person's interaction with a number of systems and subsystems. The model therefore includes a number of variables ignored by the traditional treatment model and the determinate sentencing proposals. The reintegration model is reflected in the following formula:

$$O+D+OTP+F+E+PC+CR=S/F$$

The traditional treatment model ignored, for the most part, the complex of systems in which the offender must interact. Treatment of the offender in the clinical setting tended to ignore the family (F) and almost always ignore the offender's economic situation (E), peer contacts (PC), and perhaps most important for the inmate, community reaction (CR). Our reintegration model has a number of assumptions about crime and the criminal which clearly differentiate this model from the traditional treatment model. While some criminal behavior may result from emotional problems of one kind or another, we contend that most criminals have normal psychic structures and that their involvement in criminal behavior is situational-or value-oriented.

Criminal behavior which is situational is personified in Cressy's classic work examining the crime of embezzlement.[60] Cressey found embezzlers to be generally conformist individuals who had a unique non-sharable problem, and possessed the requisite skills to engage in the act. It is important to note that the person who engages in crime which is situational in nature does not view himself as criminal. Rather, as in the case of the embezzler, he describes his behavior as "borrowing" and continues to identify with societal expectations and to see himself as essentially conformist. The fact that he fails to return the money and perhaps continues to "borrow" does not alter his self-concept as a conformist person.

Value-oriented criminal behavior is personified in systemic criminal behavior where the behavior is supported and reinforced by commitment to criminal value structures. For this person, crime is a way of life. It is highly probable that he acknowledges his behavior as criminal and defines himself accordingly. The value-oriented criminal interacts with individuals who share his perspective. Burglary is one example of frequent behavior for this person. It is important to note that the value-oriented criminal differs significantly from the situational criminal in that the probability of recidivism is great because of his commitment to criminal values. The probability of recidivism for the situational criminal is minimal. However, these two categories cannot be considered a dichotomy. That is, there are many criminals who exhibit behavior patterns which fall on a continuum somewhere between these two categories. The point that remains important is that the criminal behavior exhibited by these two types, and those who fall between, reflects situations and values, not emotional pathologies. Their's is not a disease, and they are not sick.

Our assumptions about the criminal and criminal behavior call for assessment techniques and strategies which reflect the complexities of the interaction process experienced by the criminal. Assessment procedures must go beyond the traditional battery of psychological tests sometimes administered by reception and diagnostic centers as a part of the medical model. The assessment techniques must provide data on several dimensions of each of the variables cited in our reintegration model. Each individual, after conviction of a crime, would have an extensive pre-sentence investigation which would focus on the above variables.

In applying the appropriate offender treatment program (OTP), and assuming for a moment that the decision will be to incarcerate, consideration must be given to an appropriate sentence. The complex issues in sentencing have been discussed earlier, but many of the contemporary proposals have not asked the right questions. As a result, the recommendations from the reformers and chaos to an already complex problem. The following issues must be resolved:

1. Should there be provision for discretion in the sentencing process?

2. If so, where should the discretionary power be placed?

3. How much discretionary power should be granted?

4. What kinds of guidelines, etc. should be established to regulate the discretionary power?

The sentencing process should provide for discretion, not because one approves of the concept of discretionary judgements in the sentencing process, but rather because a system without discretion is impossible. As noted earlier, it is impossible for a legislature to construct a penal code which will cover all the nuances of each crime which can occur in a variety of social contexts. Furthermore, even if it were possible to construct the perfect penal code, police and prosecutors will always exercise discretion. The decision to arrest involves a personal judgement as does the official charge which is determined by the prosecutor.

The second issue is, where should discretionary power be placed? Discretionary power should be given to parole authority, autonomous and independent from the corrections bureaucracy. Cognizant of the weaknesses in the present process, we nevertheless reject the notion that determinate sentence returns sentencing power to the legislature. Determinate sentencing reallocates the discretionary power in the criminal justice system so that the prosecutor, not the legislature, is the recipient of much of the power. Contrary to contentions made in several proposals, it is not the judge who determines the sentence. When examined from the perspective of the prosecutor, determinate sentencing undoubtedly increases his power considerably.

Analysis of the plea-bargaining process, now sanctioned by the criminal justice system, indicates that socio-economic factors play a greater role at this point in sentencing than any other time in the criminal justice process. Bargained justice is bought justice with the best bargains going to the highest bidders. It is the prosecutor who determines the price to be exacted and the final bargain. Fogel and others have noted that when the corrections process internalizes injustice, the entire criminal justice system loses credibility in the offender's eyes.[61] While we concur with Fogel's position that too much discretion in the sentencing process has enhanced the problem, his sentencing solution is short-sighted. Simply, determinate sentencing models do not appreciate the politics of prosecution and the role the prosecutor plays in the local political context. It is in this context, behind closed doors, out of public view and beyond due process, where a community's power dimensions, prejudices and politics interact. Allocations of power to this person should be reduced, not increased.

The third issue is, how much discretionary power should be granted? The amount of discretionary power should be extremely limited. The problems addressed by Beccaria in his 1764 treatise, *An Essay on Crimes and Punishments*, were not unique to the politics of that day.[62] Discretionary power, regardless of the rationale, is often a misnomer for tyranny. Whether it be tyranny of the king or the tyranny of the psychologist, the outcome is quite similar-- loss of liberty. For this reason, each criminal sanction should carry a maximum, in no case should the minimum be more than two-thirds of the maximum, and sentence ranges and lengths should be reduced. We should realize that the major function to be served by punishment is retribution, and efforts should be made to minimize its effect on persons incarcerated. To contend that punishment has more important functions is to ignore the realities of the sentencing process.

The fourth issue is what kinds of guidelines should be established to regulate discretionary power. Guidelines should be stringent, and the paroling authority should be obligated to follow the guidelines with appropriate accountability mechamisms established. That is, when parole is denied, the inmate should have the right to appellate review. Accountability for the parole process is long overdue. Sentencing time is a major component of the offender treatment program (OTP) and it is extremely important that it be equitable. The parole system, often pervaded by politics, is a serious barrier to reintegrating the offender into the community. The issue of incarceration is complex and every effort should be made to develop programming which minimizes incarceration and maximizes reintegration into community life. This is not to say that incarceration should not be used. Obviously there are a number of individuals who cannot be adequately supervised in community-based corrections systems and protection of society must be a primary goal of the process. At the same time, the irrational incarceration of thousands of convicted criminals, without differentiation between those who are a threat to society and those who are not, is a waste of resources. Furthermore, there is considerable evidence that through the incarceration process offenders often become increasingly sophisticated in their criminal behavior patterns. There is also evidence that some offenders become more violent. The criminal justice system has a number of criminogenic characteristics; characteristics of the system which enhance the potential for further criminal behavior. Unfortunately, we have ignored these issues and as a result problems have been compounded.

Beyond the issues of sentencing, delivery systems for programming must be totally restructured. The present delivery system is based on another erroneous assumption; that the interests of the warden and the inmate are the same. If you were in prison, would you hire the warden's lawyer as your attorney? Can the clinical worker who delivers the "treatment" be an employee of the prison warden and at the same time function as an advocate for the inmate? The answers are obviously, "No". Consideration should be given to a voucher system whereby inmates contract for the clinical services they believe they need. Obviously, if the inmate does not perceive a need for clinical services, none would be purchased. Parole would not be linked to the inmate's participation in programming per se, but rather to self-improvement strategies the inmate develops.

Industries in prisons, better known as "slave shops", should be contracted out to the business community. In this way, industries could be developed which would respond to market conditions for both products and employment. Wage levels should reflect realistic job market conditions with inmates reimbursing the state for at least some of the maintenance costs incurred as a result of their incarceration. Restitution programs should be established for victims as well as support programs for the offender's family. In these efforts, programming should be developed which focused on two important subsystems in which the offender must be prepared to interact: the economy (E) and the family (F).

Finally, the collateral consequences of conviction must be eliminated wherever possible. The successful reintegration of the offender, is, to a large extent, determined by the nature of the community reaction (CR) and avoidance of participation in criminal subcultures with continual interaction with former peers (PC). It is grim fact that punishment does not end when an inmate is released from one of our prisons. A study completed by the American

Bar Association found 1,948 different state statutory provisions that prohibit the licensing of ex-offenders and thereby limit career development in a number of fields.

> The public is not generally aware of the fact that at the very time when it is approving efforts to develop job skills and employment for offenders and ex-offenders there exists a major body of legal barriers to meaningful and gainful employment of persons released from correctional systems . . .
>
> We are thus involved in a system which defeats itself, in a system where through the work ethic and the values of our society, we applaud hard work and productive activity, while at the same time deny exactly that opportunity to do hard work and productive activity to persons we expect, in fact demand, to act responsibly. We try to rehabilitate, and then we place barriers to rehabilitation and in fact initiate an active impetus back to a life of crime.[63]

The resultant loss of self-esteem enhances considerably the potentials for recidivism. If we do not radically alter the legal barriers which now function to severely limit the reintegration process, the vicious cycle of incarceration-release-incarceration will continue regardless of the sentencing model used. The present community reaction (CR) to the ex-offender is often one of negativism and continued stigma. We should not be surprised that ex-offenders often return to previous life styles, maintain commitments to old values and become recidivists. The problem was identified by Frank Tannenbaum in 1938.

> The process of making the criminal, therefore, is a process of tagging, defining, identifying, segregating, describing, emphasizing, making conscious, and self-conscious; it becomes a way of stimulating, suggesting, emphasizing, and evoking the very traits that are complained of . . . The person becomes the very thing he is described as being. Nor does it seem to matter whether the evaluation is made by those who would reform . . . The harder they work to reform the evil, the greater the evil grows under their hands. The persistent suggestion, with whatever good intentions, works mischief, because it leads to bringing out the bad behavior that it would suppress. The way out is through a refusal to dramatize the evil.[64]

The advice given by Tannenbaum in 1938 has seldom been followed. The way out is to reject the retribution philosophy as it has been practiced and turn instead to the philosophies of reintegration, restitution and reconcilation. We can no longer focus our efforts on the individual offender by blaming the offender when our efforts fail.

NOTES

*Zimbardo and Ruch have described the "groupthink" process which contributes to poor decision making. "Groupthink" has a number of characteristics including the following:[65]

1. Collective rationalizations of the group's actions, which allow the group to discount any evidence that is contrary to the decision;

2. An unquestioned belief in the group's actions, which leads the group to ignore the ethical or moral consequences of the decision;

3. Stereotyped views of the enemy as weak, evil (thus ruling out negotiation) or stupid;

4. An illusion of unanimity on the decision, which is partly the result of the conformity pressures;

5. The emergence of self-appointed "mindguards" - group members who suppress inconsistent information and reproach anyone who deviates from the group consensus.

REFERENCES

1. Culbertson, R.G. Corrections: The state of the art. *Journal of Criminal Justice*, 1977, 5:1, 39-46.

2. Fogel, D. . . .*We are the living proof; the justice model for corrections.* Cincinnati: W.H. Anderson Co., 1975.

3. Mitford, J. *Kind and usual punishment--the prison business.* NY: Vintage Books, 1974.

4. Morris, N. *The future of imprisonment.* Chicago: University of Chicago Press, 1974.

5. Packer, H.L. *The limits of the criminal sanction.* Stanford, CA: Stanford University Press, 1968.

6. Mead, G.H. The psychology of punitive justice. *American Journal of Sociology*, 1918, 23:4, 586-592.

7. Durkheim, E. *The rules of the sociological method.* NY: Macmillan, 1938.

8. Mead, pg. 591.

9. Griswold, H., Misenheimer, M., Powers, A. and Tromanhauser, E. *An eye for an eye.* NY: Holt, Rinehart and Winston, 1970.

10. Schur, E.M. *Our criminal society.* Englewood Cliffs, NJ: Prentice-Hall, 1969.

11. Bacon, D. Ripoffs, new American way of life. *U.S. News and World Report,* 1976, 81:22, 29-32, and Glueck, S. and Gluek, E. *Unraveling juvenile delinquency,* Cambridge, Mass.: Harvard University Press, 1950.

12. Silberman, C.E. *Fair and certain punishment: report of the 20th century fund task force on criminal sentencing.* NY: McGraw-Hill, 1976.

13. Lipton, D., Martinson, R., and Wilks, J. *The effectiveness of correctional treatment: a survey of evaluation studies,* NY: Praeger, 1975.

14. Germann, A.C., Day, I.E. and Gullatti, J. *An introduction to law enforcement.* Springfield, Ill.: C.C. Thomas, 1975.

15. Miller, F.W. *Prosecution: the decision to charge a suspect with a crime.* Boston: Little, Brown & Co., 1969.

16. Hewitt, J.D. The effects of individual resources in judicial sentencing. *Review of Public Data Use,* 1977, 5:1, 30-51.

17. Newman, D.J. *Conviction: the determination of guilt or innocence without trial.* Boston: Little, Brown & Co., 1966.

18. Goldman, J. The sentencing hearing: forgotten phase of the sentencing process. Paper presented to the Meetings of the American Society of Criminology, Atlanta, November, 1977.

19. Dawson, R.G. *Sentencing: The decision as to type, length and conditions of sentence.* Boston: Little, Brown & Co., 1969.

20. Stanley, D.T. *Prisoners among us: the problem of parole.* Washington, D.C.: The Brookings Institution, 1976.

21. Clear, T.R., Hewitt, J.D. and Regoli, R.M. Discretion and the determinate sentence: its distribution, control and impact on time-served. Paper presented to the Meetings of the American Society of Criminology, Atlanta, November, 1977.

22. Zimring, F. A consumer's guide to sentencing reform: making the punishment fit the crime, *Hasting Center Report,* 1968, December, 13-17.

23. Bailey, W.C. Correctional treatment: an analysis of one-hundred outcome studies. *Journal of Criminal Law, Criminology and Police Science,* 1966, 57:2, 153-182.

24. Martinson, R. What works--questions and answers about prison reform. *The Public Interest.* 1974, 35:2, 22-56.

25. Robinson, J. and Smith, G. The effectiveness of correctional programs. *Crime and Delinquency,* 1971, 17:1, 67-86.

26. Kassebaum, G., Ward, D. and Wilner, E. *Prison treatment and parole survival: an empirical assessment.* NY: John Wiley & Sons, 1971.

27. Stanley, pg. 185.

28. Wright, E.O. *The politics of punishment: a critical analysis of prisons in America.* NY: Harper & Row, 1973.

29. Jackson, G. *Soledad Brother: the prison letters of* . . . NY: Bantam Books, 1970.

30. Morris, 1974.

31. van den Haag, E. *Punishing criminals: on an old and painful question.* NY: Basic Books, 1975.

32. Warren, M.Q. All things being equal. *Criminal Law Bulletin*, 1973, 9:3, 483-512.

33. Palmer, T. Martinson revisited. *Journal of Research in Crime and Delinquency*, 1975, 12:2, 230-253.

34. Adams, S. Some findings in correctional caseload research. *Federal Probation*, 1967, 31:4, 48-56.

35. Adams, S. Interaction between individual interview therapy and treatment amenability in older youth authority wards. In *Inquiries concerning kinds of treatment for types of delinquents.* California Board of Corrections, Sacremento, 1961.

36. Clear, T.R. Neo-retributionism, correctional policy and the determinate sentence. *Justice System Journal*, 1978 (in press).

37. Cole, G. Will definite sentences make a difference? *Judicature*, 1977, 61:2, 58-65.

38. Singer, N.M. The economic implications of standards for correctional institutions. *Crime and Delinquency*, 1977, 23:1, 14-31.

39. Rosett, A. and Cressey, D.R. *Justice by consent.* Philadelphia: J.B. Lippincott, 1976.

40. van Dine, S., Dinitz, S. and Conrad, J. The incapacitation of the dangerous offender: a statistical experiment. *Journal of Research in Crime and Delinquency*, 1977, 13:1, 22-35.

41. Mitford, pg. 90.

42. American Friends, 1971.

43. Stanley, 1976.

44. Mitford, 1974.

45. Kittrie, N. *The right to be different: deviance and enforced therapy.* Baltimore: Johns Hopkins Press, 1971.

46. Morris, 1974.

47. Ibid.

48. Plotkin, R. *Constitutional Challenges to Employment Disability Statutes.* Washington, D.C.: National Clearinghouse on Offender Employment Restrictions, 1974.

49. Clear, 1978.

50. Von Hirsch, A. Crime and punishment. *In Improving the criminal justice system in the United States.* Washington, D.C.: U.S. Government Printing Office, 1976.

51. Hart, H.M. The arms of the criminal sanction. *Law and Contemporary Problems,* 1958, 23:3, 399-438.

52. Silberman, Pg. 4.

53. Moberly, Sir W. *The ethics of punishment.* Hamden, Conn.: Archon Books, 1971.

54. Clear, et. al., 1977.

55. Zimring, 1976.

56. Neithercutt, M.G. Parole legislation. *Federal Probation,* 1977, 41:1, 22-26.

57. Conrad, J. We should have never promised a hospital. *Federal Probation,* 1975, 39:4, 3-8.

58. Allen, H. and Simonsen, C. *Corrections in America: An Introduction.* Beverly Hills: Glencoe Press, 1975.

59. National Advisory Commission on Criminal Justice Standards and Goals. *Corrections.* Washington, D.C.: U.S. Government Printing Office, 1975.

60. Cressey, D.R. *Other people's money.* Glencoe, Ill.: Free Press, 1953.

61. Fogel, 1975.

62. Beccaria, C. *On crimes and punishments.* Trans. H. Paolucce. Indianapolis: Bobbs-Merrill, 1978.

63. American Bar Association. *Law, licenses and the offender's right to work.* Washington, D.C.: National Clearinghouse on Offender Employment Restrictions, 1973.

64. Tannenbaum, R. *Crime and community.* NY: Ginn & Co., 1938.

65. Zimbardo, P. and Ruch, F. *Psychology and life.* (9th edition). Glenview, Ill.: Scott Foresman & Co., 1975.

TABLE I:

OPPOSING STATEMENTS ON SENTENCING REFORM SUPPORTING STATEMENTS

Area of Concern	Determinate Sentencing	Partially Indeterminate Sentencing
Effectiveness	1. In general, the "treatment approach" has failed. 2. Only voluntary treatment programs can succeed in changing offenders. 3. Parole release decisions are based on "predictions" which are highly error-prone. 4. Fixed sentencing will deter offenders by increasing certainty of punishment.	1. For certain offenders, some treatments have been successful. 2. Treatments and controls can be effective even when coercively applied. 3. Predictions are an unavoidable aspect of any penal sanction. 4. In light of unsolved crime, fixed sentencing has almost no impact on the certainty of punishment.
Humaneness	1. Rehabilitation has been used as an excuse for abuse of prisoners. 2. Judicial fixing of the sentence will eliminate the bitter, angry inmate reactions to parole release decisions. 3. Fixed sentencing will not increase prison populations.	1. Rehabilitative programs mitigate the harshness of imprisonment. 2. Any system of institutional controls over inmates will result in prisoner anger. 3. Fixed sentencing inevitably increases use and length of imprisonment.
Justice	1. Fixed sentencing affirms individual dignity and responsibility. 2. Fixed sentencing will reduce sentencing disparities. 3. Fixed sentencing will give final control over the sentence to the judge, who can best decide what punishment is desired.	1. A focus on punishment negates human dignity. 2. Fixed sentencing solidifies hidden sentence disparities. 3. Other criminal justice decision-makers will continue to influence the sentencing decision, regardless of reform.

THE FEDERAL "SPEEDY TRIAL ACT OF 1974":
PROVISIONS AND PROBLEMS
Francis Edward Devine

In *Barker* v. *Wingo*[1] the United States Supreme Court considered and rejected the contention that the right to a speedy trial under the Sixth Amendment requires that a defendant be offered trial within a fixed period of time. While pointing out that such an approach was constitutional, in use in some jurisdictions, and often advantageous, the court found no constitutional basis for mandating it. Instead, the court established a balancing test to determine violation of the constitutional right to a speedy trial. Considered in this balance should be the length of delay, the reason for delay, whether and how persistently the defendant demanded trial, and the seriousness of the prejudice to the defendant from the delay.

The congressional response to this decision was that it provided no guidance and reinforced the legitimacy of delay; Congress, therefore, felt the need to adopt speedy trial legislation "to give real meaning to the Sixth Amendment right."[2] The resulting Speedy Trial Act of 1974 - without, of course, abolishing the constitutional right as defined by the court - established a federal statutory speedy trial right defined in number of days.

The act applies, on the federal level only, to "any cases involving a defendant charged with an offense." That is, it applies only to criminal cases, but applies equally to misdemeanors and felonies. This indicated the possible necessity of utilizing the greater flexibility permitted in civil cases, in various ways, to facilitate meeting the more demanding requirements in criminal cases. Moreover, suggestions have been widespread among those charged with implementing the law that certain inherently complex categories of cases be made subject to special time limits. These include conspiracy cases, and cases with multiple defendants.[3]

In cases covered by this law, the appropriate judicial officer is required--at the earliest practicable time--to consult with defense and prosecution attorneys and set a date for trial, or at least to enter the case on a weekly or other short-term calendar. Legislative intent with regard to this provision--as established by House Report (Judiciary Committee) No. 93-1508--is to allow adequate time, within the deadline for trial, for defense and prosecution to notify witnesses of when they will be required to appear.

The following maximum periods of delay are established by this law:

BETWEEN		DAYS	EFFECTIVE
arrest	indictment	60	1 July 76
or ---	or	45	1 July 77
summons	information	35	1 July 78
		30*	1 July 79
indictment -- arraignment		10	1 July 76
information			
or			
initial appearance			
(whichever is last)**			
arraignment*** -- Trial		180	1 July 76
		120	1 July 77
		80	1 July 78
		60	1 July 79
mistrial -- retrial		60*****	******
or			
reversal****			

The effect of these limitations on delay can already be seen in the practices of many Federal District Courts. In order to comply with the interval allowed between arrest and indictment grand juries will be convened more frequently, especially in sparsely populated districts previously convening them

---

*In felony cases, if no grand jury has been in session in the federal district during this thirty day period, the delay permissible shall be extended an additional thirty days (Sec. 3161b). No similar provision is explicit in section 3161f dealing with the period between 1 July 76 and 1 July 79, but the probable intent is to provide for a similar extension.

**This contemplates the possibility that information or indictment precedes arrest.

***This applies where a not guilty plea is entered at the arraignment. Entry of a guilty plea (or *nolo contendere*) constitutes a waiver of the sanction of dismissal (Sec. 3162 or 2). If a guilty plea is entered and withdrawn, time runs from the day the order permitting withdrawal is final.
  The legislature is cognizant of, but unimpressed by, the argument that this provision will increase not guilty pleas, in the hope that the prosecution will fail to meet the deadline, where previously guilty pleas--negotiated or otherwise would have been entered (House Report No. 93-1508). The likely effect of this provision on the number of cases in which trial is demanded might profitably be taken into account.

****Whether on appeal or collateral attack.

*****The court retrying the case may extend the period for retrial up to 180 days if unavailability of witnesses or other factors resulting from the passage of time makes retrial within sixty days impractical.

******No effective date for section 3161e seems specified.

infrequently. Moreover, in some districts arrests will be delayed, whenever possible, until after indictment. In the development most effecting law enforcement personnel, United States Marshalls and other arresting agencies have been required by a number of districts to report arrests promptly to the Clerk of Courts, so that monitoring of time periods may begin--literally before it is too late. Finally, a trend toward the use of firm cut-off dates for the filing of pre-trial motions may be developing.

The Speedy Trial Act has created support for legislation to increase the powers of United States Magistrates so that they may conduct arraignments involving guilty pleas, hear some pre-trial motions, and try all misdemeanors.[4]

In computing the running of time under the provisions governing indictment or information, and trial, the statute provides for tolling under the following circumstances:

A. Any delay resulting from other proceedings concerning the defendant. This is construed to include, but not be limited to:

    1. examination of and hearing on mental competency, or physical incapacity of the defendant

    2. examination under 28 U.S.C. sec. 2902 (potentially rehabilitable drug addict)

    3. trials of the defendant on other charges

    4. interlucutory appeals

    5. hearings on pre-trial motions

    6. transfer of the defendant from another district

    7. up to thirty days when any proceeding concerning the defendant is actually under advisement.

B. Any period during which prosecution is deferred by the government for the purpose of allowing the defendant to demonstrate his innocence, pursuant to a written and court approved agreement with the defendant.

C. Any period of delay resulting from the absence or unavailability of the defendant or an essential witness. Due diligence in seeking the subject is required to justify delay.

D. Any delay resulting from the defendant's mental or physical incapacity to stand trial.

E. Any delay resulting from treatment under 28 U.S.C. sec. 2902 (potentially rehabilitable drug addict.)

F. A reasonable delay when the defendant is joined for trial with a co-defendant for whom the time for trial has not expired.

G. A period resulting from a continuance based on the judge's finding that the resulting ends of justice outweigh the interest in a speedy trial. The court must set forth in the record its reason for so finding. Potential miscarriage of justice, impossibility of proceeding, and complexity of the case are properly considered. Not to be considered are congestion of the court's calendar, lack of diligent prosecution preparation, or failure to obtain available witnesses. "The Committee cannot foresee any excuses for institutional delay which would justify granting a continuance. . . ."[5]

According to the same report, if delay is sought because of defense counsel's failure to diligently prepare his case:

The court in this situation would determine whether the defendant participated actively in the delay or whether his counsel alone was responsible for it. If the defendant did not cause the delay, he should not be penalized by being forced to go to trial with an unprepared counsel. In this case, he should be permitted enough time to seek a new counsel and to properly prepare his case for trial. In the event that the defendant actively participated in the delay, then no miscarriage of justice has occurred and the court should deny the defendant's . . . request for a continuance. . . .

The relatively short period between indictment and arraignment, when combined with the apparent failure of the legislation to apply these time exclusions to this stage, has led to suggestions for a longer time period, or explicit application of the relevant exclusions at this point.[6]

In the case of a defendant known to be imprisoned on another charge this statute provides:

A. that the prosecuting attorney shall promptly:

1. attempt to obtain the presence of the prisoner for trial.

2. file a detainer and request that the prisoner be informed of his right to demand trial.

B. that the person having custody of the prisoner shall:

1. advise him of the charge and of his right to trial.

2. if the prisoner does demand trial, so notify the attorney filing the detainer.

3. upon a properly supported request, and subject to any rights of the prisoner to contest the legality of his delivery, make the prisoner available to the attorney for the government.

No sanctions for failure to comply with the above provisions are in effect until 1 July 1979. Thereafter, the sanction is the dismissal of the case. This may be done with or without prejudice to further proceedings at the determination of the court. To be considered in this determination are:

1. The seriousness of the offense.

2. The facts and circumstances which lead to dismissal.

3. The impact of a reprosecution on the administration of justice and the administration of this statute.

The discretion of the court to dismiss with or without prejudice has probably the most extensive legislative history of any part of this law. The original Senate version provided for no prejudice. The original House version provided for prejudice in all cases. Indeed, the committee report argues strongly for such a provision. The House version was amended on the floor to provide for discretion. The flexibility thus provided, has strong subsequent legislative affirmation.

Dismissal for failure to meet deadlines is necessary but not automatic. The defendant must move for dismissal. Failure to do so prior to trial constitutes a waiver of the right to dismissal. The defense has the burden of proving a violation of a time limit; the prosecution has the burden of proving that any period should be excluded in calculating the running of time. Additional penalties for improper conduct of attorneys in relation to this law are provided by Sec. 3162b.

Special interim limits effective from 1 October 1975 to 1 July 1979 are established for detained persons held in detention solely because they are awaiting trial, and for released persons awaiting trial who have been designated by the government attorney as being of high risk.* The special interim limits have given rise to the most important litigation under the law thus far.[7] Considerable confusion has occured as to the conditions under which time may be excluded. The result has been a call for amending the law to specifically apply the exclusions applicable in other sections of the statute.

Trial of such persons must commence within ninety days of detention or designation, and sanctions exist:

1. Where neither counsel is at fault: Automatic review by the court of conditions of release, applying the principle that no such detainee shall be held in custody pending trial for more than 90 days.

2. Where a designated releasee has intentionally delayed trial: An order of the court modifying the non-financial conditions of his release, to assure his appearance for trial.

No provision of this statute is to be interpreted as a bar to asserting 6th

---

*The "high risk" designation is not popular with the courts; only five districts have used it.

Amendment Rights.*

If a district court is unable to comply with a time limit due to the status of its court calendars, although existing resources are being efficiently utilized, the chief judge, after seeking the recommendation of the planning group, may apply to the judicial council of the circuit for suspension of the time limits. The judicial council of the circuit shall evaluate the capabilities of the district, and the availability of visiting judges both from within the circuit and outside it, and make recommendations. If it finds no remedy is reasonably available, it may apply to the Judicial Conference of the United States for a suspension not to exceed one year. Such suspensions apply only to the provisions governing the period from arraignment to trial, which may be increased up to 180 days. Limited provision exists for subsequent increases.

A major requirement of the Speedy Trial Act is the formulation of a sequence of plans for the implementation of the law. According to the provisions of the act, plans governing the trial or other disposition of offenses within each district must have been effected by 1 July 1976 for the period 1 July 1976 through 1 July 1978, and by 1 July 1978 for the period 1 July 1978 to 1 July 1979 and thereafter. Ideally, the resulting accelerated disposition of criminal cases provided for in each plan must be consistent with:

1. efficient law enforcement

2. fairness to the accused

3. efficient judicial administration

4. increasing knowledge of the proper functioning of the criminal law

5. avoidance of over, under, or discriminatory enforcement

6. nonprejudice to prompt disposition of civil litigation

7. avoidance of undue pressure as well as undue delay in the trial of criminal cases

In meeting these standards, the feasibility of several fundamental reforms in the criminal justice system must be considered. Paramount among these reforms are changes in the grand jury system and in habeas corpus and collateral attack. In considering the former, the problem is how to accomodate the Fifth

---

*If the more strenuous balancing test for 6th Amendment Speedy Trial rights outlined in *Barker* v. *Wingo* 407 U.S. 514, 1972 could be met, the discretion of the court to dismiss without prejudice would be lost (*Strunk* v. *U.S.* 412 U.S., 434, 1973).

Amendment requirement of indictment by the grand jury in capital or otherwise infamous crimes. Under the holding in *U.S.* v. *Moreland*,[8] this includes all offenses punishable by death, imprisonment in a penitentiary, or imprisonment anywhere at hard labor. In reforms touching habeas corpus and collateral attack, the requirement of the exhaustion of available state remedies[9] should prove useful. Other areas needing review are pretrial diversion, pretrial detention, the excessive reach of Federal criminal law, the simplification and improvement of pretrial and sentencing procedures, and appellate delay.

Each plan for the implementation of the act must contain:

1. a description of the time limits

2. procedural techniques, innovations, systems, and methods

3. methods for gathering and monitoring information and statistics

4. information concerning the implementation of the time limits and other objectives of this section including:

    a. the incidence and reasons for, requests for, or allowances of, time beyond the statutory (or district) standard

    b. the incidence and reasons for periods of delay permitted to toll the running of time

    c. the nature and incidence of, and reason for, the invocation of sanctions or failure to invoke them

    d. new timetables set as a result of extensions

    e. the effect of time limits and sanctions on criminal justice administration including effects on: prosecution, defense, courts, corrections, costs, transfers, appeals

    f. effects on, incidence and length of, as well as reasons and remedies for pretrial detentions

    g. identity of types of cases which because of special characteristics require special treatment

    h. incidence and length of extentions on indictments due to failure of grand jury to be in session

5. Information and statistics covering but not limited to:

    a. time between arrest and indictment, indictment and trial, conviction and sentencing

    b. the number of matters presented to the U.S. Attorney for prosecution, the number prosecuted and not prosecuted

    c. the number of matters transferred to other districts or states for prosecution

    d. the number of cases disposed of by trial, and by plea

    e. breakdown of dispositions into nolle prosequi, dismissal, acquittal, conviction, diversion, or other disposition

    f. number of defendants and days in preadjudication, custody, and at liberty

6. Rule changes, statutory amendments, and appropriations necessary to carry out the plan

7. Recommendations on reporting forms, procedures, time requirements, and personnel responsibilities for the General Plan rests with the Planning Group. The district court clerk will compile all information and statistics.

Comparison of the time span of criminal cases pending, not involving fugitive defendants, between 1975 and 1976, shows a 29.6% reduction. The reduction is greatest in the 6-12 months bracket (36.9%), least in the over two year bracket (7.2%).[10] This reduction, though impressive, presumably contains most of the more easily achieved results. Further reductions can be expected to be more difficult. Moreover, if the interests of justice are not laws, particularly regarding the indictment to arraignment stage, exclusions from the interim time limits, and delegation of powers to U.S. Magistrates, is imperative.

REFERENCES

1. 407 U.S. 514, 1972.

2. House Report No. 93 - 1508.

3. Administrative Office of the United States Courts, *Report on the Implementation of Title I and Title II of the Speedy Trial Act of 1974* (Washington, 1976), p. 20.

4. *Ibid.*, pp. 21-22.

5. House Report No. 93 - 1508.

6. Administrative Office of the United States Courts, p. 21.

7. *U.S.* v. *Tirasso* 532 F. 2d 1298 (9th Cir. 1976); *U.S.* v. *Masko* N 76 Cr. 15, (W.D. Wis. 1976), and *U.S.* v. *Mejius* No. 76 Cr. 164, (S.D. N.Y. 1976).

8. 258 U.S. 433, 1922.

9. 28 U.S.C. sec. 2254b.

10. Administrative Office of the United States Courts, p. 9.

BAIL-BOND IN A CHANGING ERA
OF CRIMINAL JUSTICE
William G. Broome and William Banks Taylor

American case law of the past forty years has drifted slowly but steadily towards the realization of an all-important but ill-defined priority of the nation's founding fathers: due process of law. Often this drift has pitted hallowed traditions and institutions against newly emerging procedural rights. The result has been administrative chaos, unprecedented bickering, dramatically increased expenditures, and documented claims of escalating inefficiency within the criminal justice system. Few reasonable persons doubt, however, that the clarification of the Due Process Clause of the Fourteenth Amendment is long overdue, that this clarification is well worth the price of implementation, and that the process of clarification has hardly begun. Among the institutions and traditions which will be unable to withstand the assault is the American application of bail-bond.

The concept of bail developed in medieval England for the very practical reason that pre-trial detention was unrealistically lengthy and therefore expensive under a feudal judiciary based on traveling justices. Originally the shire-reeve was delegated the authority to release prisoners on their own surety if they were landed, or more commonly, on the surety of a landed third person. If the prisoner failed to honor the terms of his release, the forfeiture of his land or the land belonging to the third party satisfied the shire-reeve and the Crown, thus guaranteeing the triumph of "justice".

The termination of the shire-reeve's judicial function threw the administration of bail into the hands of the justice of the peace. Significantly, feudal justices were required by law to own a considerable amount of land, and bail therefore became a profoundly satisfactory medium through which the landed classes cooperated to deliver the bodies of the landless for trial. The land-lord obtained the release of his serf by posting surety in land, continued to profit from the labor of the grateful defendant, and all the while knew that the police power of the state stood as his ally in the unlikely event of flight by the serf.

Because each shire had several justices, this development also increased the use of bail, and common law rules defining bailable offenses developed over the years. Generally, the character of the accused, the charge against him, and the quality of evidence served as criterion; but in few cases indeed were those who had no stake in the land admitted to bail. Like many other English legal traditions, therefore, bail evolved as a concept peculiarly geared to the socio-economic structure of feudalism. Land and captive labor were the common denominators.

Abuses in English bail administration were not regarded as such so long as the landed classes were not abused by the practice. During the political struggles of the seventeenth century, however, it became increasingly clear that bail could be used to immobilize men of land, rank, and fortune as effectively as it had traditionally immobilized serfs. Accordingly, one of the results of the "Glorious Revolution" was the first restriction on the use of bail. After feeling the lash of Tory justice for years, the triumphant Whigs of 1689 banned "excessive bail" in the tenth article of the famous Bill of Rights.

In similar fashion, many colonists in the New World complained of the political abuse of bail administration by English jurists, and the subject became a bone of contention between Federalists and Anti-Federalists during the struggle for ratification of the Constitution of the United States. As a result, the Eighth Amendment to the Federal Constitution states bluntly that "Excessive bail shall not be required . . . ."

Notwithstanding this common heritage, the subsequent development of bail administration in Great Britain and the United States has produced wide differences in its contemporary application. Of enormous importance is the fact that English law has never regarded bail as a *right* of the accused, but instead as a discretionary privilege under judicial control. While the advantages of pre-trial release to the accused are acknowledged by English jurists, there never has been serious legal conflict on the *purpose* of bail. It exists to allow temporary freedom in those cases where the probability of the accused appearing for trial is established to the satisfaction of the judiciary; it is a legal privilege, not a legal right.

The arbitrary nature of this feudal judicial privilege was tempered by the provisions of the Magistrates' Court Act of 1952, which established the authority to grant bail and the limits on that authority. Under its provisions police are allowed discretionary but narrowly defined power to grant bail in cases where an arrest has been made without a warrant and when the arrestee cannot be brought before a magistrate within a reasonable period. This type of bail requires the suspect to return to the police station within a given period of time.* Magis-

---

*The pros and cons of this practice cannot be discussed meaningfully in the absence of a sound understanding of the considerable differences in British and American police organization and administration.

trates, of course, are also authorized to grant bail. However, the decision to release the accused is made only after a review of the totality of the circumstances involved--economic, social, and legal. If the nature of the charge and the social status of the accused do not establish a probability of appearance for trial, financial surety *based on the financial resources of the accused* may be required to establish probability. Accordingly, in many cases there is no requirement for the posting of cash or property as collateral, and in those cases in which collateral is deemed necessary, the amount of surety is usually determined by the ability of the accused to pay.[1] In this manner Great Britain has preserved the common law tradition without its feudal connotations, and also realized the provision of the Bill of Rights which bans excessive bail.

Over two hundred years of independence has seen the administration of bail in the United States take an entirely different route. The American Revolution was a repudiation of feudalism, and the republican mania which seized the new nation during the last decade of the eighteenth century damaged many ancient legal traditions while failing to provide workable alternatives. Among these was common law bail administration. Though the Federal Constitution did not alter the common law administration of bail, the long-debated Judiciary Act of 1789 provided that "upon all arrests in criminal cases, bail shall be admitted, except where the punishment may be death." This apparent concession to prevailing notions about the "Rights of Man" was a significant departure from English practice, for it established bail as a legal right in non-capital cases.

Unfortunately, when combined with several factors peculiar to America, this rather flippant bestowal of right threatened to subvert the traditional function of bail. The most fundamental problem stemmed from the American rejection of feudalism. No longer could the courts look to landlords for surety in cases involving the indigent because, with the noteworthy exception of most Negroes, American laborers were free, expected to fend for themselves, and of comparitively small value to those who employed them. Then, too, the absence of the restrictions which the feudal system had placed on the mobility of the indigent often pitted the right to bail against the common sense of the American bench. This problem was acute due to the presence of the American frontier, which provided the accused with an excellent opportunity for successful flight to avoid prosecution. Finally, the pitiful state of law enforcement gave the courts little hope of apprehending a defendant who decided to flee. All this added up to considerable judicial confusion.

As a result of this conflict between right and practicality, a demand arose for an agency to assume the function of the feudal landlord in cases involving the indigent. This demand was supplied by the professional bail-bondsman. In return for an unrefundable cash premium paid by the accused, the bondsman agreed to stand as financial surety to the court that the accused would appear at the specified time and place for trial. Failure to honor this promise held the bondsman liable to the court in the full amount of the bail. To protect his interest, therefore, the bondsman frequently required property collateral from his client in addition to the usual fee of ten percent of the bail.

Predictably, the spirit of feudal bail administration passed quickly to this peculiarly republican application of the common law tradition. It became standard practice for the bondsman to establish his office close to the jail so as to provide quick service, and the bondsman rapidly established himself as a vital cog in the machinery of American criminal justice. Unfortunately, he just as rapidly established himself as an American businessman, a fact which cast a dark shadow across the Fourteenth Amendment. To be sure, the function of the bondsman enabled the courts to grant the accused an abstract right to bail. However, the bail-bond system made the bondsman--not the court--the principal determiner of a defendant's freedom, and the right to bail came to be guaranteed *only if the defendant could meet the terms of the bondsman.* Thus, with a wink from the bench, the indigent were reduced to the state of serfdom upon which feudal bail administration had depended, and the bondsman assumed the paternal but hardly disinterested function of the feudal landlord.

RIDING THE FUEDAL HORSE

Understandably, perhaps, the federal courts have largely ignored the constitutional issues surrounding bail-bond, and today the legal status of the practice is as vague as it is dubious. In 1912, the United States Supreme Court was apparently unabashed in ruling that the bondsman's interest in producing the body of the principal in court was extra-legal, impersonal, and wholly pecuniary.[2] However, in 1951, in the case of *Stack* v. *Boyle*,[3] the High Court reviewed precedent, attempted to develop a correspondingly logical defense of the bail system, and promptly ran aground.

Interestingly, the opinion rendered in *Stack* placed far more emphasis on the right of the accused to bail than on the utility of bail in delivering the body of the principal to trial. As a departure from both common law and practicality, this construction assured chaos. The opinion pointed out that from the passage of the Judiciary Act of 1789, federal law had unequivocally provided that a person arrested for a non-capital offense "shall be admitted to

bail". "This traditional right to freedom before conviction", wrote Justice
Jackson, "permits the unhampered preparation of a defense, and serves to prevent the infliction of punishment prior to conviction." Moreover, the opinion
of the court made it clear that, although some defendants may be more likely
to take flight than others, speculation on the probability of flight did not
justify the denial of bail in non-capital cases:

> Admission to bail always involves a risk that the accused will
> take flight. This is a calculated risk which the law takes as
> the price of our system of justice.

Apparently, however, the court was unwilling to demand such a price of the system of justice, for it ruled that "The right to release before trial is con-
ditioned upon the accused's giving adequate assurance that he will stand trial."
In effect, therefore, the court spoke double-talk and dodged the serious constitutional issue at hand. It forgot that rights are meaningless without clearly
established principles and procedures of operation, and it ignored the fact
that either the accused or the State had to be given priority before the interests
of either could be served. Sadly, the court upheld the abstract right to bail;
it closed its eyes to the realities of bail administration; and it then, in
effect, maintained absurdly that the right of the accused to bail was no more
substantial than his ability to meet the terms of a private businessman who existed to exploit him.

Of equal concern is the repeated assumption of the United States Supreme
Court[4] that the threat of the forfeiture of bail is an effective deterrent to
flight under the professional bail-bond system. Undoubtedly, this was true in
feudal England. Today, however, the only party who stands to lose money by
the failure of the accused to appear in court is the bondsman, for the money
paid by the defendant to obtain the bond is lost in any event.

Also disconcerting is the failure of the federal courts to give meaning
to the clause of the Eighth Amendment which bans excessive bail. To be sure,
in requiring that the accused post only ten percent, professional bail-bondsman
often have served to inflate the amount of bail set by the courts. In large
part, this accounts for the considerable difference in the amount of bail set
by English and American judges. Yet, while ruling that judges were not "free
to make the sky the limit" in setting an amount "reasonably calculated to hold
the accused individual for trial", *Stack* failed to consider the reasons why
judges felt obliged to make the sky the limit. Indeed, so ill-developed is
this clause of the Bill of Rights that it was not until 1963 that a United
States Circuit Court was forced to *take it for granted* that the federal excessive

bail provision applied to state and federal prisoners alike.[5]

This confusion on the part of the federal courts has allowed the separate states such a degree of latitude that the much-ballyhooed right to bail has been seriously compromised. At the present time, thirty-nine states* guarantee the right to bail in non-capital cases. Four states** limit the power to deny bail to cases of treason and murder. Three states*** grant an absolute right to bail only in misdemeanor cases. And four states**** allow judges almost complete discretion, thus following both common law and contemporary English construction.

In defense of the courts, one must note that distinctly practical reasons for the retention of the professional bail-bondsman have been advanced. Possibly the most seductive of these has been the contention that the bondsman is an agent whose financial interests are bound to the interests of the judiciary. Not only does the bondsman spare the state a most demanding administrative burden, it is argued; he also is an agent who, at his own expense, complements the police power of the state by tracing and taking into custody those who have fled from justice.

A closely related argument comes with the fact that the peculiar status of bondsmen has allowed the courts to give them police powers which are constitutionally denied formal law enforcement officers. Bondsmen enjoy virtual immunity from the legal procedures associated with the processes of arrest and extradition. In *Taylor* v. *Taintor*,[6] the Supreme Court of the United States bestowed upon the bondsman the same privileges that England's feudal lords enjoyed in bail administration involving their serfs:

> (The sureties) whenever they choose to do so may seize him and deliver him up in their discharge; and if this cannot be done at once, they may imprison him until it can be done . . . . They may pursue him to another state; may arrest him on the Sabbath, and, if necessary, may break and enter his house for that purpose. The seizure is not made

*Alabama, Alaska, Arizona, Arkansas, California, Colorado, Connecticut, Delaware, Florida, Hawaii, Idaho, Illinois, Iowa, Kansas, Kentucky, Louisiana, Maine, Minnesota, Mississippi, Missouri, Montana, New Hampshire, North Dakota, Nevada, New Jersey, New Mexico, Ohio, Oklahoma, Pennsylvania, Rhode Island, South Dakota, Tennessee, Texas, Utah, Vermont, Washington, Wisconsin, and Wyoming.

** Indiana, Michigan, Nebraska, and Oregon.

*** Georgia, Maryland, and New York.

**** Massachusetts, North Carolina, Virginia, and West Virginia.

by virtue of new process. None is needed. It is likened to
the rearrest by the sheriff of an escaping prisoner.

This right actually supercedes the rights of the states and becomes the
right of the surety in a contractural sense. *In re Van der Ahe*[7] adds: "Needing no process, judicial or administrative, to seize his principal, jurisdiction does not enter into the question." This elevates the custodial authority of a professional bondsman to a position superior to either the judicial
or executive authority of one state over another. A practical consideration
indeed!

Yet another argument supporting the professional bail-bondsman is usually
advanced in the form of a question: "Where else would an indigent man accused
of committing a crime secure surety for the court?" Assuming that the states
will be as reluctant to adopt English theory on bail administration in the
future as they have been in the past, this is no mean question. Consequently,
for years the bondsman has successfully represented himself as a struggling
entrepreneur, a public servant, and a friend of the poor and unfortunate in
their hour of need.

Several of the arguments put forward in defense of the professional
bondsman are worth consideration in a practical (as opposed to a legal) context. Others are highly suspect. And still others are nonsense. First, so
long as the provisions of common law, the Eighth and Fourteenth Amendments to
the Federal Constitution, and the Judiciary Act of 1789 remain unclarified
on the function of bail, it can be argued that the bondsman performs a vital
service. Even on those terms, however, there are those who question his
usefulness. For example, in 1970, a committee of the Illinois Legislature made
the following points about the bondsman's extra-legal police function:

> As to the value of bondsmen being responsible for the ap-
> pearance of accused and tracking him down and returning him at
> the bondsman's expense - the facts do not support this as an
> important factor. While such is accomplished occasionally with-
> out expense to the county, the great majority of bail jumpers
> are apprehended by the police of this and other states. Since
> bail jumping is now a distinct and separate crime, and with the
> nation-wide exchange of information between law enforcement
> agencies and the F.B.I., the average bail jumper has little
> chance of escape. The facts show that most of them are re-
> captured in this state, and even in the same county where they
> are to appear.[8]

These are arguments worth considering. Granted, American history confirms the
utility of both professional bondsmen and bounty hunters as extra-legal police.
The American frontier, however, is but a memory, and cooperation among formal

police organizations is good and getting better with the expenditure of every federal dollar. Consequently, a prop which has traditionally supported the bondsman is sagging badly.

There is also reason to suggest that the professional bail-bond system promotes crime among those who are granted bail. When freedom is obtained through bail-bondsmen, the accused is primarily under obligation to the bondsman for his freedom, instead of to the court. This state of vassalage, of course, inclines the accused to stay on good terms with the bondsman and to pay his bond payments promptly, for the bondsman may terminate his freedom and return him to jail at any time. Not only does this place the accused in a vulnerable and legally dubious position before a private businessman; it also puts enormous pressure on the accused to raise money *come what may*. Common among law enforcement officials are accounts of criminals who were arrested in bondsmen's offices while making payments from the proceeds of crimes committed within the previous few hours.

Equally disturbing is the corrupting influence of the bail-bond system. Clearly, it is organized and operated in a manner which creates opportunities for abuse and provides almost irresistible temptations for illegal profits at all levels of the criminal justice system. Documented practices include policemen hired by bondsmen to arrest defendants who jump bail, desk clerks and jail officials who receive a commission for each arrestee they refer to a bondsman, process servers who are paid by bondsmen to avoid immediate arrests of indicted clients, and a requirement by a policy game operator that a condition for employment as a runner or collector was to agree to a contract for bail-bond service to insure quick release if arrested. The list goes on to include standing arrangements between small time violators such as prostitutes, floating gambling rings, bookmakers, and the like. Not related to personal financial gain is the still disgusting practice of some magistrates and judges imposing unreasonably high bail to give the accused a "taste of jail" or to attract favorable public attention in cases of publicly abhorred crimes. A New York City bar report of 1964 contained a list of abuses including the frequent requirement by bondsmen that particular defense attorneys be selected. Kickbacks by attorneys to bondsmen were common.[9]

Finally, the hypocrisy which shrouds the notion that bondsmen stand as public servants and friends of the downtrodden is chimerical, for the notion is founded on nothing but the disarray of American Law. The fact is that the bondsman, like the feudal landlord before him, has a great stake in this brand of paternalism. A sense of civic responsibility may creep into the transaction, but never at the expense of ten percent of the bail backed by one hundred per-cent collateral. "If a person comes in and I don't know him or his lawyer," notes a New York bondsman, "we look for collateral; if they don't have it, we don't bother with them."[10] It has been observed that capitalism's greatest weakness lies in the fact that it has no heart. To say the least, it seems paradoxical to base a crucial aspect of due process on such an institution.

It becomes increasingly clear that the last bastion of the professional bail-bond system lies in the political punch inherent in the wealth it gener-ates. Today's bondsmen are engaged in a very lucrative operation supported by long-standing statutory incentives. The capital required for licensing is miniscule in comparison to the bondsman's potential income. The bondsman's fees, if compared to sales tax or interest on short term loans, are positively exorbitant. And bondsmen ply their trade under almost ideal arrangements with the courts. Special arrangements for the bondsman to pay forfeitures range from a ten day "grace" period in Florida to ninety days in New Jersey. Even after forfeiture payment is made, the amount is usually remitted upon producing the defaulter. Florida gives the bondsman up to two years to produce the body of the accused without financial penalty, and New Jersey allows four years. Not surprisingly, the Surety Association of America reports that losses from bond forfeiture among all bail-bond companies are less than 2.4 percent.[11] As a result, this legally dubious but financially rewarding feudal enterprise is protected by a powerful lobby generally supported by bondsman association mem-bers from the various states.

CRACKS IN THE FEUDAL ARMOR

Serious interest in bail reform began to develop in the 1920's, and several independent studies were conducted at that time by legal scholars across the country. These and subsequent studies produced a normative body of truth which caused the first cracks to appear in the feudal armor of the professional bail-bondsman.

A very comprehensive study of the bail system in Chicago was conducted by Arthur Lawton Beeley in 1927. Beeley analyzed the procedures for granting bail and reported some very shocking statistics. He found that the system operated basically on a "station-house" schedule related to the offense with little or no regard for the social status of the accused. Release on personal recog-nizance was permitted in only five percent of the cases studied, and these were all for minor offenses. Bail-bondsmen held the key to release, with the result that twenty percent of the accused remained in jail awaiting trial simply because they could not raise the fee necessary to pay the professional bondsman. Many of those so detained were released without trial in a month or two.

The study also pointed out that ninety percent of the unsentenced jail population had lived in Chicago for over a year, that seventy percent had families there, and that fifty percent had no record of previous convictions. Beeley offered three recommendations:

(1) greater use of the summons to avoid unnecessary arrests,

(2) a Constitutional Amendment to permit denial of bail to hardened offenders, and

(3). the inaugeration of fact-finding investigations so that bail determinations could be tailored to the individual.

The last of these recommendations goes to the heart of the system. This principle would place reliance for appearance on the individual's reputation, place and length of residence, family and friends, and employment. If these matters indicate a reliability factor assuring appearance in court at the appointed time, there is little or no justification to apply a bail-bond.[12]

A comprehensive study of the administration of bail in Philadelphia was conducted in 1954 by a group of law students at the University of Pennsylvania under the direction of Professor Caleb Foote. Their findings paralleled many of the Chicago discoveries. Two-thirds of the bail cases reviewed showed that bail was set in the station-house with no investigation beyond the charges except the identification of name, address, and occupation. Judges seldom entered into the investigation. When they did, it was not to determine the advisability of granting bail, but instead to set bail at a level capable of denying the accused a reasonable opportunity for freedom. In serious offenses requiring a magistrate's intervention, an average of five days was spent in jail by those awaiting trial.

The detention of accused persons without benefit of bail in Philadelphia produced some frightening statistics. Fifty-two percent of those who were eventually released on bail were not convicted. And of those convicted, the ones who had been denied bail got prison terms two and one-half times more often than those who had been granted bail. It became increasingly evident that denying bail resulted in not only prejudicial incarceration prior to trial, but also a longer sentence. If the legal implications of these findings did not impress officialdom, the financial implications did. Foote concluded that unnecessary detention cost the city $300,000 per year.

The Philadelphia study concluded with three recommendations:

(1)   use of more releases on personal recognizance,

(2)   a statute to penalize failure to appear as a criminal offense, and

(3)   lowering the standard amounts of bail.[13]

Two important studies were made of the bail system in New York City. The first was conducted under the guidance of Professor Foote in 1957,[14] and the other in 1963, by the Judiciary Committee of the New York Assembly.[15] The latter concentrated its investigation into the practices and procedures of the unified Criminal Court of the City of New York.

Among the critical remarks of this investigation was the observation that a "large segment of the Bench and the Criminal Bar had forgotten - or never really learned - *that the only permissible function of bail is to assure reappearance.*" It further concluded that the bail hearings were limited to facts concerning the alleged offense or the accused's criminal record, and completely disregarded personal qualities of the defendant that may have indicated he was a good risk. The committee also reported they had found evidence that some judges used bail to give defendants a "taste of jail".

One important conclusion of the committee, which offers further corroboration to other independent studies, was that during the period of their study (1963) forty-five percent of the city's prison population was made up of pretrial detainees. The cost of detaining this large number of prisoners was in excess of $5,000,000 per year!

The Junior Bar Section of the Washington, D.C. Bar Association made a cursory study of bail in the District of Columbia in 1962. In analyzing 250 consecutive bail cases on the docket of the United States District Court they found that only ninety-seven of 285 eligible defendants posted bail. The remaining 188 (two-thirds of the total) spent all their time from arrest to trial in jail. Again, as in previous independent studies elsewhere, evidence from this study clearly showed a much higher incidence of convictions and a lower incidence of probation for those detained as compared to those released on bail. The reasons offered for this included the inability of accused persons to assist in the preparation of a defense, the increased difficulty of locating witnesses, the promotion of speedier trials, and the adverse effect on the jury produced by seeing the defendant entering the courtroom from the jail escorted by a marshall.[16]

This study played a major part in other investigations which ultimately resulted in the passage of three very significant acts in the Federal Congress. The first of these was Public Law 89-465, an act to revise existing bail prac-

tices in courts of the United States, popularly referred to as the Bail Reform
Act of 1966. This act established the statutory right for release on personal
recognizance or on unsecured bond in an amount specified by a judicial officer.
Of interest is the stipulation that the magistrate can deny bail if he feels
that it will not assure the appearance of the person as required.

The magistrate is permitted judicial discretion in making this decision,
but he is bound by further provisions of the act to impose as small a restriction
on the person's liberty as is consistent with a reasonable assurance of his
appearance. In making his determination of conditions for release, the magistrate is required to take into account the nature and circumstances of the
offense, the weight of the evidence against the accused, family ties, employment, financial resources, character, mental condition, length of residence
in the community, record of prior convictions, and record of previous reliability in appearing in court.

In the event the magistrate determines the need for imposing a cash or
surety bond, the amount of the bond is normally set at ten percent but may require a fully secured bond with collateral of solvent securities or cash. In
any event, however, the amount of surety required is deposited in the registry
of the court - not in the eager hands of a bail-bondsman. Violation of the
conditions of bail can lead to amended conditions by the court. Failure to
appear as required carries a potential penalty of $5,000 or not more than five
years in prison if the accused is charged with felony. In addition, the defendant may be fined the maximum allowable for misdemeanor charges, imprisoned
for up to one year, or both. This legislation virtually duplicated England's
Magistrates' Court Act of 1952.

A companion act was passed July 26, 1966, ad Public Law 89-519. It established the District of Columbia Bail Agency. This act levied the requirement
upon the bail agency to "secure pertinent data and provide for any judicial
officer in the District of Columbia reports containing verified information
concerning any individual with respect to whom a bail determination is made."
This applies to any person arrested in the District of Columbia, or any material
witness in any criminal proceeding in a court (in the District of Columbia) for
trial or pending appeal.

Inquiry also extends to intoxication offenses and traffic violations. The
procedure to be followed in obtaining the information for the court is clear:
interview the defendant, attempt to verify the information obtained by preference
to any other available sources, check the criminal records of the Metropolitan
Police Department for previous offenses, and render a report to the court. If

it desires, the agency can include a recommendation for release on personal
recognizance, personal bond, or other non-financial conditions; but no other
recommendations. Copies of the report are to be submitted to the appropriate
judicial officer, the U.S. Attorney, and the defense counsel for the accused.
The information contained in the report is to be used only for bail determination and otherwise handled as confidential information. The agency is
charged with the responsibility of preparing and submitting its report at the
earliest practicable time.

This act, in conjunction with the Bail Reform Act of 1966, creates a
system whereby the determination for the release of any person awaiting trial
or appellate hearing is made by a judicial officer based upon information
relative to the reasonable expectation of the defendant's likelihood of appearing in court as required. Taken together, the acts place this responsibility in the hands of individuals not having any financial interest in the
decision. The release of a large percentage of persons awaiting trial or
pending appeal has resulted in substantial savings to the public.[17]

The third statute emanating in connection with the bail system in the
District of Columbia is Public Law 91-358, passed July 29, 1970. This statute
amends and expands on the provisions of the public laws discussed above. Among
other provisions, it requires the D.C. Bail Agency to:

(1) supervise all persons released (under provisions of cited
     statute),

(2) notify persons released when to appear, and

(3) assist released persons in securing employment.

The law also requires a pre-trial detention hearing to determine that there is
"clear and convincing evidence" in regard to the defendant's pattern of behavior
which would serve to deny release. A provision is also included to permit and/
or provide counsel during these hearings, and to expand conditions applicable
to appeal to bail determinations.

In light of these developments, it is safe to say that the Federal Congress
has outlined a workable alternative to the professional bail-bond system. This
alternative gives the accused a legal right to pre-trial release under conditions
that favor the innocent. In addition, freedom is denied to recidivists, corruption encouraged by the professional bail-bond system is discouraged, and the
taxpayer is spared the burdensome costs incurred by the unnecessary detention
of a majority of accused persons.

The legal and financial advantages of this congressional action have not been ignored by all state legislatures. Action was taken to revise the rules of civil procedure by a committee of the Tennessee Legislature in 1975. Part of the committee's proposed reforms was a call for the adoption of "Rule 46" of the Federal Rules of Criminal Procedure, which incorporates 18 U.S.S. 3156, 3148, and 3149. Under this rule, the accused is presumed innocent until proved guilty, and it is established that, whenever possible, the accused will be released before trial. Along with this recommendation came several revisions through which the committee sought to implement reforms in the administration of bail-bond.

Under the proposed system, the accused would sign a bail-bond and deposit ten percent with the court. If the conditions of the bond were fulfilled by the accused, the court clerk would return ninety percent of the deposit to the accused and retain ten percent as an administrative fee. Fifty percent of this administrative fee would be submitted to the State to cover the expense of apprehending those defendants who fled to avoid trial. If the defendant forfeited his bail, a judgment *nisi* would be made against him for the full amount of bail. In cases where the defendant posts bond, complies with its terms, is convicted, and a fine and/or costs is adjudicated, the deposit would be used to pay the fine and/or costs.

Also under the plan was a stipulation allowing the defendant to meet the requirements of the bond by posting a deed of trust on real estate one and one-half times the value of the bond. All preparation and recording costs would be paid by the defendant. In the event the defendant complied with the conditions of the bond, the deed of trust would be released with the defendant paying the cost of the release.

It is clear that this proposal offered the State of Tennessee an opportunity to make direly needed changes in its archaic system of bail administration. It is also clear, however, that the proposal was compromised to such an extent as to draw criticism from both right and left. On the one hand, it did not seriously address the constitutional issues, only the practical ones. On the other hand, in broaching the practicalities of bail administration, it called for the State to assume a considerable administrative burden without providing adequate constitutional or financial justification. Of crucial importance was the timidity of the committee in addressing the future of the professional bail-bond system. The professional bondsman was not to be eliminated, only crippled by State competition. These weaknesses made the proposal extremely vulnerable under the fire of a powerful lobby, and the Tennessee Supreme Court omitted "Rule 46" from the proposed rules submitted to the Tennessee

General Assembly on January 28, 1976.[18]

Similar events transpired in Illinois when the Legislature attempted to eliminate the abuses of a professional bail-bond system under which the bondsman charged ten percent of the amount of bail, none of which was returned regardless of whether the accused satisfied bail conditions. Reform was attempted through a statute providing that the accused could obtain pre-trial release by depositing ten percent of the amount of his bail with the court clerk. As in the Tennessee plan, upon meeting the conditions of bail the accused was returned ninety percent of the deposit and the clerk retained ten percent to cover costs.

Ironically, while the old system had never sparked meaningful litigation, the reforming statute produced a class action originating in the Circuit Court of Saint Clair, Illinois. The plaintiffs based this contention on other Illinois statutes which declared that no charge could be imposed by the State in cases where the accused was released on personal recognizance or in cases where bail-bond was posted in full by cash, securities, or realty worth twice the amount of bail. In addition, the statute was attacked for permitting a court retention charge against a defendant who was ultimately found innocent.

These were strong arguments, and the class action was affirmed in favor of the plaintiffs by both the Illinois Supreme Court and the United States Supreme Court.[19] As in Tennessee, meaningful bail reform was checked in Illinois by compromise and the formulation of a half-measure. However, this decision set important precedent relative to state-managed bail-bond, and by implication it brought the entire superstructure of bail-bond under question.

Kentucky is perhaps the only state to confront both the constitutional and practical implications of bail-bond in a responsible manner. On February 10, 1976, her General Assembly passed House Bill 254. Section One of the act abolished the commercial bail-bond business, and Sections Two through Nine created or amended rules pertaining to the rights and conditions or pre-trial release.

The statute permitted the courts to grant release on personal recognizance, on unsecured bail-bond, or on any of several other conditions including third person custody, travel restriction, ten percent deposition bond, or cash/property bond. Limitations were placed on the imposition of bond. These limits took into account the nature of the offense, the criminal record of the accused, the anticipated behavior of the accused if bailed, and the financial abilities of the accused. A bond higher than the statutory limits of the potential fine and costs was specifically prohibited.

The statute placed the execution of bail-bond in the hands of the court clerk. Bond was limited to ten percent of the bail, but was never to be less than $10. When the accused satisfied all conditions of the bail, he was guaranteed a ninety percent refund of the deposit, with the court retaining the other ten percent but never less than $5.

A provision of the statute invited the Kentucky Supreme Court to prescribe by rule or order a uniform schedule of amounts of bail for designated misdemeanors and violations. Moreover, penalties were established for a defendant who willfully failed to appear in court or in any way failed to comply with the conditions of his release. Finally, the statute established that persons who violated any provision of the act which was not otherwise punishable by law or statute would be guilty of a Class "D" felony, and that each violation would constitute an additional offense. With a bold stroke, therefore, the Kentucky General Assembly assaulted the commercial bail-bond system and offered a distinctly practical and more constitutionally germane alternative.

Shortly after the passage of this historic act, litigation was initiated in Jefferson Circuit Court to test the constitutionality of several provisions. Directly challenged was Section One, which uncompromisingly dismantled the commercial bail-bond business. Not surprisingly, the suit was initiated by three bonding companies. With little ado, the court held that H.B. 254, as it related to the prohibition or abolition of the bail-bond business, was unconstitutional because it was "unreasonable and arbitrary", and thus in violation of both the Fourteenth Amendment and Section One of the Constitution of the Commonwealth of Kentucky.[20]

Undaunted, the Commonwealth Attorney and the Attorney General of the Commonwealth appealed the case to the Kentucky Supreme Court. With the issue revolving around the constitutionality of Section One of H.B. 254, the Plaintiffs argued before the Supreme Court that the Commonwealth could not legally abolish, through legislation under its police power, an entire business not inherently injurious to the public or demoralizing in its activities. Plaintiffs argued further that their business could be continued and regulated under existing statutes. Finally, they contended that H.B. 254 was an unreasonable act with no substantial public purpose.

The Commonwealth countered with the argument that the public interest in bail reform as provided in H.B. 254 outweighed the private pecuniary interest of the compensated surety constituted a reasonable exercise of the Commonwealth's police power.

The Supreme Court held[21] that the policy to be followed in matters affecting the public welfare was a legislative matter; and that if this involved the application of police powers, it should be applied as broadly and comprehensively as the demands of society make necessary. The opinion took cognizance of the evils and abuses of the practice of compensated surety inherent to the commercial bail-bond system, and the court reached back a century to cite precedent:

> Whilst it was evidently the intention of the framers of the Kentucky Constitution to secure prisoners the inestimable privilege of bail, it was not intended to declare the qualifications of the bail, but to leave to the lawmaking department the power, unabridged who should be deemed sufficient bail.

The court pointed out that the commercial bail-bond business was neither an ancient, honorable, nor necessary calling; but rather, that it was one whose evils had been tolerated because no better system had been provided. The court pointed out that in regulating certain other businesses, government entities could forbid activities and compel the public to use public facilities to the exclusion of private. And in reversing the trial court's decision, the Supreme Court of Kentucky responded to the appealant's plea that their business not be allowed to "die on the vine". The passage of H.B. 254 severed the life-sustaining cord from the respirator, observed the court, and this severence forced the professional bondsman to go "quickly and gently into that good night".

DELIVERING THE COUP DE GRÂCE

"If it is true that the quality of a nation's civilization can be largely measured by the methods it uses in the enforcement of its criminal law, then the American Bail System as it now operates can no longer be tolerated", wrote former Associate Justice Goldberg. "At best, it is a system of checkbook justice; at worst, a highly commercialized racket."[22] This opinion is shared by the American Bar Association. In a study of 1968,[23] the Association observed that the professional bondsman had become an anachronism serving no major purpose that could not be served better by public offices. And yet this feudal holdover remains largely intact in an age of legal history which has produced *Mapp, Escobedo, Miranda, Gault,* and a host of other judicial decisions that have served to make due process a largely definable aspect of American criminal justice.

When will the long-delayed coup de grâce be delivered? Clearly, no sooner than the legislatures of the separate states realize that not only constitutional considerations but also the interests of the state demand reform. Clearly, not before logic outweighs tradition for the sake of tradition; not before half-measures succumb to measures; and not before the seductive charm of the lobbyist falls before the majesty of the law.

How will the coup be delivered? Tennessee and Illinois have displayed the mechanics of failure, and Kentucky--endorsed by judicial review--has displayed the mechanics of success. In light of these precedents, certain truths become discernable, and a blueprint for effectual bail reform emerges. *Sine qua nons* appear to be:

1. Improved fact-finding mechanisms under the direction of the Judicial System to verify information relative to the defendant's employment, residence, family, character, and prior criminal record (if any).

2. A policy of quick release on personal recognizance in cases of misdemeanors and traffic offenses (not involving homicide), and felonies (excepting capital offenses) unless there is clear and justifiable evidence that the accused will attempt to flee to aboid court appearance as directed.

3. A policy and procedure of summons in lieu of arrest in all less serious offenses, both as a principle of justice and a means of avoiding the unnecessary costs of pre-trial detention. As an example, in the Federal System a summons may be used for any crime on the recommendation of the U.S. Attorney under Rule 4, or by a judge under Rule 7. All defaults on summonses in the Federal System in 1963 totaled forty-four.

4. Release to a third party. In many jurisdictions, and especially in juvenile cases where runaway flight is not uncommon, the release of a defendant to the supervisory custody of an attorney, minister, employer, friend, or close relative has worked very well. A large scale program has worked satisfactorily in Tulsa, Oklahoma involving release of a defendant to his attorney.

5. Day-time or supervised release. The loss of salary or even employment as a direct result of pre-trial detention is a most unfair punishment prior to conviction. The defendant is not only unjustly (and perhaps unconstitutionally) punished, but also his family suffers financial loss, injury to social prestige, and a lasting stigma even if the accused is subsequently found not guilty. Immediate release (without pre-trial arrest publicity) should become common practice whenever not contra-indicated by developed facts, so as to allow the uninterrupted employment of the accused. This can be accomplished in most cases by either day-time or supervised release programs.

6. Lower amounts of bail. The United States presents a most unenviable system of excessive bail that flies into the face of our Constitutional right against unreasonable bail. Experience does not support any proof that high or excessive bail adds any efficacy to insuring appearance of the accused at trial. The payment of the bail-bondsman's fee is lost from the defendant at the moment it is paid, so he has no more to lose. Under the Kentucky System, a cash amount is required almost as a last resort, and all but ten percent of the deposit required is refundable upon court appearance. Certainly this is a better incentive to appear. Bail should be set by a magistrate, or by a court appointed agent, at the absolute minimum amount appropriate to the circumstances.

In criminal matters, mankind has seldom succeeded in finding solutions which are at once economically feasible, socially productive, and morally acceptable. But surely we can do better in our administration of bail-bond.

REFERENCES

1. Delmar Karlen, *Anglo-American Criminal Justice* (New York: Oxford University Press, 1967), pp. 136-143. Note, "Bail: An Ancient Practice Reexamined", 70 *Yale Law Journal*, 966 (1961).

2. *Leary* v. *United States*, 224 U.S. 567, 575, 32 S. Ct. 599, 56 L. Ed. 889 (1912).

3. *Stack* v. *Boyle*, 342 U.S. 1, 72 S. Ct. 599, 96 L. Ed. 3 (1951).

4. *Bandy* v. *United States*, 81 S. Ct. 197, 5 L. Ed. 2d 218 (1960); *Pannell* v. *United States*, 320 F. 2d 698 (D.C. Cir. 1963).

5. *Pilkinton* v. *Circuit Court*, 324 F. 2d 45, 46 (8th Cir. 1963).

6. *Taylor* v. *Taintor*, 16 Wall. 366, 21 L. Ed. 287, 290 (1873).

7. *In re Van der Ahe*, 85 F. 959 (C. C. W. D. Pa. 1898).

8. *Illinois Annotated Statutes*, CF 38, p. 300 (Smith-Hurd, 1970).

9. "Bail or Jail", 19 *The Record* 11 (Jan. 1964).

10. *New York Times*, Dec. 22, 1961.

11. D.J. Freed, et al, *Bail in the United States: 1964*, (New York: Vera Foundation, 1964), p. 29.

12. Arthur Lawton Beeley, *The Bail System in Chicago*, (Chicago: Beeley and The Chicago Community Trust, 1927).

13. C. Foote, "Compelling Appearance in Court: Administration of Bail in Philadelphia", 102 *University of Pennsylvania Law Review*, 1031 (1954).

14. C. Foote, "A Study of the Administration of Bail in New York City", 106 *U. Pa. Law Rev.* 693 (1958).

15. New York State Assembly Judiciary Committee, *Bail . . . Special Investigation of Practices and Procedures in the Criminal Courts of the City of New York*, Leg. Doc. No. 37, ch. 3 (1963).

16. District of Columbia Junior Bar Association, *The Bail System of the District of Columbia*, (Jr. Bar Sect., D.C. Bar Association, 1963).

17. J. Freed, pp. 30, 40-42.

18. Letter to the authors from Robert E. Kendrick, Tennessee Deputy Attorney General, State of Tennessee, September 8, 1976.

19. *Schilb* v. *Kuebel*, 404 U.S. 357, 92 S. Ct. 479, 30 L. Ed. 2d 502; reh den. 405 U.S. 948, 92 S. Ct. 930, 31 L. Ed. 2d 818 (1971).

20. *Stephens* v. *Bonding Association of Kentucky*, 538 S.W. 2d 580, 581 (Kentucky 1976).

21. *Stephens* v. *Bonding Association of Kentucky*, 538 S.W. 2d 580, 583 (Kentucky 1976).

22. Ronald Goldfarb, *Ransom: A Critique of the American Bail System* (Ronald Goldfarb, 1965), preface.

23. ABA Project on Standards for Criminal Justice, *Pretrial Release, Tentative Draft 1968*, (New York: Inst. of Judicial Administration, 1968).

THE INVESTIGATION OF PUBLIC ASSISTANCE FRAUD
Vernon B. Wherry

INTRODUCTION

Our founding fathers believed that all men were created equal. Most Americans, similar to Abraham Lincoln, believe that involuntary servitude is abhorrent to our society. "The Great Emancipator" did something about the great problem of his time by freeing the slaves in the Confederate States in 1863. The several states did something about that same problem in ratifying the Thirteenth Amendment to the Constitution in 1865. Those acts of the nineteenth century were intended to purge our society of all forms of involuntary servitude for all times.

Today, in the twentieth century, we find ourselves confronted with yet another form of involuntary servitude, that of an economic nature. If not controlled, abuses of our welfare system will result in involuntary servitude in a more subtle and sophisticated form, but equally odious and contemptible. Any system which requires one segment of the population--the working people--to support another segment of the population--those who may be able to work, but won't--is nothing short of involuntary servitude. To the extent that one man is required to work one hour to support another man who won't work, though able to do so, the former is an economic slave to the latter, in violation of the spirit, if not the letter of the Thirteenth Amendment.[1]

Welfare fraud, or public assistance fraud as it is frequently referred, includes the receipt of monetary assistance or services through such Federal/ State programs as Aid to Families with Dependent Children, Foodstamps, and Medicaid to which the recipient is not entitled or greater than that to which the recipient is entitled.

This paper has been designed to (a) describe the magnitude of the problem, (b) illustrate what is being done to eradicate the problem, and (c) indicate how these successful results may be applied to other areas of fraud investigation.

The National Scene

According to U.S. Department of Health, Education, and Welfare statistics, approximately 116,700 cases reported by State public assistance agencies as involving a question of recipient fraud were disposed of by administrative action during fiscal year 1973.

For almost one-half (48.2%) of the cases disposed of by administrative action, a decision was reached that the facts were insufficient to support a question of fraud.

Of the 59,300 cases in which information was sufficient to support a question of fraud, 30,200 cases or 50.9% were referred to law enforcement officials for action; 17,700 cases were not referred; and 11,500 cases were reported to have been pending a decision as to referral to law enforcement officials.

Disposition of cases with sufficient facts to support a question of fraud per 1,000 cases opened for maintenance assistance increased in fiscal year 1973 over fiscal year 1972 as follows: total, 4.6% to 7.3%; adult programs (old-age assistance, aid to the blind, and aid to the permanently and totally disabled), 1.5% to 2.2%; and AFDC (Aid to Families with Dependent Children), 7.8% to 12.2%.

AFDC comprised less than one-half of the cases open for maintenance assistance but 85.1% of the cases involving questions of fraud disposed of during the year.

The number of cases disposed of by legal action totaled 25,000, an increase of 8,800 cases or 54.3% above the corresponding number in 1972; of the total, 9,900 cases were prosecuted, and the remaining 15,100 cases were disposed of without prosecution.[2]

According to U.S. Department of Agriculture figures, the number of people receiving food stamps jumped from 6.5 million in 1970 to 10.5 million in 1971; went to 12.4 million in mid-1973, and to 19.2 million in June, 1975. In some areas--Puerto Rico, for example--half of the population is receiving the stamp subsidies. Errors were found in 56.1% of cases looked into. Of these, 12.2% of households were really ineligible for stamps; 37.9% were issued too many or too few, and 6% were incompletely registered. Of the food stamps issued, 15.2% went to ineligible households. Among eligible households, stamp allotments were found to be 23.2% more than the amounts they were entitled to.

Judging by estimates of Government miscalculations--by both the Agriculture Department and the Department of Health, Education, and Welfare--some officials figure that nearly 1 out of 5 food-subsidy dollars is being issued improperly. That would put overpayments in the neighborhood of 800 million dollars during fiscal year 1974![3]

The Florida Situation

State Auditor General's Report No. 8057, dated October 23, 1973, revealed that 60.1% of 136,651 public assistance warrants issued to AFDC Program recipients during a three month period ending May 31, 1973, contained payment errors. Additionally, it was reported that a significant amount of potential welfare recipient fraud was contained in the 60.1% error rate. It was concluded for that period in those counties reviewed, that one out of every four warrants issued to AFDC welfare program recipients was obtained by apparent misrepresentation of facts by the recipients. This potential fraud accounted for approximately $2,559,446 for a three month period based upon fifteen (15) counties reviewed within the state.[4]

Audit Report No. 8207, dated June 24, 1974, revealed that a review of the food stamp program in 26 counties for the month of December, 1973, indicated that one out of three households who purchased food stamps for that month received all or part of their food stamps by what appeared to be misrepresentation of facts by the purchasers of the stamps as to their household's eligibility. The potential fraud rate of 34.8% indicated a projected dollar value of $668,017 for those households that purchased food stamps for the month of December, 1973, in the 26 counties reviewed![5]

Unique Aspects of Investigating Welfare Fraud Cases

The investigation of public assistance fraud matters poses difficulties unlike those of traditional criminal cases. Traditional crimes such as a homicide, a robbery, or a burglary involve one singular event and include the involvement and actions pertinent only to that specific act. For example, in homicide cases the corpus delecti (body of the offense) centers upon the victim, how the body got to its present state, what instrument or means was used to cause death, and the investigation is usually centered upon a singular crime scene in an attempt at determining the reason(s) for the act and the gathering of evidence in locating the perpetrator of the offense. In a crime such as this, there is no limit to the statute of limitations which is the maximum time period in which criminal charges must be lodged against the accused.

Public Assistance Fraud cases, on the other hand, often involve numerous corpus delicti and the statute of limitations is usually limited to a two year period prior to the date that the case is referred to the office of the State Attorney for prosecution. Acts of fraud are based upon the perpetrator signing a document in which he certified that the information pertaining to his eligibility is correct at the time of executing same and agrees to report any changes which will affect the amount of monetary assistance awarded him. Any act of omission (failing to fully disclose his accurate financial resources or income, for example) or commission (securing increased income after executing the document) is prima facie evidence of having committed fraud.

Investigation of welfare fraud is based almost solely on circumstances and is dependent upon entries made in the normal course of business as evidence.

Criminal intent must be contrived from a pattern or chain of events from which
is implied that the person knew their rights and responsibilities and failed to
carry them out, and thus knowingly and willingly, as a result of their failure
to carry out certain responsibilities, received or attempted to receive benefits
to which they were not justly entitled. Normal procedures call for the recipient to execute documents during a recertification process at least every six
months to remain eligible for continuing assistance, therefore one investigation
frequently involves four separate documents, each of which must be scrutinized
for intent to defraud.[6]

FRAUDULENT PRACTICES

By Recipients

Between 80% and 90% of all fraud cases uncovered in the State of Florida
relate to the improper reporting of income.[7] Non-reported income could include
earnings from employment by the recipient or a member of the household, income
derived from unemployment or workman's compensation by a member of the household, income received through child support payments or other contributions
made by the child's father, lump-sum payments as the result of insurance set-
tlements, sale of property, inheritances, pari-mutual winnings, rentals, divi-
dends or proceeds from the sale of stocks and bonds, military allotments, veteran's benefits, retirement benefits, cash assistance from other agencies, or
income derived from illicit enterprises such as prostitution or gambling.

Another major factor relating to the fraudulent receipt of welfare is the
underreporting of income as derived from the aforesaid sources. Many cases
have been uncovered in which the recipient of public assistance reports correctly her earnings from one employer and makes no mention of income derived
from a second job.

Another fraudulent practice committed by persons seeking assistance to
which they are not entitled includes improperly reporting deprivation of children. In these cases, the father may be reported to have deserted the household
or divorce proceedings purported to have taken place when in actuality the
father is continuing to live in the household or a planned separation was agreed
upon in order for the recipient to qualify for assistance.

Failure to correctly report household composition is yet another fraudulent practice. In cases such as these, the recipient will attempt to disguise
the actual number of children present in the home by adding children of friends,
neighbors, and relatives in the hope of increasing her monthly grant.

Finally, attempts are frequently made by recipients to receive additional assistance by under-reporting or non-reporting owned assets such as residences and other property such as land and automobiles, in addition to overstating their cost of living, rental, transportation, and child care expenses.

The foregoing are examples of how public assistance recipients attempt to receive benefits to which they are not entitled in the AFDC, Food Stamp, and Medicaid programs. A major fraud abuse committed within the Food Stamp program involves groups of persons who travel Florida's arterial highway system stopping in several food stamp offices each week and who purchase food stamps by using false identification and by providing false information at each office. Within the Food Stamp program, many investigations have successfully culminated in referring State employees to the appropriate authorities for converting stamps to their own use and for certifying and issuing stamps to friends and other persons who are not eligible. One Food Stamp Supervisor was found to have been providing food stamps to young females in payment for sexual favors which took place in the Food Stamp Office! Another worker was discovered to have embezzled some $9,000 in a 12-month period by juggling the official food stamp records.[8]

Aiding and Abetting

Persons charged with aiding and abetting recipients in the receipt of public assistance are considered principals under Florida law.[9] The means by which this is carried out are numerous. Any person within the recipient's household who affixes his signature attesting to the veracity of the recipient's statement of circumstances, knowing them to be false, has aided and abetted the client in receiving assistance to which they are not legally entitled.

Similarly, an employer who completes a verification of a recipient's earnings knowing that the amounts indicated on the form which are used to compute the client's grant are false is guilty of aiding and abetting. Public assistance workers who intentionally make commissions or omissions within a recipient's file resulting in the client receiving assistance greater than that to which they are legally entitled are aiding and abetting.

Initiating the legal process against those persons accused of aiding and abetting has a great deterrent effect. Often employers who complete earnings verification forms for recipients have, in their employ, many other public assistance recipients for whom they provide false information enabling the client to receive more assistance. From a practical standpoint, however, it is very difficult for an investigator to be able to prove that these persons knowingly and intentionally committed an act designed to defraud the State as opposed to making clerical errors and other miscalculations.

Providers

Vendors and persons authorized to provide health care for public assistance recipients are in a unique position to commit fraud. Included are providers of Medicaid services such as pharmacists, doctors, nursing homes and hospital staffs.

Under contractual agreements, these vendors are authorized by the State to provide medical services for qualified public assistance recipients and to submit scheduled costs periodically to the State for reimbursement. The amount of fraud and the regularity of commission is the subject of intensive review by agencies responsible for accountability in the Medicaid program. Only through a well devised system of audit review and inspection can legislation relating to such abuse be enforced.

In 1974, an Orlando, Florida, pharmacist was adding onto recipient's Medicaid cards sums of money for non-prescribed drugs and was billing the State excessively for several months prior to discovery and his subsequent conviction.

A Tampa, Florida, nursing home operator was convicted, in 1976, of improperly maintaining in-trust accounts involving patients of his nursing home. In this case it was discovered that the only person who had access to the account was the nursing home operator!

Allegations persist that medical doctors frequently overcharge the State for services provided to Medicaid recipients. Included among these practices are billing for non-provided services, duplication of services, and billing for services not actually required (e g , X-rays).

Due to the intricacies and individual guidelines established for each service provided, investigators encounter considerable difficulty in attempting to unravel potential overcharging by these vendors.

INVESTIGATION OF ABUSES

The success of any effort to reduce fraudulent practice by public assistance recipients is predicated upon legislative, executive, and judicial partnership which has as its goal the improvement of services and benefits to the genuinely needy by eliminating the greedy.

The State of Florida has implemented an agressive and highly effective system for detecting and prosecuting individuals who commit fraud in the receipt of money and/or benefits through State administered public assistance programs.[10]

The Division of Public Assistance Fraud

In 1972, Florida Legislature charged the Auditor General, a legislative officer, with the responsibility of investigating on his own initiative, eligi-

bility and payments in the Public Assistance, Food Stamp and Medicaid programs.
The Division of Public Assistance Fraud (DPAF) was created within the Officer
of the Auditor General to investigate and refer for prosecution cases of suspected fraud.[11] The Division has established eleven (11) field offices throughout the State of Florida to facilitate the investigation of welfare fraud
cases. These offices are located in Pensacola, Tallahassee, Jacksonville,
Gainesville, Orlando, Tampa, St. Petersburg, Fort Meyers, West Palm Beach, Fort
Lauderdale, and Miami. There are presently seventy-nine (79) investigative
positions within the Division of Public Assistance Fraud.[12]

The philosophy of DPAF is "low-key" and its members are not responsible
nor empowered to act as law enforcement agents of the State. They are an investigative body charged with the primary mission of ascertaining facts and
circumstances surrounding alleged fraud in the payments and receipt of monies
and/or benefits within state administered welfare programs. Investigators also
work closely with the State Attorney's Office, assisting them in obtaining
evidence, testifying in court, and discussing the intricacies of welfare policy.

The goal of the Division is to raise the level of benefits available to
legitimate clients by reducing the number of persons receiving assistance to
which they are not legally entitled.[13]

Welfare Fraud Statute

State Law: According to Section 409.325 of the Florida State Statutes,

> Whoever knowingly obtains, attempts to obtain, or aids
> or abets any person in obtaining or attempting to ob-
> tain, by means of a false statement or representation,
> by false impersonations, or by other fraudulent device,
> assistance or service to which he is not entitled or
> assistance or service greater than that to which he is
> justly entitled; or whoever willfully makes an unauthor-
> ized disposition of any food commodity . . . shall be
> guilty of a misdemeanor of the first degree . . .

Effective October 1, 1976, if the assistance or service obtained fraudu-
lently is of an aggregate value of $200 or more in any twelve (12) consecutive
months, the person is guilty of a felony in the third degree. Additionally,
provisions within the new legislation provide for misuse of public assistance
monies by recipients and contain similar penalties depending on the amount of
misuse within a twelve (12) month period.[14]

Income Verification System

The income verification system, developed by the Division of Public Assistance Fraud, was designed to match the wage files reported by employers to

the State of Florida, Department of Commerce, on a quarterly basis and earned by the recipients of public assistance with income reported by welfare recipients to the Department of Health and Rehabilitative Services.

When a social security number from the Department of Health and Rehabilitative Services file matches a social security number contained within Department of Commerce records, the name and employment earnings as well as other vital information will appear on a computer printout. In the event that the wages reported to DHRS by the recipient do not coincide with what the employer has reported to the Department of Commerce, the system then acts as an indicator of possible welfare fraud.

In addition to providing income derived from employment, the income verification system also includes income received by the client's household in the form of unemployment compensation and workman's compensation.

EVALUATION OF INVESTIGATIVE EFFORT

For purposes of evaluating the effectiveness of the Division of Public Assistance Fraud's effort in the investigation of welfare fraud, the activity of the Division for the period January 1, 1976, through June 30, 1976, will be analyzed.

At January 1, 1976, the Division had a total of 2,481 welfare fraud cases under active investigation. During the six-month period between January 1, 1976 and June 30, 1976, an additional 4.763 cases were assigned for field investigation, making a total of 7,244 cases under active investigation. Investigation was completed on 3.975 of these assignments, leaving 3,269 cases under active investigation as of June 30, 1976.

The 3,975 completed case assignments resulted in referral of 1,277 cases to the prosecutive authorities. The remaining cases (2,698) were not referred due to insufficient facts to warrant referral.

Referrals

The 1,277 cases referred for prosecution during the six-month period may be categorized as follows:

- Aid to Families with Dependent Children	1,047
- Food Stamp Program	221
- Non-recipient Cases	6
- Medicaid Program Providers (Vendors)	3
TOTAL	1,277 referrals

Included among the six non-recipient cases were three Department of Health and Rehabilitative Services, Food Stamp Program employees. Two of the three were suspected of falsely certifying persons as being eligible for food stamps. The third worker was suspected of being involved in embezzlement. This worker was accused of falsely preparing food stamp authorizations for purchases and then collaborating with the people who used the authorizations for personal gain.

The three State Medicaid Program providers (vendors) referred by the Division to prosecutive officials during the six-month period were two pharmacies in the Prescribed Medicine Program and one Nursing Home.

Prosecutive Action

During the described six-month period, the State Attorneys in 20 Florida Judicial Circuits took action on a total of 1,276 cases. These actions involved both prior period referrals and current period referrals.

Of the 1,276 cases, charges were brought on 1,180 of which 49 were nolprossed. The remaining 96 cases did not result in charges being filed. This reflects that 92% of the referrals made by the Division resulted in formal charges being filed.

During the same six-month period between January 1, 1976 and June 30, 1976, of the 1,128 cases which the State's Attorney had filed, 1,015 resulted in convictions for a 90% rate.

Of the 1,015 guilty verdicts handed down during the six-month period ending June 30, 1976, sentences imposed involved jail terms, probation, monetary fines, restitution, or a combination thereof.[15]

These impressive statistics detail the success of the Division of Public Assistance Fraud and reflect a tremendous savings to the taxpayers within the State of Florida. In addition, one cannot estimate the added preventative effect such a program has by deterring potential fraud recipients through vigorous investigation and prosecution.

CONCLUSION

This paper has attempted to show a practical method with a 'tool and technique' approach to the investigation of one aspect of fraud, that pertaining to public assistance. It is the author's contention that the same application may be made toward successfully investigating other areas of fraud by governmental agencies charged with this responsibility. Abuses are rampant in the Educational Assistance Program within the U.S. Veteran's Administration, the Vocational Rehabilitation Program, the Unemployment Compensation Program, and numerous other well-intended efforts designed at aiding individuals.

Governmental funding for these programs is not analogous to a bottomless well. Those responsible for overseeing budgets and various citizen's groups are increasingly calling for more accountability toward spending on such outreach programs. Agencies are being forced to meet several criteria, including control mechanisms, in order to become or remain eligible for participation.

Administrators in agencies providing monies and/or services to persons from public funds have the obligation to establish anti-fraud investigation units designed to eliminate those recipients who are not legally eligible to receive benefits in order to enable qualified persons to enjoy, fully, those provisions.

REFERENCES

1. Ross G. Tharp, "A View From the Bench" (paper presented at the meeting of the California District Attorney Association, Oakland, California, October, 1972, p. 1.

2. U.S. Department of Health, Education, and Welfare, National Center for Social Statistics, *Disposition of Public Assistance Cases Involving Questions of Fraud*, (Washington: Fiscal Year, 1973), p. 2.

3. U.S. News and World Report, "Food Stamps Out of Control?" September 1, 1975, pp. 12.13.

4. State of Florida, Office of the Auditor General, Division of Public Assistance Fraud, *Public Assistance Programs Administered by the Department of Health and Rehabilitative Services, Division of Family Services and Related Activities of the Office of the Auditor General, Division of Public Assistance Fraud* (Jacksonville: April, 1975), pp. 3-4.

5. Ibid.

6. State of Florida, Office of the Auditor General, Division of Public Assistance Fraud, *Manual of Field Investigations* (Jacksonville: 1976), Chapter IX, p. 3.

7. U.S. Congress, Senate, Subcommittee on Agricultural Research and General Legislation, Proposed Food Stamp Reform, Hearing, November, 1975 (Washington: Government Printing Office, 1976), p. 10.

8. Ibid., p. 64.

9. Florida, *State Statutes* (1976), Sec. 409.325.

10. U.S. Department of Health Education and Welfare, *Florida Welfare Fraud and Abuse System* (Atlanta: March, 1976), p. 1.

11. Florida, op. cit., Sec. 11.50.

12. State of Florida, Department of Health and Rehabilitative Services, Division of Family Services, *Assistance Payments Manual* (Jacksonville: 1972-76), p. 2.

13. State of Florida, Office of the Auditor General, *Manual of Field Investigations*, Chapter II, p. 2.

14. Florida, op. cit., Sec. 409-425.

15. State of Florida, Office of the Auditor General, Division of Public Assistance Fraud, *Activities of the Office of the Auditor General, Division of Public Assistance Fraud, for the Period January 1, 1976 through June 30, 1976,* (Jacksonville: August, 1976), pp. 2-4.

DISPOSITION OF PERSONS UTILIZING THE
INSANITY PLEA IN A RURAL STATE
Richard A. Pasewark and B. Wayne Lanthorn

There are few reported empirical studies concerned with the competency of
criminal defendants to stand trial,[1] and those dealing with the insanity plea,
the topic of the present paper, are even more limited. Surprisingly, in the
case of the NGRI plea, little information is available regarding the extent to
which it is employed and the degree of success once the plea is entered. For
example, Simon states that it is "generally estimated at about 2 percent for
criminal jury trials."[2] Yet, while her analysis of pre and post-Durham decision trials in the District of Columbia indicates that approximately .24% of
criminal defendants are found NGRI in the four years preceding Durham and 2.29%
determined NGRI in six years following its adoption, she is unable to report
the number of defendants entering the plea, because of trial procedures employed
in the district. Foster[3] erroneously reports that, in New York State during
the 1960's, there were but eleven successful NGRI pleas, a figure markedly divergent from the 294 cases found in New York during the period 1965-75 by the
senior author in a study currently in progress.

Matthews, reporting upon the American Bar Association study of the insanity
plea, remarks that in a four month period in Chicago and San Francisco in 1963,
there was but one NGRI plea in each jurisdiction. Each was to a charge of
murder and each proved successful. In a three-month period in the city of New
York, one unsuccessful plea was made to a homicide charge. In three and two
month periods in Detroit and Miami respectively no insanity plea was entered;
and, in a two month period in Michigan but one such plea was recorded. According to Matthews, the insanity plea was made but 464 times (1.3%) in 34,643
felony dispositions made by California courts during 1965. In 213 of these 464
cases, the plea was subsequently withdrawn. Another 56 cases were dismissed
or withdrawn from the court calendar. Thus, the 195 NGRI pleas remaining represented .53% of all felony dispositions. Of these, 109 were acquitted and 86
convicted. Unfortunately, because of California's bifurcated trial system in
which guilt is first established and responsibility considered at a secondary
trial, Matthews was unable to determine the number of persons actually acquitted
by reason of insanity.

Studies by Walling,[4] Quinsey, *et al*,[5] and Coone and Sikorski[6] are concerned
with individuals committed to mental health facilities following an NGRI adjudication and are therefore unable to provide data upon the extent of the plea

and its success.

The present study reports upon all 102 persons making the insanity plea in Wyoming during the two year period July 1, 1970 to June 30, 1972, a time frame chosen to allow adequate disposition of cases prior to the period in which data were collected.

In contrast to other investigations in which the insanity plea has been studied, Wyoming is a highly rural area. Approximately twice the size of Pennsylvania, Wyoming contains but 332,000 persons and has a density of 3.40 persons/square mile.[7] At the time of the study, Wyoming had two cities of about 40,000 people, one city of 25,000, and two towns of between 10,000 and 12,000 persons. The remaining populace were distributed fairly evenly throughout the state in towns of 2000 to 7000 persons and surrounding ranches and farms.

Essentially, in its law Wyoming adheres to the principles embodied in the modified McNaughton rule: (1) presence of mental disease, (2) presence of defective reason, (3) lack of knowledge of the nature or wrongness of the act, and (4) incapacity to refrain from the act.[8]

Typically, in Wyoming, the defendant who relies upon the insanity defense enters the tri-parte pleas: "not guilty", "not guilty by reason of insanity", and "not triable by reason of present insanity". Following such pleas, by law, the defendant is committed to the Wyoming State Hospital, or such other facility authorized by the trial judge, for a period not to exceed 60 days for determination of sanity.[9] In practice, however, all such cases are committed to the State Hospital, and thus the present study provides data on all persons in a given state who have made the insanity plea.

CHARACTERISTICS OF SUBJECTS

Of the 102 subjects, 98 were male, and four were female. Ages ranged from 18 to 68 with a mean age of 32.09 years. A surprisingly large number of the population were out of state residents. Thirty-one (30.30%) were non-residents, while 71 (69.61%) resided in Wyoming. Those who were residents lived in 18 of Wyoming's 23 counties.

The most frequently occurring marital status was married (42.16%), followed by single (27.45%), presently divorced (23.53%), and, widowed (6.86%). Of the 102 subjects, 69 had no dependent children; 17 had one child; six had two; four had three; two had five; and, one had nine. A comparison of subject's marital status with that of Wyoming's general population is revealing and suggests them to be a group characterized by difficulty in establishing and maintaining close

interpersonal relationships. Comparative statistics for the state's population in the same time period are: married (66.7%); single (27.0%); presently
divorced (3.9%); and, widowed (2.4%).

Educational level of the population ranged from two to fourteen years with
a mean of 10.11 years. Median years of educations completed was 11.01, and
the mode, 12.0 (35 cases). Median school years completed for the general
Wyoming population is 12.2.[10]

Employment records of subjects were quite marginal. Only 28.43% had a
history of continuous employment; 46.08% were unemployed sporadically; and
25.49% were chronically unemployed.

PREVIOUS CRIMINAL HISTORY

Of the 102 subjects, 63 (61.77%) had previous arrests. Of these, 44.12%
had prior convictions. (See Table 1.)

ALLEGED CRIMES

Alleged crimes were categorized using a three-fold classification: (1)
crimes against property (51.95%); (2) crimes against people (42.15%); and,
(3) crimes without victim (5.88%). The majority of subjects, 91 (89.21%),
were charged with only one crime at the time of observation. Table 2 contain
the listing of the specific primary crimes of which subjects were accused and
compares their alleged crimes with arrests and indictments among the general
Wyoming population. (See Table 2.)

From Table 2, it is obvious that all of the crimes of which subjects are
accused, excepting fraud, are over-represented in the insanity group when compared to the general distribution of arrests and indictments within the state.
Thus, for example, while check offenses represent but .31% of the total 26,567
felony arrests and 38% of 22,102 felony indictments in Wyoming, persons charged
with that crime comprise 15.69% of the NGRI group. Similarly, while rape and
homicide constitute .34% and .17% of Wyoming arrests and .35% and .15% of indictments, persons alleged to have committed these offenses make up 12.75% and
8.82% of the study population.

Of those crimes of which subjects are accused, there are certain criminal
charges to which a defendant appears more likely to enter the NGRI plea. For
example, of all homicide indictments in Wyoming, 26.47% of the defendants plead
NGRI; in the case of arson 20.00% make the plea; to check offenses 19.28%; and,
to rape 14.61%. Contrastingly, in fraud charges but .24% of those indicted
utilize the plea; to larceny .68%; to burglary 1.65%; to family and child offenses,

1.90%; and, to aggravated assault, 1.78%.

NGRI RATES

During the study period, there were 26,567 felony arrests in the state and 22,102 resulting indictments. Thus, the NGRI plea represented .38% of all felony arrests and .46% of felony indictments and the single NGRI court verdict represents an inconsequential proportion (.05%) of the 2021 felony cases acquitted or dismissed by the courts. These figures, however, probably represent an underestimation of the effectiveness of the plea. For it is seen that the percentage of dismissals and acquittals of the NGRI plea group (21.51%) far exceeds that of those persons indicted for felonies in Wyoming (9.14%). Essentially, it would appear that although but a single NGRI verdict resulted from the entered plea, other events and considerations were set in motion on behalf of the study group defendants which led to a different set of outcomes for this group as compared to those indicted persons not utilizing the insanity plea.

SITE OF ALLEGED CRIME

Although 18 of the state's counties accounted for one or more cases, three (Natrona, Laramie, and Carbon) contributed 53 (52%) of those committed to the State Hospital for observation. (See Table 3.)

UTILIZATION RATES

For each county, Table 3 presents the population; arrest rates per 10,000; and, a utilization rate. The utilization rate was computed by dividing number of NGRI pleas by number of arrests in a given county. As such, the derived utilization rates provide a comparative estimate of the extent to which the NGRI plea is employed in the 23 counties.

From Table 3, it is apparent that wide discrepancies prevail among counties as concerns employment of the NGRI plea. Thus, in Big Horn County, the NGRI plea is involved in 8% of arrested cases while in four counties it was never used in the two year study period. Rank order correlations suggest that use of the plea is not related to county population (rho=-.05) but that there is a negative association between county arrest rates and employment of the plea (rho=-.47). A possible explanation for this negative relationship, and one which we shall attempt to substantiate in a follow-up study being undertaken, is that as the justice system becomes encumbered by higher arrest rates, an unconscious adjustment is made to this situation by defense attorneys and/or jurists by a reduction in the proportion of NGRI pleas. Contrastingly, in those counties with lower arrest rates, and where "business is less brisk", judges and attorneys are more prone to explore more fully potential psychological and social factors that may have contributed to the defendant's alleged crime. A second hypothesis, and one for which supporting or rejecting data are not available in the present study, is that disparity in utilization rates results from some counties having particular attorneys who are more prone to encourage use of the plea by clients.

PROCESSING TIMES

A current goal in the administration of criminal justice is to ensure that the alleged criminal receives rapid processing through the justice system and an early verdict as to guilt or innocence.

Results indicate that the initial phases of legal action in the cases studied occurred comparatively swiftly. Forty-nine percent of the population were arrested within one day of the commission of crime; and, mean arrest time was 28.14 days. Similarly, processing time surrounding hospitalization for evaluation is consistently expedient. Average time from arraignment to hospital commitment was 4.53 days. Length of hospitalization was 32.77 days or about half the legally allotted 60 days.

Judicial actions taken following the hospital's disposition were the most lengthy and variable in terms of time. For example, the mean interval from hospital disposition to final court disposition was 87.25 days, nearly three months; and, the length of this interval contributed greatly to the mean of 172.91 days from the date of crime commission to final court disposition. As this time period is somewhat inflated by the inclusion of time periods during which the alleged criminal had yet to be apprehended, a more revealing interval, as a temporal measure of judicial processing, is time between arrest and final court disposition. This averaged 146.00 days. The period from arrest to hospital disposition is 58.24 days; whereas, the period from hospital disposition to court disposition, consumed 87.25 days.

EVALUATION RESULTS

Physical and neurological examination for all subjects, including EEG and spinal tap, were negative.

Table 4 presents the final psychiatric diagnosis accorded subjects. Eighty-nine (87%) of the individuals were diagnosed as personality disorders; ten as schizophrenic reactions (10%); one as a psychosis associated with alcoholic deterioration (1%); and, two as mental retardates (2%). (See Table 4.)

Of the 102 defendants, two were found to be insane at the time of the commission of the crime, and untriable due to present insanity. The remaining 100 cases were found to be sane upon commission of the alleged crime and presently competent to stand trial. The two individuals found insane received the same psychiatric diagnosis, Schizophrenia-chronic undifferentiated type. Following this hospital diagnosis, both cases were retained at the hospital for a period. Subsequently, their trials were dismissed and they were transferred to a mental hospital in another state.

Of the 102 cases, 96 were returned by the hospital to custody of the district court having jurisdiction. The remaining six were retained at the State Hospital, with court permission. As previously noted, two of those retained were transferred to institutions in their state of residence. The remaining four were retained for treatment under court order and eventually returned to custody of the court.

DISPOSITION OF COURT

Subsequent court action in the 102 cases with regard to trial is contained in Table 5. From Table 5, it can be seen that 74 of the cases were tried and 19 cases dismissed. (See Table 5.)

TRIAL RESULTS. Of those 74 defendants tried, 73 were convicted and one acquitted. In the single case of acquittal, the jury determined that the individual was insane at the time of the crime (murder), a finding at variance with the hospital's determination of sanity at the time of the act.

SENTENCING. As a wide variety of felonies were represented in the population, a relatively wide range of sentences were meted out by the court. These sentences are given in Table 6. Data on final court disposition for one case could not be obtained. For the remaining seventy-two cases, sentences ranged from less than one year to 35 years. (See Table 6.)

SUSPENDED SENTENCES. Of the 73 persons whose sentences were known, 14 (19.72%) had their sentences suspended and such suspension always entailed probation. Of the 14 persons receiving suspended sentences, five were ordered to the State Hospital for treatment. One person was returned to undergo the hospital's drug abuse program; one was returned to participate in the alcoholic program; two were ordered returned without a specific therapy program recommended; and, one was ordered returned to the hospital prior to trial date and later received a suspended sentence.

DISPOSITION OF SUBJECTS DIAGNOSED AS PSYCHOTIC. Of the eleven receiving a final psychiatric diagnosis as medically psychotic, the following occurred: two were determined to be insane, their trials dismissed, and subsequently transferred to a hospital in their home state; one was retained for treatment at the State Hospital, eventually having his trial dismissed; one was returned to the custody of the court, but ultimately had his trial date deferred and was returned to the State Hospital for treatment; one was tried, found guilty, and received a suspended sentence if he would "voluntarily" enter the hospital for treatment; and six were tried, found guilty, and incarcerated.

SUMMARY AND DISCUSSION

Results indicate that the use of the NGRI plea in a rural state like Wyoming is extremely limited and represents but .38% of all felony indictments. This figure is much lower than that reported by Matthews[11] for Washington, D.C. and California and probably considerably higher than that reported by him for Michigan, Detroit, Miami, and New York City.

While the general state rate for the plea is low, it is apparent that it is entered proportionately more in some counties. This differential rate is not related to county population but is related to county arrest rate, suggesting that, as the business of the criminal justice increases, there is a lesser likelihood for prosecutors, attorneys and judges to add to their workload by encouraging the employment of the insanity plea by defendants.

Generally, results suggest that most persons utilizing the insanity plea in Wyoming are neither medically psychotic nor legally insane. Of the 102 subjects, only two were determined insane, and 11 diagnosed as medically psychotic by the State Hospital and another found insane by the court. This finding is consistent with Wyoming's use of the McNaughton Rule in that the presence of a "disease of the mind", *per se,* is not sufficient to warrant a determination of legal insanity. Although this is the case, it would nevertheless appear by the disproportionate number of dismissals in the study group that the process involved in the plea does result in differential treatment for this class of defendant as compared to indicted persons not entering the plea.

Demographic characteristics of the 102 subjects suggest that the population may be classified, in general, as "adaptive failures" with the probability of future criminal recidivism and/or psychological difficulties likely.[12] As a group, they display poor marital, employment, and educational histories in comparison to the general Wyoming population, and a large proportion had previous criminal records.

One further observation seems generated by the results. In Wyoming, the
insanity plea is employed as a defense to a wide variety of criminal charges
and not restricted in use, as in some areas, to more serious crimes such as
murder and manslaughter.[13]

REFERENCES

1. Vann, C.R. "Pre-trial Determination and Judicial Decision Making: An
   Analysis of the Use of Psychiatric Information in the Administration of
   Criminal Justice." *University of Detroit Law Journal*, (1965), 43, 13-33.

2. Simon, R.J. *The Jury and the Defense of Insanity*. Boston: Little, Brown
   & Co., 1967, p. 8.

3. N.Y.U. Colloquium. "President Nixon's Proposal on the Insanity Defense."
   Journal of Law and Psychiatry, (1973), 1, 297-334.

4. Walling, L.D. *A Follow-up Study of Persons Adjudged Criminally Insane,
   Treated and Released - Colorado State Hospital, 1961-1964*. Denver: Grad-
   uate School of Social Work, University of Denver, 1965. (mimeographed)

5. Quinsey, V.L., Pruesse, M., and Fernley, R. "A Follow-up of Patients
   Found 'Unfit to Stand Trial' or 'Not Guilty by Reason of Insanity'."
   Canadian Psychiatric Association Journal, (1975), 20, 461-467.

6. Cooke, G. and Sikorski, C.R. "Factors Affecting Length of Hospitalization
   in Persons Adjudicated Not Guilty by Reason of Insanity." *Bulletin of
   the American Academy of Psychiatry and the Law*, (1975), 11, 251-261.

7. *U.S. Census Bureau*. (1970).

8. State v. Pressler, 92. 806 (1907); 16 Wyoming 214, 15 Anncas. 93; Flanders
   v. State, 195, 156 p. 39; 24 Wyoming 81, rehearing denied 156 p. 1121, 24
   Wyoming 81; State v. Brown, 1944, 151 p. 2d 950 60 Wyoming 379.

9. Laws 1939, CH. 83, 3; *Compiled Statutes 1945*, and Laws 1951, C.H. 87, 3;
   Compiled Statutes 1957.

10. *U.S. Census Bureau*. (1970)

11. *Id.*, Matthews.

12. Phillips, L. *Human Adaption and its Failures*. New York: Academic Press,
    (1968).

13. *Id.*, Matthews.

TABLE 1

Previous Arrests and Convictions

Previous Arrests	N	%	Previous Convictions	N	%
0	39	38.24	0	57	55.88
1	20	19.61	1	18	17.65
2	17	16.67	2	7	6.86
3	4	3.92	3	7	6.86
4	9	8.82	4	6	5.88
5	3	2.94	5	2	1.96
6	3	2.94	6	4	3.92
8	2	1.96	8	1	.98
9	1	.98	-	-	-----
10	1	.98	-	-	-----
17	1	.98	-	-	-----
20	1	.98	-	-	-----
24	1	.98	-	-	-----
TOTAL	102	100.00	TOTAL	102	99.99

TABLE 2

DISTRIBUTION OF ALLEGED OFFENSES OF PERSONS PLEADING INSANITY AND ARRESTS OF THE GENERAL WYOMING POPULATION

OFFENSE	Insanity Group		Wyoming Arrests		& Arrests Making NGRI Plea	Wyoming Indictments		& Indictments Making NGRI Plea
	N	%	N	%	%	N	%	%
Crimes Against Property								
Larceny-theft	16	15.69	2759	10.39	0.58	2363	10.69	00.68
Check	16	15.69	83	00.31	19.28	83	00.38	19.28
Burglary - B & E	13	12.75	1051	3.96	1.24	788	03.57	01.65
Forgery	4	3.92	200	0.75	2.00	153	00.69	02.61
Arson	3	2.94	32	0.12	9.38	15	00.07	20.00
Fraud	1	0.98	513	1.93	0.19	424	01.92	00.24
Crimes Against People								
Rape	13	12.75	89	0.34	14.61	77	00.35	16.88
Criminal homicide	9	8.82	44	0.17	20.45	34	00.15	26.47
Assault, aggravated	8	7.84	512	1.93	1.56	450	02.04	01.78
Sex, excluding rape	5	4.90	116	0.44	4.31	77	00.35	06.49
Robbery	4	3.92	121	0.46	3.31	78	00.35	05.13
Family, children	2	1.96	145	0.55	1.38	105	00.48	01.90
Kidnapping	1	0.98	*	*	*	*	*	*
Hit-run	1	0.98	*	*	*	*	*	*
Crimes Without Victim								
Drug	5	4.90	1187	4.47	0.42	795	03.58	00.63
Jailbreak	1	0.98	*	*	*	*	*	*

*Not included as offense category in Wyoming crime statistics

TABLE 3

NGRI Pleas, Population, Arrest Rate
and Utilization Rate by County

County	NGRI Pleas	1970 Population	Arrest Rate	Utilization Rate
Albany	4	26,431	257	.0029
Big Horn	6	10,202	36	.0810
Campbell	4	12,957	139	.0111
Carbon	13	13,354	440	.0110
Converse	2	5,938	306	.0055
Crook	0	4,535	115	.0000
Freemont	7	28,352	433	.0028
Goshen	0	10,885	446	.0000
Hots Springs	0	4,952	398	.0000
Johnson	0	5,587	227	.0000
Laramie	17	56,360	393	.0038
Lincoln	1	8,640	125	.0046
Natrona	23	51,264	473	.0047
Niobrara	2	2,924	68	.0500
Park	6	17,752	194	.0087
Platte	4	6,486	111	.0278
Sheridan	2	17,852	516	.0011
Sublette	2	3,755	256	.0104
Sweetwater	1	18,391	492	.0006
Teton	3	4,823	535	.0058
Unita	3	7,100	139	.0152
Washakie	2	7,569	513	.0026
Weston	0	6,307	339	.0000

TABLE 4

PSYCHIATRIC DIAGNOSIS

		N
I.	PSYCHOSIS	
	Alcoholic Deterioration	1
	Schizophrenia-latent	6
	Schizophrenia-schizo-affective	1
	Schizophrenia-chronic undifferentiated	3
II.	MENTAL RETARDATION	
	Borderline	1
	Mild	1
III.	PERSONALITY DISORDERS	
	Schizoid	7
	Explosive	1
	Hysterical	1
	Anti-social	20
	Passive-aggressive	32
	Inadequate	8
	Passive-dependent	8
	Sexual deviation	1
	Pedophilia	1
	Exhibitionism	1
	Alcohol addiction	6
	Drug dependency	2
	Drug dependence-psycho-stimulants	1

TABLE 5

SUBSEQUENT COURT ACTION TOWARD THE SUBJECTS

OUTCOME	N	PERCENT
Defendant tried	74	72.55
Trial dismissed	17	16.68
Dismissed, transferred to another institution	2	1.96
Trial deferred	7	6.86
Suicide prior to trial	1	.98
No information available	1	.98
TOTALS	102	100.01

TABLE 6

SENTENCES IMPOSED IN YEARS

SENTENCES	N	%
35	1	1.37
30	1	1.37
24	1	1.37
18	1	1.37
15	2	2.74
14	2	2.74
13	1	1.37
10	5	6.85
9	1	1.37
8	1	1.37
7	4	5.48
6	5	6.85
5	5	6.85
4	3	4.11
3	7	9.59
2	8	10.96
1	23	31.51
1	1	1.37
Unknown	1	1.37
	73	100.01

AN OVERVIEW OF VICTIMOLOGY
John P. J. Dussich

The State of the Art

The definition of the term victimology varies among a number of authorities. Some see it as restricted to crime victims, some to a broader category of injury and suffering, others point to its roots in religious rites and yet others are content with leaving it vague and flexible. By comparison, it is significant to note that this nation's leading law dictionary does not even have the word victim, or any words derived from it, mentioned in its pages.[1]

At the first International Symposium on Victimology held in Jerusalem, Israel, it was concluded that "Victimology may be defined as the scientific study of victims."[2] Stephen Schafer defined victimology as "the study of criminal-victim relationships."[3] Benjamin Mendelsohn, one of the fathers of victimology, defined it as "the science of victims and victimity."[4] According to the Webster's Third New International Unabridged Dictionary, the word victim is defined as:

> 1: a living being sacrificed to some deity or in the performance of a religious rite, 2: someone put to death, tortured, or mulcted by another: a person subjected to oppression, deprivation, or suffering, 3: someone who suffers death, loss, or injury in an undertaking of his own, 4: someone tricked, duped, or subjected to hardship: someone badly used or taken advantage of."[5]

Not only has this emerging field produced a variety of definitions but it has also spawned many new terms. *Victimity* refers to the phenomena that characterizes all categories of victims, not just those involved with crime.[6] *Victimization* refers to the social process a person is subjected to when he or she is victimized.[7] *Victimogenesis* refers to the natural process of becoming a victim.[8] *Victimogen* refers to variables that are characterized as contributing to victimization.[9] *Victimhood* is the state of being a victim.[10] *Victimize* means to make a victim by an act, to slaughter as in a sacrifice, to subject to deception or fraud, or to destroy entirely.[11]

Until recently the term victimology was familiar only to a small group of people within the discipline of criminology. Today the number of *conoscenti* (people in the know) has greatly increased. It has become known to criminologists, those in related disciplines and to many laypersons as well. Zvonimir Separovic notes that while victimology started as a part of criminology, it need not be bound by it, for its limits have not yet been clearly defined.[12]

While the definition of victimology denotes the study of victims, its connotation goes well beyond. It includes such traditional topics as the victim/ offender relationship, rape, restitution and compensation; newer topics as victim assistance programs, spouse abuse, child abuse, victim rights, victims as witnesses, victimization surveys, accident proneness; and, in general, attempts to provide a greater humanization of society by recognizing the plight of all victims.

Less than a decade ago only a handful of people were working in the field of victimology. Today that figure easily exceeds two thousand.[13] Perhaps the three most heartening areas of recent development are in the development of theory, in conducting victim-centered research (victimization surveys, case studies, descriptive and inferential studies and systems analysis), and in assisting victims with their recovery (compensation, restitution, and victim services).

Theoretical Considerations

To speak of theory in victimology is to address only a few scattered postulates, for a comprehensive theory does not yet exist. Numerous writers and researchers have provided valuable insights into the phenomena of victimity, but no one has yet developed a complete theory in this field of study. As the study of victims continues, the literature increases and the need for the emergence of an integrating theory becomes more evident.

Some of the major areas of theoretical endeavor thus far have focused on typologies, victim precipitation, the offender/victim relationship, the dynamics of victimization and the vulnerability to victimization.

Ideally, typologies should meet at least four basic criteria: they should present categories that are comprehensive and exhaustive, should be mutually exclusive, and, they should be utilitarian (have value as a heuristic device in research or serve some diagnostic value for treatment), and should reflect a particular theoretical or philosophical perspective.

The two earliest typologies were developed by Hentig in 1948 and Mendelsohn in 1956. Hentig, using thirteen categories, and drawing characteristics from psychology, sociology and biology, set up the following typology:[15]

1. the young
2. the female
3. the old
4. the mentally defective and other mentally deranged
5. immigrants
6. minorities
7. dull normals
8. the depressed
9. the acquisitive
10. the wanton

11. the lonesome and the heartbroken
12. tormentors
13. the activating sufferer

Mendelsohn focused on the issue of culpability and classified his victims according to the degree of their guilt:[16]

1. the completely innocent victim
2. the victim with minor guilt
3. the victim as guilty as the offender and the voluntary victim
4. the victim more guilty than the offender
5. the most guilty victim and the victim who is guilty alone
6. the simulating victim and the imaginary victim

Sellin and Wolfgand developed five special analytical categories primarily for research purposes in victimization.[17] Fattah also came up with a classification of five major types of victims based on the nature of the victim-offender interaction which is sociopsychological in perspective.[18]

1. Nonparticipating victims
2. Latent or predisposed victims
3. Provocative victims
4. Participating victims
5. False victims

Another recently developed typology uses as its differentiating and classifying factor the "role of the victim." This typology was proposed by John Mack and placed the typology within a continuum of six gradations with the "traditional criminal-victim relationship" at one end and "victimless crimes" at the other.[19]

Typologies reflect particular perspectives and serve to give order to those perspectives. Thus the number of possible typologies could be numerous indeed. A logical other possibility could be based on the crime involved: Murder, Rape, Assault, Robbery, Theft, Larceny and Auto Vehicle Theft (the FBI's seven Index Crimes). Another typology might be based on the extent and nature of injury: fatally injured, permanently crippled, mentally disabled, temporarily injured, permanent emotional damage, temporary emotional trauma, no injury, etc. As the study of victims evolves, whether in services, or theory, it will become increasingly necessary to have functional typologies to organize our respective approaches to the plight of victims.[20]

The area of victim precipitation is one of the more traditional and older subjects written about in victimology within the last three decades. The basic notion is that the victim in some way and to some degree contributed to the victimization that befell him/her. One of the first significant references to victim precipitation was made by Hentig in 1970 in a paper discussing the victim-offender relationship. He was also impressed with a novel by Franz Wertel, *The Murdered One Is Guilty*.[21] He later elaborated on this topic in his book *The Criminal and His Victim*. Some others to first discuss variations of this relationship were Fattah, with his "victim-induced criminality"[23] and Fooner, with his "provocative victim."[24] The identification of these related concepts prompted researchers to investigate the phenomena further. Wolfgang studied victim precipitated homicide,[25] Amir studied victim precipitated forcible rape,[26] Mulvihill *et al* studied precipitation in crimes of violence,[27] Holyst studied victim provocation in homicide in Poland,[28] Johnson *et al* studied the recidivist victim,[29] Conklin studied victim invitations to potential robbers.[30] Victim precipitation continues to intrigue serious scholars and researchers, for its understanding could provide significant insights into the very genesis of crime.[31]

The victim-offender relationship is another salient topic of victimological inquiry. Closely related to the study of victim precipitation, it has also generated much research activity. In every component of the criminal justice system the administrative distinction between the victim and criminal is made very clear. Yet those who have studied the dynamics of crime know the distinctions are not clear, but usually overlap in a blend of interaction. Schafer felt that "the criminal-victim relationship may point to the genesis of a crime and to a better understanding of its development and formation.[32]

Hentig alluded to a reciprocity that exists between the perpetrator and victim, manifest in the terms he used to characterize these two persons, "doer-sufferer".[33] Mendelsohn was early to identify the significance between victim and offender in the use of his term "the penal couple."[34] Reckless was also aware of this important relationship and frequently used the terms "victim-doer-victim" in many of his criminological writings.[35] In a more diagnostic vein, the Italian psychologist-lawyer Guglielmo Gulotta wrote about the "offender-victim system" as a system's model, which focuses attention, not just on the victim's personality, but on the "diad criminal-victim."[36] Another psychodiagnostic approach was proposed by Joachim Weber who makes an attempt of qualifying the descriptions of the offender-victim relationship (OVR) in algebraic fashion. He offers four standard procedures as a means of understanding the attraction between these special "partners."[37]

The importance of being sensitive to this relationship goes well beyond its diagnostic value, but also has significance to the practical application of criminal justice. Romine Deming points to the unique integrating qualities of the victim-offender relationship as a concept that enhances a wide variety of

concerns, to include theory construction, research and program development.[38]
LeRoy Schultz, in a somewhat related tone, points to the importance of the
concept in the administration of the parole and probation process. He says
"probation and parole officers must understand victim-offender relationships."[39]
Numerous others have found that to restrict one's perspective to just the offender is not only unjust but inaccurate in understanding the dynamics of crime
and its causes. Thus a new and important era has been ushered in by a handful
of writers who have provided us with yet another dimension to the theory and
practice of criminal justice.

A closely related concept to the two previous ones discussed is that dealing with the dynamics of victimization. Various persons have made attempts at
explaining how and why victimizations occur. Some explanations are psychological, some psychiatric and some are sociological. Whatever the orientation,
understanding victims in their own right is a fertile area for research and
study. Heretofore victims have been largely excluded from the realm of investigation and as a result explanations of the phenomenon of crime have been
sterile and incomplete. This added perspective now provides students of crime
with a more total view, a Gestalt of the crime problem . Richard Ball, in a
recent article, comprehensively assimilated an excellent theoretical model to
examine the dynamics of victimization.[40] Focusing on microprocesses and macro-
processes, the concept of the victimological cycle is approached from the perspective of mutual victimization at the individual level and at the societal
level. His basic processes are regression, aggression and resignation. Using
these three basic categories, he describes and analyzes nine cyclical forms of
mutual victimization cycles. His approach is unique, logical and functional
in providing a basis for understanding the dynamics of the phenomenon victimization.

In the victimological literature from the early works of Mendelsohn and
Hentig, victimization has been presented as an activity occurring along a continuum with total responsibility of the victim at one end, and total innocence
of the victim at the other. In order to more accurately depict the dynamics
of victimization, David and Claster extend the limits beyond total innocence
to "the resisting victim."[41] This treatise explores the specific behavior of
resisting as it applies to the elderly particularly and the population generally, as a function of prevailing social attitudes. The behavior of victims,
especially victims ov violent crimes follows similar patterns. The first
immediate response is momentary shock and disbelief, quickly followed by a
"frozen-frighten" response. This response, according to psychiatrist Martin

Symonds, "is so profound and overwhelming that the victim feels hopeless about getting away." The logical consequence for survival is to appease the criminal.[42] Based on his findings at the Karen Horney Clinic, he notes that survival in a stress situation is a function of attitudes, "adaptive behavior from early childhood."

One of the most complete works dealing with the dynamics of victimization is by Canadian criminologist Ezzat Fattah. His major premise is that victim behavior is an inseparable component of a dynamic total situation involving also the criminal and the act itself. Fattah attempts to integrate the "motivational, interactional and victimological approaches in order to better understand criminal and delinquent behavior."[43]

Hentig, in the final sentence of his book, *The Criminal and His Victim,* stated "Crime will become a problem of dynamics, and we will build our systems of treatment and prevention around the most seizable and workable of the accusative forces.[44]

There are numerous other topics which fall within the theoretical rubric of victimology, such as vulnerability, recidivism, culpability, responsibility, to mention a few. Like in other emerging disciplines, hypotheses, postulates, facts and theories must be generated and integrated before a body of knowledge may be called a discipline. Today, there is a fast growing body of knowledge in victimology. One of the important ingredients of this growth is empirical research, without which victimology as a separate area of study would not exist.

Research Efforts

Some of the early studies conducted were meager attempts at objectifying and measuring the victimization phenomenon. One of the earliest recorded studies can be traced to 1720 in Denmark. Researchers in Aarhus conducted household interviews to measure the extent of actual crime.[45] Adolphe Quetelet, in 1853 at the First Session of the International Statistical Congress in Brussels used statistics to better understand the crime situation.[46] Each of the early fathers of this field collected data in his own fashion. Mendelsohn as a practicing attorney in Rumania used the legal case method. Hentig, a psychiatrist, used a type of medical case study method, as well as collecting mostly descriptive data. A number of the later founders of victimology were also lawyers who used (for the most part) the legal case study method and descriptive measures (Ellenberger, Schafer, Fattah and Koichi Miyazawa).

In this century some of the earliest victimization statistics appeared in this country in the twenties. Murder victims were counted in Memphis, Tennessee in 1920-25 by Bruce and Fitzgerald,[47] and later in Birmingham, Memphis, New

Orleans and Boston by F.L. Hoffman in a 1932 publication.[48] Victim statistics were also often found as part of annual crime reports published by police departments of major cities.

Of more recent vintage, Marvin Wolfgang, in 1957, studied homicide victims in Philadelphia,[49] and in 1962-63 Stephen Schafer conducted a study of victims and offenders in Florida.[50]

In Europe there were also a number of victim studies. In the early 1930's the German journal *Kriminalstatistik* compiled victim statistics.[51] In London, William East made comparisons of victims from sane and insane murderers,[52] and somewhat later E. Gibson and S. Klein of the Home Office Research Unit conducted an analysis of murder victims and offenders in England and Wales from 1952 to 1960.[53]

Victimization studies, in their present form are a recent development, having been generated only about ten years ago. Their main purpose was to measure the extent of unreported crime so as to expand the existing statistics on reported crime. The first of this new generation of victimization surveys was conducted in 1966 in Washington, D.C. by the President's Commission on Law Enforcement and the Administration of Justice. Numerous other victimization surveys have evolved both in this country and abroad, and have become sophisticated instruments of measurement. So far, these surveys, while not perfect, do give the closest indication of the actual incidence of crime available.

Beyond the confines of descriptive research, numerous recent studies have been conducted that explore victimization with new and more refined methods of research. Today the study of victims may involve program evaluation, system analysis, cost-benefit analysis, a variety of inferential methods, factor analysis, path analysis, multivariate analysis, etc. The full armament of empirical tools is being brought to bear on the study of victims. Clearly the empirical study of victimization is one of the major focal areas in victimology today.

Victim Assistance

For the most part, victims are assisted in three major ways. Some governments award amounts of money to help cover medical and other expenses resulting from a crime victimization. This is called compensation. Another way, usually at the local level, is where a judge, a parole officer, a probation officer or a correctional counselor may decide to have the offender pay back the victim for any expense incurred as a result of the crime as part of the correctional process. This is called restitution. The most recent form of victim assistance is generally referred to as victim services. While there are many types of victim service models, they are all concerned with rendering a variety of services to the victim of crime in a direct and immediate manner.

Forms of victim compensation can be traced back to the time of Hammurabi in ancient Babylonia dating to about 1775 B.C., but it was not until the 1960's that major national and state programs (as we know them today) finally were established. Perhaps the first person in this century to focus attention on this issue was Margery Fry. She was greatly disturbed at the way victims of crime were being treated, and in 1957 wrote a persuasive article in London's *The Observer* proposing that governments ought to establish national compensation programs that would restore a sense of justice to the judicial process by giving innocent monetary recompense for their losses as a result of a crime.[54] The first country to try her proposal was New Zealand in 1964, and California was the first state in America to try the concept in 1965. Today some twenty-two states in this country and some fifteen countries have some form of national victim compensation program established.[55] The two most often heard criticisms of victim compensation is that it will be unjustifiably expensive and it will lead to extensive fraud. The programs in existence today do show that at least partial compensation can be made to the more serious victimizations without exorbitant expenses or risks of fraud incurred by the government.[56] In the United States Congress for the past seven years various types of bills have been presented in both the House and the Senate. Thus far, both houses have not been able to agree on a bill that is mutually suitable. Today many states and many countries are debating the issues of compensation, and every year the number of established programs increases. In an effort to carry on the compensation movement and to provide a forum within which to learn, the International Association of Crime Victim Compensation Boards meets annually. This association is composed of persons who manage compensation programs, scholars and other interested persons all concerned with improving the state-of-the-art in this fast changing area of victim compensation.

The next area of victim assistance is restitution. It is also of ancient origin, and was inextricably part of the earliest form of punishment. Punishment meant payment back to the victim; retribution was of lesser importance than the restoration of the status quo through indemnification to the victim. In the Middle Ages the system of "composition" represents the historical origin of restitution found in the Germanic common laws.[57] Various forms of restitution can be found throughout history. Among the Semitic nations, in the Turkish Empire, in India, Greece, and in Roman Law, as civilization evolved vengeful retaliation gave way to composition. Composition was a way of satisfying the victim not only through monetary recompense but also through a degree of humiliation. Eventually as kings took over the responsibility of punishing for their subjects who were wronged, the fines and penalties that once went to the victim, were turned over to the state. Finally the rights of the injured were separated from penal law and the obligation to pay damages became part of civil law. After a period of decline starting in the Middle Ages, restitution began a slow resurrection. In 1847 Bonneville de Marsangy devised a scheme for reparation and throughout the later 1880's various international congresses on prison reform made restitution an important issue in their agenda.[58] The role of restitution as an extension of the correctional process had to be justified within the framework of punishment. Hentig, in 1937 thus stressed that "In many cases payment to the injured party will have a stronger inner punishment value than the payment of a sum to the neutral state."[59] Other responses resulted in such terms as "creative restitution,"[60] "correctional restitution" and "punitive restitution."[61] Today restitution is fast becoming a common sentencing option for judges, and a favorite rehabilitative tool for reform minded correctional administrators. In 1975 the Minnesota Department of Corrections and the Law Enforcement Assistance Administration jointly sponsored the First International Symposium on Restitution in Minneapolis.[62] Since then numerous conferences, forums and symposia both nationally and internationally have produced a wealth of new writings and research on the subject of restitution. Compared to the criminal it appears that the balance of concern is finally returning to the victim again to some semblance of importance in the criminal justice process.

The recent newcomer to the area of victim assistance is victim services. The origins of victim services are numerous. Services have traditionally evolved from a concern for a specific category of victims: rape victims, elderly victims, child abuse victims, etc. Not long ago most victims of crime were dealt with primarily as medical patients in hospital settings. If other problems developed, not much else was available except perhaps family and friends.

The greater majority of current programs can trace their roots to the last decade. The earliest of these was in the area of child abuse, in New York, in 1964. At this time New York passed the child abuse law in the nation, later, 1969) giving way to the establishment of the Mayor's Task Force on Child Abuse and Neglect in 1969.[63] The traditional approach to child abuse and neglect has been and still is social work. Today many states have enacted legislation aimed at preventing and treating child abuse. At the federal level, the Child Abuse Prevention and Treatment Act (P.L. 93-297) was signed into law on January 31, 1974. This resulted in the establishment of the National Center on Child Abuse and Neglect in the Children's Bureau, Office of Child Development, U.S.

Department of Health, Education and Welfare.[64] Next came the rape movement in
New York. This gave rise to WAR (Women Against Rape) and in 1972 the establishment of rape crisis centers in Los Angeles, Washington, D.C., and Ann Arbor.[65]
In 1972 this writer published the Victim Ombudsman, which was the first attempt
to focus attention on a comprehensive approach to victim services by including
all victims as clients based on need rather than type.[66] The concept, revised
and renamed the Victim Advocate, was first implemented in Fort Lauderdale,
Florida, in April or 1974.

Another important related development occurring almost simultaneously was
the start of the National District Attorneys Association Commission on Victim
Witness Assistance in October of 1974. This development focused principally on
victims who were witnesses and dealt primarily with the problems encountered in
having to testify for the prosecution. Two other special categories of victim
service programs were: for elderly victims, of which only a few exist nationally; and, for spouse abuse, which have also primarily been a product of the
feminist movement. Thus, in retrospect, it is clear that each kind of service
program; while coming from a wide variety of sources, is concerned with the
lasting and complete recovery of the crime victim as early as possible.

Recovery from victimization may be short-term or long-term. It could look
at physical, emotional and/or financial problems. It could be concerned with
the victim's life style or personality, or the victim's environment, or both.
Most functions can be divided into primary, secondary, and tertiary.

Primary functions are those that are common to most models, are immediate
in nature, and are aimed at delivering a narrow range of direct services to the
client. Secondary functions are usually those that are of lesser importance,
have long range system's import, and are broad in scope. Tertiary functions are
usually unique to specific victim categories, may be either long or short range,
and have more relevance to planners, educators and the community at large rather
than to victims or agents of the criminal justice system.[67]

With regard to types of victim service models, most are described in terms
of their host agency, or in terms of their clients. The structural characteristics vary considerably from a loose ad hoc structure at one extreme to a highly
organized, comprehensive, formal structure at the other extreme. Usually these
different structures represent different time points in the evolution of victim
service programs, fairly common throughout the nation. That is, as an effort
loses its newness, it tends to become more organized, more formal, and more comprehensive in scope. Within the above parameter, three general approaches to
service delivery are identifiable: the "additional duty" approach, the "volun-

teer services" approach, and the "comprehensive program" approach.[68]

All of the above models have strengths and weaknesses, each occurring at one or more of the stages in the evolutionary process of program implementation. Implementation is a dynamic process that includes the following major stages: "selling the idea," "staffing up," "organizational acceptance," and "institutionalization."[69] In order to realize some degree of success, a project director must anticipate the variety of problems, associated with each of these phases.

The result of victim service programs, in spite of some vain attempts, has been toward increased community awareness, more victims receiving assistance, and greater sensitivity of the criminal justice system to the plight of victims. Perhaps the most important point to realize in considering the variety of victim service models is that each community must tailor its program to the unique needs of its victims. This may mean the development of large, fully staffed programs or just the issuance of extra guidelines for existing personnel to follow. For what is important is the quality of the community's response, not the size or structure of the program. The future direction of victim services must be toward greater legitimacy within the system. Victims must be accepted as bona fide clients and play a greater role in the total criminal justice process.

REFERENCES

1. Black's Law Dictionary, Revised Fourth Edition, St. Paul, Minnesota, West Publishing Company, 1968, p. 1739.

2. First International Symposium on Victimology, *Victimology: A New Focus*, "Conclusion," I. Drapkin and E. Viano, editors, Vol. 1, Lexington Books, 1974, p. 209.

3. Stephen Schafer, *The Victim and His Criminal*, New York, Random House, 1968, p. 9.

4. Mendelsohn, Beniamin, "Victimology and Contemporary Society's Trends", *Victims and Society*, E. Viano, editor, Visage Press, Inc., Washington, D.C., 1976, p. 8.

5. *Webster's Third New International Unabridged Dictionary*, G. & C. Merriam Co. Publishers, Springfield, Massachusetts, 1971, p. 2550.

6. Mendelsohn, Beniamin, "Victimology and the Technical and Social Sciences: A Call for the Establishment of Victimological Clinics," *Victimology: A New Focus*, Vol. 1, I. Drapkin and E. Viano, Lexington Books, Massachusetts, 1974, p. 25.

7. Smith, David Lewis and Weis, Kurt, "Toward an Open-System Approach to Studies in the Field of Victimology" in *Victims and Society*, edited by E. Viano, Visage Press, inc., Washington, D.C., 1976, p. 44.

8. Mendelsohn, *Ibid.*, 1976, p. 8; (and also Ellenberger).

9. H. Ellenberger, "Relations Psychologiques Entre la Criminel et la Victim," Revue Internationale de Criminologic et de Police Technique, Paris, France, 8, 1 (January - March: 1954) pp. 103-121.

10. Webster, *Ibid.*

11. *Ibid.*

12. Separovic, Svonimir, "Victimology: A New Approach in the Social Sciences," I. Draphin and E. Viano, editors, *Victimology: A New Focus*, Vol. 1, Lexington Books, Massachusetts, 1974, p. 15.

13. Dussich, John P.J., "Victim Programs Directory, National Organization of Victim Assistance, NOVA, Hattiesburg, 1976.

14. Anttila, Inkeri, "Victimology: A New Territory in Criminology," I. Drapkin and E. Viano, editors, *Victimology: A New Focus*, Vol. 1, Lexington Books, Massachusetts, 1974.

15. Hans von Hentig, *The Criminal and His Victim: Studies in the Sociobiology of Crime*, Hamden: Archon Books, 1948, pp. 404-438.

16. Beniamin Mendelsohn, "The Victimology," *Etudes Internationales de Psycho-Sociologic Criminelle* (July-September 1956), pp. 25-26.

17. Marvin E. Wolfgang, *Analytical Categories for Research in Victimization*, Germany: Kriminologische Wegzeichen, 1967, and in T. Sellin and M. Wolfgang, *The Measurement of Delinquency*, New York: John Wiley and Sons, 1964.

18. Ezzat A. Fattah, "Towards a Criminological Classification of Victims," *The International Journal of Criminal Police*, No. 209, 1967.

19. John A. Mack, "A Victim-Role Typology of Rational-Economic Property Crimes" in *Victimology: A New Focus* Vol. 1, Theoretical Issues in Victimology, editors I. Drapkin and E. Viano, Lexington Press, 1974, pp. 127-135.

20. For an excellent critique of victimological typologies see Richard A. Ball, "The Victimological Cycle," *Victimology: An International Journal*, Fall, 1976.

21. Hans von Hentig, "Remarks on the Interaction of Prepetrator and Victim," *Journal of Criminal Law and Criminology*, 31 (September - October 1970). pp. 303-309.

22. Hentig, 1948, *Ibid.*

23. Fattah, *Ibid.*

24. M. Fooner, "Victim-Induced Criminality," *Science*, 155, 3770 (September 2, 1966) pp. 1080-1083.

25. Marvin E. Wolfgang, *Patterns in Criminal Homicide*. New York: Science Editions, 1966; and "Victim Precipitated Criminal Homicide," *Journal of Criminal Law, Criminology and Police Science*, 48, 1957.

26. Menachem Amir, "Victim Precipitated Forcible Rape," *Journal of Criminal Law, Criminology and Police Science*, Vol. 58, No. 4, 1967: 795-802.

27. D. Mulvihill, M. Tumin and Lynn A. Curtis, *Crimes of Violence*, Washington: National Commission on the Causes and Prevention of Violence, 1949.

28. B. Holyst, "The Victim Role in Homicide," (Rola ofiary w genezie Zabojstwa). Lodz Panstwoi Prawo (Warsaw) 19/1, pp. 746-755. Excerpted in Excerpta Criminological 5 (1964): 325-326.

29. Joan M. Johnson, Hazel B. Kerper, Dorothy D. Hayes, and George G. Killinger, the Recidivist Victim: A Descriptive Study, Criminal Justice Monograph, Vol. IV, No. 1, Institute of Contemporary Corrections and the Behavioral Sciences, Sam Houston State University, Huntsville, Texas, 1973.

30. J. Conklin, *Robbery and the Criminal Justice System*, Philadelphia: Lippencott, 1972.

31. For an excellent discussion of victim precipitation, see: Robert A. Silverman, "Victim Precipitation: An Examination of the Concept" in *Victimology: A New Focus* Vol. 1, *Theoretical Issues in Victimology*, edited by Israel Drapkin and Emilio Viano, Massachusetts: Lexington Books - D.C. Heath and Co., 1973.

32. Schafer, *Ibid.*, p. 39.

33. Hentig, 1978, *Ibid.*, p. 388.

34. B. Mendelsohn, "The Origin of the Doctrine of Victimology" Excerpta Criminologica, Vol. 3, No. 3, 1963, pp. 239-244.

35. Walter Reckless, *The Crime Problem*, New York: Appleton-Century-Drafts, 1967.

36. Guglielmo, Gulotta, "The Offender-Victim System" in *Victims and Society*, editor Emilio C. Viano, Washington, D.C.: Visage Press, Inc., 1976, p. 50.

37. Joachim Weber, "On the Psychodiagnosis of the Offender-Victim Relationship: An Approach to a Quantifying Description" in *Victimology: A New Approach*, Vol. 1, editors I. Drapkin and E. Viano, Lexington Press, 1973, pp. 155-167.

38. Romine R. Deming, "Advocating the Concept of the Victim-Offender Relationship" as presented to the Second International Symposium on Victimology, Boston, Massachusetts, 1976.

39. LeRoy G. Schultz, "The Victim-Offender Relationship" *Crime and Delinquency*, No. 14, April, 1968.

40. Ball, *Ibid.*

41. Deborah, S. David and Daniel S. Claster, "The Resisting Victim: Extending the Concept of Victim Responsibility," as presented at the Second International Symposium on Victimology, Boston, Massachusetts, September 5-11, 1976.

42. Martin Symonds, "Victims of Senseless Violence," *Psychiatric Worldview*, Vol. 1, No. 1, Jan/Mar, 1977.

43. Ezzat Fattah, "The Use of the Victim as an Agent of Self-Legitimization: Toward a Dynamic Exploration of Criminal Behavior," in *Victims and Society*, editor Emilio Viano, Washington, D.C.: Visage Press, Inc., 1976.

44. Hentig, *Ibid.*, 1978.

45. Finn H. Lauridsen, "Tyverier i 1720' erne," in Nød og Brøde Ulykke, eds Aarhus Byhistoriske Udvalg. Begiveuheder i Aarhus, Universitets forlaget in Aarhus, 1969.

46. Bulletin de la Commission Centrale de Statistique, Brussels, Vol. VI, 1855.

47. Andrew A. Bruce and Thomas S. Fitzgerald, A Study of Crime in the City of Memphis, Chicago, 1928.

48. H.C. Brearly, *Homicide in the United States*, University of North Carolina Press, Chapel Hill, 1932.

49. Wolfgang, *Ibid.*, 1957.

50. Stephen Schafer, "Criminal-Victim Relationships in Violent Crimes," Unpublished Research, U.S. Department of Health, Education and Welfare, July, 1965.

51. Hentig, *Ibid.*, 1967.

52. William N. East, *Medical Aspects of Crime*, J. and A. Limited, London, 1936.

53. Evelyn Gibson and S. Klein, "Murder," Home Office Studies in the Causes of Delinquency and the Treatment of Offenders, 7, London, 1961.

54. Margery Fry, "Justice for Victims," *The Observer* London, 1957.

55. For a comprehensive overview of the theory and practice of victim compensation, see Leroy L. Lamborn, "Crime Victim Compensation: Theory and Practice in the Second Decade," *Victimology: On International Journal*, Vol. 1, No. 7, Winter, 1976, pp. 503-516.

56. Lamborn, *Ibid.*

57. Stephen Schafer, *Compensation and Destitution to Victims of Crime*, Patterson Smith: Montclair, N.J., 1960, p. 3-5.

58. *Ibid.*

59. Hans von Hentig, *Punishment: Its Origin, Purpose and Psychology*, London, 1937.

60. A. Eglash, "Creative Restitution: Some Suggestions for Prison Rehabilitation Programs," *American Journal of Corrections*, 20 (6): 20-34, 1958.

61. Stephen Schafer, "The Victim and Correctional Theory: Integrating Victim Reparation with Offender Rehabilitation," *Criminal Justice and the Victim*, editor William F. McDonald, Sage Publications: Beverly Hills, 1976, pp. 227-235.

62. Joe Hudson and Burt Galaway, "Introduction," *Restitution in Criminal Justice,* editors J. Hudson and B. Galaway, Lexington Books, D.C. Heath & Co.: Lexington, Massachusetts, 1975, p. 1.

63. Vincent O. Fontana, *Somewhere a Child is Crying,* Macmillan Publishing Co.: New York, 1973, pp. 171-172.

64. Child Abuse and Neglect: The Problem and Its Management, Vol. 3, The Community Team, An Approach to Case Management and Prevention, U.S. Dept. of H.E.W., 1976.

65. Mary Ann Largen, "History of Women's Movements in Changing Attitudes, Laws and Treatment Toward Rape Victims," Marcia J. Walker and Tanley L. Broadsky, editors, *Sexual Assault,* Lexington Books: Boston, 1976, p. 69.

66. John P.J. Dussich, *The Victim Ombudsman,* The Governor's Council on Criminal Justice, Tallahassee, 1972.

67. John P.J. Dussich, Models of Victim Service Programs, in *Perspectives on Crime Victims,* editors Joe Hudson and Burt Galaway, C.V. Mosley Company, 1978.

68. *Ibid.*

69. *Ibid.*

PART II: THE POLICE

THE ROLE OF PSYCHOLOGISTS IN A POLICE DEPARTMENT
S. A. Somodevilla

STRESS IN POLICE WORK

A Police Officer lives and performs under more stress than members of any other profession. He is exposed to situations that the average citizen never even hears about. He risks his life as a matter of daily routine. He is expected to be at all times appropriate; always make the right decision; use only the correct quantity and quality of force; and never make a mistake. If a laborer or a white collar worker makes a mistake, he will probably receive, at most, a reprimand and wrist-slap from the supervisor. In police work, there are no minor mistakes since any slip-up can result in harm to self, partners, or citizens, as well as major legal implications. Even though police work is not the most physically dangerous profession, it certainly is the most emotionally dangerous of all professions.

In addition, the Police Officer is expected, by himself and society, to carry on the business of living his life in a fulfilling manner; bringing satisfaction to self and family, and being able to deal with everyday problems as in the field, faultlessly. Any sign of anxiety, fear, or uncertainty becomes a highly undesirable trait, for many officers feel they must be at all times a "Superman", always in control

Due to the suppressive nature of police work (a Police Officer is expected to deal with all situations regardless of degree of danger in the same methodical manner) the officer develops a "mask" that serves to maintain an "image" as well defend himself from the horrors he is exposed to. Many times this "mask" becomes so ingrained that the officer incorporates it into his personality at work and at home, and usually without his awareness. Thus a protective device becomes a liability, and can be a causative factor of emotional and physical problems that, in many cases, the officer in question is the last one to recognize.

Police Officers have one of the highest rates of divorce of all professions (75%); problem drinking (20%); and suicide (6½ times higher than average population). Cardiovascular disorders and other health problems are also very frequent and psychomatic illnesses in general are rampant in Police work. There are many other problems, less obvious and probably less dramatic that plague a Police Officer and can contribute to his physical and emotional deterioration.

It is an accepted fact that a Police Officer is under stress and pressure unequaled by any other profession. Even though a Police Officer has been compared to a combat soldier as to the amount of stress experienced, a combat soldier is "unleashed" whereby he can totally and completely let go and behave quite violently within extremely broad parameters. A Police Officer's "unleashing" almost always involves highly controlled violence within very strict parameters that, if violated, may bring about internal and/or external investigations, as well as negative publicity and disciplinary action.

In a profession where stress is rampant; where accurate selection and effective maintenance of personnel is a key in the perpetuating of the smooth functioning of the Department; where unpredictability is the only thing predictable; a psychologist can provide services in a multitude of areas towards the improvement of the human dimension of Police work. The next section will deal with those services.

PSYCHOLOGICAL SERVICES

One of the many services a psychologist can provide to a Police Department is that of *diagnostician*. In this role, the psychologist can be of service in the evaluation of applicants as to emotional stability, intellectual, and interpersonal skills. He can perform behavioral cause investigations when an officer is behaving in a way that is suggestive of emotional problems as being reflected in his poor performance. He can also perform psychodiagnostic evaluations on officers who are seeking counseling as any psychologist in private practice or a clinic setting would on a client or patient.

As a *counselor*, the Police Psychologist has a wide open field to employ his abilities. The disorders usually seen in working with Police Officers and their families involve marital problems, sexual problems, family problems, excessive drinking, displacement of aggression, authority problems, psychosomatic problems, problems with children, as well as all the usual neuroses and personality problems seen in a Counseling Center. The most common methods of treatment are individual therapy and conjoint marital therapy, but biofeedback can be an asset in the treatment of psychosomatic disorders, such as migraine and tension headaches; cardiovascular dysfunction, and gastrointestinal problems.

As a *researcher*, the psychologist can provide both pure and applied research that will be useful and relevant to the functioning of the Department. With recent court decisions and Equal Opportunity Commission (E.E.O.C.) guidelines, psychological testing used to deselect applicants must be validated. The psychologist can provide the Department with data collection, manipulation, and interpretation of results, as well as recommendations for implementation. Research in most any area of Police Psychology is wide open. Validation studies are quite common and necessary but by no means limit the research potential of the Psychologist. Some of the research undertaken by the Dallas Police Department's Psychological Services Unit (P.S.U.) involves development and validation of a Physical Fitness Test; a study of accident-proneness in Police Officers; personality variables associated with marksmanship; personality characteristics of members of several departments or sections such as Vice, Motorcycle officers, and Tactical (SWAT); the use of biofeedback in treatment of musculo-skeletal disorders; etc. As can be seen, the potential is almost limitless and the needs are great.

The Police Psychologist is also a *teacher* who can become involved in the training of Apprentice Police Officers and rookies at a grass-roots level, as well as veterans. Teaching classes in the Police Academy can serve two (2) purposes, one, it can provide the students with exposure to psychological weapons to use in the field such as recognition and handling of the mentally disturbed individual and other interpersonal skills. The second purpose is that of exposing the Psychologist to those individuals who in a few months will become officers. By doing so, the students will meet the Psychologist early in their career and some of the "spookiness" about the "shrink" will be dispelled.

Another form of teaching takes place in workshops and seminars conducted by the Psychologist for different sections of the Department and for all ranks of personnel. One of the most productive is the Supervisor's Seminar where officers from the rank of Sergeant and above are exposed to the many signs of stress-related problems that may be exhibited by their subordinates. They are also taught how to deal with the individual and relate to him in a meaningful, helpful, and supportive manner as well as how to perform the touchy task of referring them for counseling if the problem requires the involvement of a professional therapist.

A Crisis Intervention Program was developed by the Psychological Services Unit of the Dallas Police Department and it is a compulsory part of the Police Academy. This program trains officers to deal with family disturbances in an effective, safe manner with a minimum of danger, since many officers are injured yearly in such family disturbances.

Much of the work of the Police Psychologist is that of *consultant* to all sections of the Department. This can be in the form of formal meetings and presentations but more often than not, it takes the form of an informal, single session or conversation with an officer of any rank and status in the Departmental hierarchy. The problems may be personal, job-related, or even having to do with helping an officer find an article in a psychology journal for a paper he is writing in college. It is obvious that as a consultant, the psychologist must be flexible and a good generalist.

Another role that the Police Psychologist is becoming more and more involved in is that of "*crime solver*." Psychological profiles of criminals can be helpful to detectives working a difficult case. Interrogation of victims of crimes is an area where the psychologist provides significant help to the investigation since a good psychologist should be skillful in interviewing techniques as well as helping the anxious person (as most victims are) become more relaxed and less anxious. In this last area of victim-interviewing, hypnosis has become a relatively new procedure and one that a psychologist should be able to perform as well as train detectives in its use for investigation purposes. Dr. Martin Reiser of the Los Angeles Police Department has been the leader of this endeavor.

Finally, the psychologist should be on call for emergencies such as a shooting where an officer has been wounded, shot someone, or his partner has been injured and has to deal with anxieties, fears, and guilt. Situations where there may be a suicidal person who may be helped by a psychologist; as well as other situations less explosive but just as meaningful to individual officers and the Department at large.

PROBLEMS AND PITFALLS

As is true of any new undertaking in a virgin field, there are many "bugs" that need working out. Most are easy to work out, but some are inherent in the system and require constant awareness. One of the latter is that of *confidentiality*. The Police Psychologist does not have the same freedom his counterpart in a non-police environment has. This is strictly this writer's opinion after three (3) years of experience in such matters, but it becomes much more gray than black or white when dealing with a population of Police Officers rather than the average citizenry. One way to deal with this problem is to inform the officer, on the first session, what the ground rules are. Any mention of planned violence, self, or other directed, will be reported to a supervisor. This, of course, does not mean that the officer won't be able to ventilate and enjoy his catharsis, but it is up to the psychologist to evaluate the verbal and non-verbal messages and decide whether the officer is talking about what he would like to do as opposed to what he is going to do. It should be easy to realize that we are dealing with a sworn officer who has the means and the ability to inflict harm on others, thus the Department has to maintain its liability at a minimum;

not only for legal reasons but also for moral reasons.

A temporary problem facing the Police Psychologist is the *initial distrust* that is present in the first stages of his contact with the Department. This is a mutual distrust that requires honesty, tact, and understanding on both sides before it can be turned into an open, mutually satisfying relationship. Since much of the involvement of behavioral scientists in Police work has been negative and highly critical, there is an understandable reaction against openly accepting a psychologist as a member of the team until he proves himself as trustworthy.

Peer reaction can be a slight problem especially if those involved get hung-up in stereotypes. A Police Psychologist may be seen by colleagues as "one of the pigs" and he will see his colleagues as just a bunch of "liberal bleeding-hearts." This is a petty conflict and one that requires both sides to be involved, one side can't by itself,

Another problem that is highly improbable but ever-present, is that of working with an *armed clientele*. The Psychologist cannot be obsessed with this possibility or he will become ineffective. He must be aware of it however, and if in his opinion his client could become violent during a session, he may ask the client, before the session, to please leave his weapon outside and clearly explain why and hopefully work through the problem.

The final problem that comes to mind is that of being relatively *unprotected* due to the absence of ivory towers and lovely private offices. "Professional tact" between psychologists isn't present in a Police Department. The honesty of Police Officers can be quite frightening to a neophyte in the field of Police Psychology. I have found this very refreshing (after the initial shock!) in that I have learned to appreciate the straightforwardness and lack of hazy jargon; the unanswering answers, and the hypothetical issues. "What is the sound of one hand clapping?" is not as important in a Police Department as to "How can we diffuse a family disturbance in a way that no one will get hurt?"

QUALIFICATIONS OF A POLICE PSYCHOLOGIST

The person who chooses Police Psychology as a career must be aware that one of its main advantages is also one of its disadvantages, namely the novelty a Police Psychologist is and the lack of role definition this novelty entails. Working under such conditions can be a fulfilling, challenging experience in that the Police Psychologist would in effect be writing his own role definition. On the other hand, due to that same novelty, many individuals within the Police hierarchy are reluctant to become involved with the psychologist and although they may not actively interfere with his work, they may be indirectly interfering through their resistance and lack of involvement. The best way to combat this attitude is through exposure and availability of the psychologist to all levels of the organization.

The Police Psychologist must be a generalist. He must possess expertise in all the traditional services (testing and individual and group therapy) as well as consultation, teaching, and research skills. Unless the Department can provide positions for several psychologists or has a large enough budget for specialized consultants, the Police Psychologist needs to be able to work with all populations and possess enough flexibility to provide the whole spectrum of services required. He must also have at least a working knowledge of organizations and management in order to understand and be of assistance to the hierarchy. One of the key aspects of being accepted by the line officers as well as obtaining first hand knowledge about the life of an officer is to spend some time riding in squad cars with officers. During the initial stages of employment it is advisable to ride as often as possible. Afterwards, periodic rides are recommended to maintain awareness as well as keep up to date with field nuances and provide exposure to field officers.

The last issue is whether a Police Department should have psychologists who are Police Officers, or civilian, or should rely on outside consultants. It has been the experience of the Dallas Police Department that a blend of officer-psychologists and civilian psychologists is the best solution. Such arrangement provides the Department with an in-house nucleus of behavioral scientists on a full-time basis that is able to deal with most situations. The officer-psychologist can provide a dimension unique to his profession. Many officers will rather see this individual than a civilian. On the other hand, many others, and especially spouses, will rather see a non-police psychologist. Thus both can cover the whole gamut of services necessary.

Consultants are the last choice due to their usual lack of police knowledge and typical short-time involvement in projects and other contracted services. Consultants are used by the Dallas Police Department, but with the full-time Psychological Services Unit, their use has been brought down to a minimum.

LOGISTICS

The Police Psychologist should ideally be totally and exclusively involved in his job. Private practice, various consulting or part-time positions, should be avoided due to the splintering effect they may have on the efforts of the psychologist.

Being on call twenty-four hours will warrant the easy accessibility of the psychologist to the Department and vice-versa. The most practical way to accomplish this is through the use of pagers or beepers that will allow for the contacting of the psychologist at all times. If involved in private practice in addition to the main job, a conflict in loyalty may develop which will be detrimental to all involved.

Consequently, the Police Psychologist should be provided with an adequate enough salary that will warrant his wholeheartedly dedication to the job. The better a psychologist is, the more chances he will have to make a high salary through multiple jobs. Thus a Police Department must be aware of this fact and act accordingly.

A Police Psychologist should also be provided with a city automobile equipped with a police radio. This would facilitate contacting him as well as his contacting police personnel; it would help in his identification by police officers who will see him in such a vehicle; and would eliminate the tedious task of keeping a milage log for the psychologist's private car.

Finally, it goes without saying that the Police Psychologist should have the freedom to exercise creativity and innovative thinking and research. At the Psychological Services Unit of the Dallas Police Department, a Sergeant is the Administrative Coordinator and this has been a very satisfactory arrangement since it provides the psychologist with an easily accessible consultant and advisor about police work proper. It is quite helpful if, as in our case, this Sergeant is well read in psychological issues and flexible enough to allow for professional freedom and expansion.

SUMMARY

There is no doubt that the psychologist who wants to have a career in the area of Police Psychology has a wide open field ahead of him. The need for psychological services is real and obvious and the types of involvement are as numerous as the psychologist is willing to puruse. There are some pitfalls and problems inherent in a new situation where there is no "book" to go by. However, it can be extremely exciting and fulfilling to be a part of the first group of psychologists in a brand new field.

ENTRY LEVEL POLICE ASSESSMENT
Don Ellis and Bill Kennedy

While having a long-standing common interest in human behavior, industrial psychologists and professional police seldom have approached the subject
from the same vantage point. In recent years, however, both groups have shown
an increasing awareness that job performance can be predicted to a great extent
through the observation of job-related behavior. Spurred by the mandates of
Federal law, this awareness has led to the development of new and improved
devices for predicting competency. One of the more recent and promising methods
is the assessment center technique.

Assessment centers have their roots in the techniques employed by both
the German and British armies to select officers during World War II. The
pioneer of the technique in industrial usage, however, was Dr. Douglas Bray
of the American Telephone and Telegraph Company, who successfully entrenched
the concept in modern personnel selection.

The term "assessment center" stimulates thoughts of a room or place. In
truth, however, it is a testing process which can be conducted wherever the design of the examination may dictate. Assessment centers are a direct outgrowth
of the behavioral approach which dominates American psychology. Consequently,
the technique places little emphasis on the mind or the personality and even
less on hypothetical concepts such as id, ego, and superego. It is based on
the assumption that actions and general behavior in given situations--regardless
of the reasons for that behavior--constitute the criteria for success and failure
in job performance.

In an assessment center, certain dimensions representative of the *total job*
for which an assessment is to be conducted are determined by a precise and exact
job analysis. This analysis is followed by the formulation of simulation exercises, performance tests, structured interviews, and job knowledge tests geared
to provide an opportunity for the applicant to demonstrate behaviors which can
be rated under standardized conditions to the predetermined dimensions of the
job. A dimension may be representative of knowledge, skill, ability, or an employee characteristic necessitated by the elements, tasks, or duties of the job.
A judgment of each applicant's performance in relation to the requirements of
the various dimensions of the job is made by trained assessors. Job dimension
ratings are complemented by an overall job rating. It is considered to be an
estimate of an applicant's performance not unlike that obtained by scoring and
weighing the components of a battery of tests. An assessment center properly

developed, staffed, and conducted can produce results of great validity.

Recently the City of Fort Worth, Texas established an assessment center as a supplement to its already well-developed program of entry level police screening. The Fort Worth process begins with an initial screening test called the BASIC OCCUPATIONAL LANGUAGE for POLICE OFFICERS or "BOLPA" examination. This examination has been thoroughly tested by a group of qualified psychologists working under a grant to upgrade the screening systems used in the cities of Arlington, Fort Worth, and Wichita Falls, Texas. The BOLPO test was validated through the testing of working police officers in the field and by the testing of applicants who had been accepted as trainees but had not yet received any police training.

The BOLPO test is followed by a "job related" Strength and Agility Test which has been validated for the department. This agility test consists of a series of action events designed to closely resemble incidents that might occur in the field: transporting a person to a place of safety, a street chase, climbing backyard fences and other barriers successfully, climbing stairs, ladders, and other obstacles. Each activity in the strength and agility test is designed to be totally job related. Consequently, one readily recognizes the advantage of this procedure over the traditional police agility tests that required push-ups, sit-ups, weight lifting, etc., all of which are relatively subjective and pseudo job related at best.

Following the Physical Agility Test, the screening process requires police applicants to submit statements of personal history. These statements are checked to assure validity. Presently the polygraph examination only includes selected questions to verify certain points in the background investigation. The polygraph test is followed by a rigid physical examination by the City Health Director based on physical criteria that is necessary for the successful performance of required duties.

Upon successful completion of the Physical Examination, the Background Investigation, and a legal review, six applicants are notified to be present at 8:00 a.m. on the day selected for the assessment center evaluation process, and they are advised to be prepared to spend a full day for the exercises. At the same time three trained assessors are notified to be present also. The assessors are picked as an assessment team from a pool of approximately thirty assessors, each of whom has previously completed sixty hours of assessment training. They have themselves undergone each of the exercises and have experience in the proper evaluation and documentation of the behavioral indices of effective job performance.

Assessment day begins with a brief orientation for the applicants conducted by an assessor. Both applicants and assessors are in casual dress so as to make the exercises as informal as possible, thus permitting the applicant to be at ease so that he may do his best in a relaxed atmosphere. Applicants and assessors are furnished a name tag and first names are used where appropriate. The applicants are told that they are in competition with one another. They are assured that no previous knowledge of the law or of police procedure is necessary during the exercise beyond what the ordinary citizen would normally possess through some knowledge of current events and life in general.

The Work Simulation Exercise then begins. This is the equivalent of the "in-basket" exercise which other assessment centers utilize for managerial positions. The applicant is seated at a desk and is furnished the equipment and materials necessary to complete the exercise. These include: headphones, cassette recorder, emergency call folder, routine assignment folders, and the help file.

The applicant, through a head phone set, receives instructions from a two-hour tape on which the entire exercise is pre-recorded. Following the initial instructions, the applicant is told that he is to consider himself a police officer assigned to a particular numbered unit and when he hears a call for that unit, he is to respond and perform the task which he is given. In the meantime while waiting for a call, he will hear a series of other broadcasts which simulate the "chatter" normally heard on a police radio frequency. While waiting for a call, he is instructed to proceed to accomplish other routine police tasks such as the sorting and filing of very simple arrest cards, the sorting and correlation of stolen property and recovered property records, and the completion of an arrest procedures checklist on specific data. These tasks are made to simulate tasks that an officer assigned to headquarters duty encounters on the job. They are of a very simple nature and a person who had little or no knowledge of office procedures can very quickly discern the proper way to accomplish them.

When he does receive a call for his police unit, he does as the voice on the tape instructs and opens the specific folder indicating the type of call and street address. Upon opening this set of instructions, he finds there are certain situations which exist and he is expected to arrive at some plan of action for coping with the situation. The primary consideration here is basic common sense, sensitivity to the feelings and needs of other persons, and a certain amount of perception in recognizing what the problem actually is. After the candidate has been given time to decide upon his course of action, he is then directed to make a short written report about the action he has taken. After a short interval, he is told to activate the cassette recorder which is furnished on the desk and dictate a report on the work he has done. This type of activity continues for approximately two hours. During this work, the candidate is observed by one of the assessors. At the conclusion of the tape, he is given a short break and returns to write a comprehensive report on one of the police incidents he had handled.

The writing of this report gives the assessor time to collect the other work the applicant has completed, listen to his reports which he has dictated on the cassette recorder, and to complete his own assessment checklist on the exercises during the 45 minutes allotted for writing the comprehensive report. Upon submission of the written report, the applicant is released for a one-hour lunch break and told the time he is expected to return for the remainder of the assessment exercises.

After the lunch break, the applicant participates in a group exercise. Candidates first view video-taped police incidents and write short responses to questions relating to their recommended handling of the incidents. Once again, the incidents are of a very common nature and many courses of action are open for the applicant to choose in the handling of them. Little or no prior knowledge of how police technically handle such incidents is required. What is required and assessed is regard for the feelings and needs of people, common sense, good judgment and perception of what actually has occurred. All applicants then participate in a leaderless group discussion of the incidents while being observed by the assessors.

During this group discussion, the applicant is allowed an opportunity to present his viewpoints on a specific written response he has given to one of the previous questions over the video skits. He then leads a group discussion about his viewpoint, and after a specified time he is to seek the approval of the group relative to the best course of action to follow. He must ask each of them to sign a consensus agreement over the question and signify that they agree with him. The discussion continues until each applicant has had an opportunity to act as a group leader and participate in a discussion led by each of the other applicants until all six questions have been discussed pertaining to the video-taped vignettes.

During this group exercise the applicants are assessed on their independence, perception, sensitivity to people, ability to follow directions, judgment, leadership, oral communications, tolerance for stress, decisiveness, and written skills. This exercise permits assessment of the applicant's ability to speak and interact in a group of peers who are in most cases strangers to each other until the exercise starts.

At the conclusion of the group exercise, a short coffee break is permitted and the assessment room is rearranged for the final exercise which is the face-to-face, structured oral interview between the assessor and the applicant. Each assessor interviews two applicants. The assessor asks a set of structured questions of each applicant. The applicant's responses again are assessed as to their impact in matters of judgment, perception, ability to follow directions, sensitivity to people, leadership, oral communications, tolerance for stress, decisiveness, and independence.

Following the completion of the interview, the applicants are brought together in a group and are permitted a question and answer period with the assessors concerning the complete day. They are told that they will be informed by mail of the results of the assessment within two weeks. They are then released.

On the following work day, the assessors meet and share opinions of the individual applicants. During the assessment, each assessor has seen each applicant in one or more of the exercises. Since he has been responsible for evaluating two applicants in work simulation, two others in group exercise, and has personally interviewed the two remaining applicants, he should have adequate insights into the potential of each applicant. The assessors then collectively arrive at one "team" rating per applicant on his showing in each dimension and his overall effectiveness.

A report to the Chief and his staff is then prepared describing the ratings and their rationale. A much briefer letter summarizing this same information is sent to the applicant.

The Assessment Center of the Fort Worth Police Department is designed to measure the applican'ts demonstrated abilities in the following areas:

I. Cognitive Dimensions
   A. Judgment - Makes sound and logical decisions based on available facts.
   B. Perception - Can quickly identify and interpret the significant details and concepts in a situation.
   C. Follows Directions - Follows oral and written directions promptly and accurately.

II. Interpersonal Dimensions
   A. Sensitivity to People - Considers the feelings and needs of others when dealing with people.
   B. Leadership - Influences the behavior of others through persuasion and reason rather than force and coercion.
   C. Oral Communications - Has command of the spoken language and can be easily understood by others.

III. Effective Dimensions
    A. Tolerance for Stress - Maintains poise and performs tasks under stressful conditions.
    B. Decisiveness - Acts quickly and surely when the situation demands it.
    C. Independence - Can solve problems and make decisions without repeated instructions or close supervision.

IV. Written Skills
    A. Can communicate effectively in written English.

Some of the dimensions are measurable in each of the three exercises and the remainder are measurable in at least two of the other exercises. The ratings for performance in the individual dimensions are described as follows:

Numerical Rating	Definition
1	Outstanding
2	More than acceptable
3	Acceptable (This candidate performs at a level on this dimension which is adequate for an entry level police officer)
4	Barely adequate
5	Unsatisfactory

The overall effectiveness rating of each applicant for the complete Assessment Center is also computed by the assessors. It is a numerical index of the ten (10) dimensions showing overall performance and relative strengths as well as weaknesses in critical categories such as judgment, sensitivity to people, tolerance for stress, independence, decisiveness, leadership, following directions, perception, oral communications and written skills. Each of these dimensions are considered in arriving at the overall effectiveness rating shown below.

OVERALL EFFECTIVENESS

Numerical Rating	Definition
1	Demonstrated outstanding potential to be a police officer
2	Demonstrated more than good potential to be a police officer
3	Demonstrated good potential to be a police officer
4	Demonstrated the minimum potential necessary to be a police officer
5	Did not demonstrate potential to be a police officer

The overall effectiveness rating of applicants will be used as a selection list for employment as a Police Trainee and for assignment to the Police Academy.

In the case of ties on the Overall Effectiveness Ratings, positions are filled by placing the applicants on the selection list according to their BOLPO test grades.

Since we are now in a period of having ample applicants to fill vacancies, it becomes even more important to select the applicants who show the greatest potential for success in the Academy and on the job. It is felt that the Assessment Center enables selecting officials to see the applicant actually performing tasks, to listen to his verbal responses when under stress, and to examine written responses in a way that they have heretofore been unable to achieve through the traditional screening steps. The most advantageous aspect of the technique is that it becomes possible to accomplish this prior to a trainee being entered in the Police Academy and prior to actual employment.

The Assessment Center program has already shown that it is a more appealing method of selection to minority applicants than the oral interview board step. Several minority police officers are trained assessors and are very enthusiastic about the opportunity for minority applicants to be able to functionally demonstrate a degree of ability to perform their duties in competition with other applicants rather than having their selection depend upon a personal appearance before a Police Review Board.

The ultimate measure of effectiveness for the Assessment Center Program is, of course, successful police officers in the field. A study of the individual progress of police officers who have been selected by this method will be an on-going study.

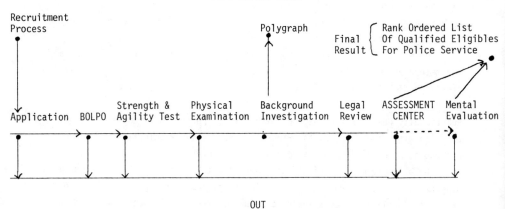

SELECTION MODEL FOR

FOR ENTRY LEVEL POLICE OFFICERS

Fort Worth, Texas

NOTE: Selection of all candidates for police training is to be based upon the
       ranking of eligibles which is representative of an individual appli-
       cant's demonstrated abilities as measured along valid, job-related
       dimensions of an entry level police officer's job.

DEVELOPMENT OF A MENTAL HEALTH SCREENING PROGRAM
FOR A LARGE METROPOLITAN POLICE DEPARTMENT
Lawrence S. Schoenfeld

It has become increasingly obvious in recent years that successful preventive work in the mental health area often revolves around the appropriate
selection and training of individuals whose roles have the greatest impact on
social units. As Caplan has so thoroughly discussed, the development of such
a program demands the active cooperation of those institutions and agencies
which are most capable of identifying and working to meet the needs of a
community.[1] In most cases local police represent, potentially at least, the
most appropriate medicine. Contemporary policemen are involved in a myriad of
social service functions and are, by job function if not by design, the largest
group of indigenous mental health paraprofessionals in any given community.
This short article deals with my experiences with a police department that has
attempted to realize this potential.

Late in 1969 I became head of the consultation and education division of
a large community mental health center. Although this center was designed to
serve only one quarter of a city of 800,000, it represented the only center
that was available to the entire community. As has been the case of most
others involved in the community mental health movement, I found myself the
only professional within the consultation and education division. Undaunted,
I set out to learn about the community agencies and then introduced the concepts of consultation and community mental health to a number of individuals.

Prior to my joining the center, it had held a workshop exploring conditions
in the Barrios, a large ghetto. Represented was the housing authority, the
police department, community workers, Barrio citizens, and mental health center
personnel. This meeting was called in order to facilitate communication and
thus prevent open, violent confrontation between the residents of the Barrio
and the represented agencies. Many recommendations were made. Those appropriate for mention here were: (1) Communication was pointed out as the main
problem and was especially felt to be needed between the police and housing
project residents; (2) The mental health center was urged to become involved
in the selection and training of police and in the training of housing officials; and (3) The police department should always be on the look-out for the
policeman who "goes bad", and also take measures to insure a better image for
the police as a whole.

As a follow-up to this conference and to my initial letter to the police department explaining consultation and education, I planned to talk with the Chief of Police. This turned out to be more difficult than I anticipated. I found it necessary to identify an influential person who might secure the appointment for me. I have learned over the years that it never hurts to have a wide network of associates who are willing to put in a good word for you.

After a most cordial meeting with the chief it was mutually agreed that I would write him, summarizing our conversation and listing the proposals that we had discussed that might be mutually beneficial to the police department and to the mental health center. He then would discuss these proposals with appropriate management and we would then negotiate for particular projects. The letter that was sent summarized the philosophy behind the community Mental Health Center movement and outlined six areas that had been discussed and seemed of mutual interest. These were:

1. The mental health center consult with the police academy in the preparation and presentation of the police trainee curriculum.

2. The mental health center provide mental health screening evaluations of police cadets or probationary patrolmen when indicated.

3. The mental health center provide a satellite clinic in the police department for the evaluation, treatment, and referral of police department employees who requested help with emotional problems.

4. The mental health center provide consultation to policemen requesting assistance in dealing with interpersonal problems they encountered in their daily work.

5. The mental health center provide group consultation to police department bureaus on problems idiosyncratic of their bureaus.

6. The mental health center make available to police administrators consultation when mental health information was needed before policy decisions could be made.

To establish additional proximity and develop a felt need for consultation, a follow-up visit was arranged with the Community Relations Division of the Police Department in order to observe a half-day of academy training. No reply was received despite numerous phone calls and occasional follow-up letters. Later it was learned that this was probably the result of two factors:

1. The conference that the police attended in 1969 which involved the mental health center and which has previously been described, and;

2. A prior experience with a mental health consultant.

The department apparently felt that the mental health center's involvement in the 1969 conference left the center prejudiced against the police department and identified with the Barrio--or radical elements in the community. Perceived lack of trust and potential conflicts of interest, therefore, threatened progress. In addition, one year earlier the police department had hired a mental health consultant to hold a human relations laboratory seminar with a specific, agreed upon outline. After beginning that seminar, the consultant had decided to involve himself in "the myriad of issues and problems relating to the internal affairs of the department." This had occurred without a renegotiation of sanction and had left the chief administrative officers questioning the trustworthiness of mental health professionals. Obviously, my predecessor had forgotten that a consultant cannot assume to have free reign within an organization. Sanction is for a particular activity and contracts must be renegotiated so as not to place any future consultative attempts in jeopardy.

Late in 1970 I received a request to orient all patrolmen concerning emergency mental health procedures. It was decided that I respond favorably to this request, for it provided the opportunity to re-establish some proximity and possibly build a reputation of competence. This also represented the first actual need of the department that received appropriate sanction. It is of interest that this request required the consultants to work almost around the clock, for patrolmen were to be oriented prior to going on shifts. This service was provided according to the department's usual work schedule and represented a considerable time inconvenience for the consultants. However, the orientations were well received by the police patrolmen, and many myths concerning mental health professionals were exploded through the informal discussions that occurred around coffee prior to or after the formal presentation. It was also learned through this educational contract that the request for the service had been directed to the medical school and not to the mental health center despite the fact that the mental health center was administered by and staffed by medical school personnel. Apparently, the concept of "Medical School" connoted more trust and competence than "Mental Health Center". This led us to believe future contacts should be made through the medical school rather than the mental health center even though the same personnel would be involved.

The passing of a year brought major changes in high ranking city staff personnel. A new City Manager was hired and a new Chief of Police appointed. The mental health personnel interested in consultation and education spent considerable energy meeting and consulting with different departments within the city government structure. Working with the department of human resources, we had the occasion of meeting with the Associate Manager for Management and Planning Services. He had been trained at the Master's level in Psychology and felt that it would be advantageous for the city to begin to consider a mental health screening program for the police department. His positive view toward mental health professionals and interest in human resources led to a meeting between the Chief of Police and the Chairman of the department of Psychiatry for preliminary discussions. This led to an informal request that the medical school consider assisting the city in the selection of police officer candidates.

In response to this informal request a meeting was arranged with the Associate City Manager responsible for the police department, the Director of Personnel, and the Assistant Director of Personnel to discuss the selection process and to seek sanction for mental health consultation in the police screening process.

At that time the process of selection involved a written screening test, police cadet capacity questionnaire, an agility test, a driver's test, a physical examination, a screening board examination, a background evaluation, and then final review by the Chief of Police. At each step in this process an applicant could be eliminated. In order to become familiar with this process and to seek sanction throughout the screening process most of the individuals involved with the various steps were interviewed and the possibility of beginning a mental health screening process discussed. Additional time was spent interviewing patrolmen, line supervisors, and administrative police officers in an attempt to identify the goals that each of these groups might have for a mental health screening program. The consultant also rode with police officers on all shifts in order to become intimately acquainted with the role function of the patrolman as well as to get assistance in identifying personality traits that might be both advantageous and disadvantageous for police cadets.

A review of the literature concerning the mental health screening of police cadets was undertaken. It was accompanied by an intensive review of the personnal folders of those police officers identified by supervisors as falling into two groups: (1) the best patrolman on the force, and (2) those patrolmen the supervisors would have preferred eliminated during the screening process due to what they considered emotional instability.

This review of personnal folders formed an impression that there was a significant difference between "good" verses "poor" police officers. The personnel folders seemed to suggest the differences along a number of dimensions:

disciplinary action, citizen complaints, car accidents, injuries, and days off job due to extenuating circumstances. These impressions were later subjected to research and will be reported at a later date.

A review of the literature revealed that in 1957 fewer than 16% of police departments surveyed indicated a usage of psychological tests.[2] Six years later, a survey reported that almost 39% of the respondents used a psychological method in evaluating applicants,[3] while in 1972 Murphy reported almost 40% usage of some sort of psychological examination.[4] The Minnesota Multiphasic Personality Inventory seemed to be the most prevalent personality test. The next most frequently used personality method seemed to be the psychiatric interview. There seemed to be a trend over the years to a multiple selection procedure and growing popularity of what has been referred to as "Situational Testing" for the applicants.

This preliminary exploration led to the City Manager requesting a formal written proposal for police cadet psychiatric screening. The proposal was submitted and accepted by the city and the police department. The proposal made it clear that the selection was a difficult and complicated problem. It was felt that we could be of assistance in the selection process through a psychiatric screen by making one of two recommendations ("High-risk" or "Passable") to the Chief of Police after the applicant had passed the screening board, but prior to his/her appointment by the Chief of Police. It was understood at the time that a recommendation of "High-risk" did not necessarily carry with it the impression of "deviate" or "totally unsuitable" but that the applicant appeared to have traits that might not make him/her an optimal risk for the public responsibility that a police officer must assume. It was our recommendation that the mental health screening be based on: (1) evaluation of personnel file, which would include, a) screening examination, b) agility testing, c) physical examination, d) background investigation; (2) information obtained by observation of the screening board or through written comments by the screening board; (3) review of the Minneapolis Multiphasic Personality Inventory; (4) an individual psychodiagnostic interview; and (5) the use of individual psychodiagnostic testing when indicated. The procedures as outlined were based on:

1. The literature review which reflected that a psychiatric interview and Minneapolis Multiphasic Personality Inventory were the most used screening devices.

2. The belief that prior experiences as represented in the background examination probably represented the best single predictor for subsequent performance.

3. An attempt to get a broad base of data in order to develop the evaluator as the instrument of screening.

This program was begun in 1972 and has continued since that date. The department has made available all information that has been requested in order to make the recommendations, and at times the consultant has provided more intensive evaluation of particular candidates when this was deemed necessary.

In the first year of operation 144 applicants were evaluated and nine found to be "high-risk". Of these nine, seven were hired by the department. In the second year of operation 142 applicants were screened and thirteen were felt to be "high-risk". Of these thirteen, only two were hired.

In addition to the screening of hundreds of applicants, this arrangement has made an educational and scientific contribution. Psychology residents have been trained in this model of selection by participating in the psychodiagnostic interviews. Evaluation of this screening program has been intrical to it. This has been reflected in a Master's thesis and a number of papers.

This paper has tried to primarily focus on the method of entry in the establishment of a consultation program with a metropolitan police department. It has also highlighted a particular method of screening. It is felt that this screening program is a benefit to the department, to the citizens of the community, and to the research and educational mission of our institution. Such a method of consultation and screening is recommended with caution: any program involving the mental health screening and selection of police officers must have a research component as an integral part to validate or invalidate its existence.

REFERENCES

1. Caplan, Gerald. *The Theory and Practice of Mental Health Consultation*, New York, Basic Books, Inc., 1970.

2. Oglesby, T. "Use of emotional screening in the selection of police applicants", *Pub. Personnel Rev.*, 18, 1957, pp. 228-231.

3. Narrol, H.G. and Levitt, F.F., "Formal assessment procedures in police selection," *Psychological Reports*, 12, 1963, pp. 691-694.

4. Murphy, J.J., "Current practices in use of psychological testing by police agencies," *Journal of Criminal Law, Criminology and Police Science*, 63, 1972, pp. 570-576.

ASSERTION IN LAW ENFORCEMENT
James T. Turner

Current literature in both professional and lay circles reflects a growing interest in assertive behavior as a means of increasing personal and/or professional effectiveness, enhancing self-esteem, and protecting individual rights.[1,2,3,4] Unfortunately, all too often assertiveness has been pictured--especially in the popular press--as a license for the release of aggressive, damaging behaviors. Assertiveness, on the contrary, affords a means of forceful, direct, but non-aggressive behavior in a variety of stressful situations.

Given the unique personal stresses that the law enforcement officer experiences on the job, as well as the high public visibility which goes with the job, it is important that the distinction between assertion and aggression be clear. To act appropriately, the officer needs to have a comfortable repertoire of assertive behaviors to utilize in a variety of interpersonal encounters. One example of such an approach to law enforcement training is the crisis intervention training by Goldstein.[5]

Responsible assertive behavior can lead to an improvement in the relations between an officer and the public he serves. Officers experience increased feelings of personal effectiveness and a decrease in public complaints. For while the individual may not like the law-related action, i.e., receiving a speeding ticket, he/she will respect the manner in which the situation is handled. Finally, an officer can enhance personal safety by defusing potentially violent, emotional situations through the professional manner in which the work is performed.

Assertive Behavior

Assertive behavior involves both the behavioral and emotional freedom to enhance self-respect through standing up for one's own rights and when necessary the rights of others.

Studies have applied assertive training to a variety of interpersonal problems, i.e., dating anxiety,[6] males with difficulties toward authority,[7] and professional groups such as dental students.[8] In general, the results of such studies indicated increased assertive skills resulting in improved interpersonal relations and self regard. In addition, it appears that professional performance can be enhanced when the difficulty is primarily interpersonal in nature.[9]

The basic components of assertive training have been developed over a period of years. Alberti and Emmons outlined not only procedures but a philosophical

rationale based on human rights.[10]   The methods of assertive training have been
spelled out in basic research.[11,12]   A self-help manual by Fensterheim and Baer
outlined applications of assertive training to a variety of personal/interpersonal
areas.[13]   This was followed by a manual for trainers by Lange and Jakubowski.[14]
This book introduced the concept of responsible assertion.   Responsible assertiveness stresses not only standing up for one's own rights through direct, honest
and appropriate interpersonal behavior, but also using one's own assertiveness
to help others stand up for their rights.   The implications arise that assertiveness is a mutual endeavor in which the self respect of both persons involved is enhanced.   This, then, appears to be a major distinction between assertion and aggression.

Assertiveness is sometimes rejected by law enforcement officers.   These
officers fear that being assertive rather than aggressive would give the appearance of vulnerability and cause them to lose control over other people.   On
the contrary, the ability to act assertively in a situation increases one's
control over oneself and others.   The variety of options available to handle
the job in a professional manner are increased over the stereotyped usage of
aggressive behavior.

The use of assertive behavior parallels the concept of minimal force usage.
That is, the officer utilizes the minimally assertive behavior possible to
correct a situation.   The degree of force is then escalated in steps until the
situation is satisfactorily resolved.   At all times the officer is conveying
respect toward the other person as a human being with certain rights.   The maintenance of this assertive behavior in the face of aggression may be a difficult
task.

Aggression

In a single isolated confrontation a variety of factors may come into play
producing an aggressive response.   This is especially true in law enforcement
situations.   In addition, these factors apply equally to the law enforcement
officer as well as the public with which the officer deals.   Hopefully, adequate
training separates the officer from the public.

Five specific factors have been outlined as occurring in general interpersonal interactions by Lange and Jakubowski:[15]

1) Powerlessness/Threat
2) Overreaction
3) Beliefs
4) Prior nonassertion
5) Skills deficit

This list seems to be especially important in law enforcement incidents. In law enforcement incidents the individual who feels powerless or threatened may engage in "flight or fight" behavior. The individual feels as if he/she has no recourse even before the face to face interaction has occurred with the law enforcement officer. On the other hand, it may be the officer who falls into this situation. When threatened by feelings of incompetency and doubt, the officer may overcompensate by acting aggressively, bullying the individual.

Closely related is the possibility of aggression produced by overreaction in a given situation. On the part of the public it may arise from difficulties with authority figures or a build-up of emotional stress. On the part of the officer overreaction may occur as a result of poor judgment, his own stresses or as an interaction of the other factors discussed here.

Beliefs are one of the strongest factors in aggressive behavior. The public may be reacting on the basis of stereotypes and expectation developed by a variety of sources, i.e., friends, television portrayals of law enforcement personnel. The officer may believe that an aggressive response is the most effective. Important to both but especially to the law enforcement officer are beliefs outlined by Albert Ellis as "shoulds and oughts."[16] The belief that people should behave in a certain way and if they don't then they deserve what they get is extremely detrimental to performance. Respect for the individual must be maintained by the officer in the face of aggression. In some ways this is much akin to Roger's unconditional positive regard.[17] Maintenance of such an attitude is a monumental task and needs to be supported through training to reinforce the concept of professionalism.

Aggression may also occur as the result of repeated violations of an individual's personal rights. The individual may see the law enforcement officer's action as the proverbial "straw that broke the camel's back." Such a situation is likely to lead to an overreaction to the particular situation. The same phenomena can occur with the officer especially if in the working situation he/she has personal rights repeatedly violated.

Finally, aggression occurs when an individual has no other behavioral patterns with which to deal with the situation. Once again this is a case where training must supply alternative professional behaviors and the opportunity to develop these skills.

Social Skills Training Program

The basic format of the program is based upon a ten-hour training program. An emphasis is placed upon role-playing, behavioral rehearsal, and modeling.

The basic learning points outlined by Goldstein, Monti, Sardino, and Green serve as a framework for the participant conceptual organization.[18] There are four general learning points:

1) Observing and protecting oneself against threats

2) Calming the situation

3) Acquisition of relevant information

4) Appropriate action for disposition and/or resolution of the situation

Different from Goldstein, et al's approach these points are used as a graded series of action which are used in situations not typically labeled as crisis intervention. Some of the role-playing situations are listed below.[19] In addition, the participants usually generate a number growing out of their own experience.

1) Routine traffic stop

a) High ranking official (officer, mayor, congressman)

b) Angry wife/refusal to comply

c) Cooperative individual

2) Possible driving-under-the-influence violation

a) Outcome negative

b) Outcome positive

c) Outcome borderline

3) Routine stop leading to probable search for drugs

a) Outcome positive

b) Outcome negative

4) Assault-type situations

a) Drug usage involved

b) Racial

c) Stress factors

5) Family disturbance

The situations listed above have been placed in order of increasing risk to the individual officer's safety. Thereby, the attempt to change behavior in a situation of minimal danger is encouraged.

This program is presented to the police involved as a means of increasing their personal safety. That is, the use of responsible assertive behavior will prevent escalation of interpersonal conflicts and place the officer in control of the situation. This maintenance of control is an important factor in personal safety. Aggression, following the differentiation of Hollandsworth, is defined as the use of threats or punishment; more specifically, the use of nonverbal physical threats and/or verbal indications of rejection or negative evaluation.[20]

The program also gives some training in the role of skills in nonwork situations. A formal rationale of why people act aggressively is explored with the police officers. They are encouraged to not only apply these concepts to other persons under stress but also to examine their own reactions under stress. The course is presented as a short-term intervention which will give them some skills but is by no means an end. Rather they can role-play with each other and rehearse their own behavior during lulls in work or even on their own time, thereby continually upgrading their own skills without dependence upon detailed training programs. The key is for him/her to improve his/her own skills. As a side benefit supervisors seem to gain insight into how role-playing and modeling can be used as a tool for sharing experience.

Studies, in general, have indicated that law enforcement personnel do not differ extremely from the general population in personality characteristics.[21,22,23] These findings include:[24]

1) Average on personality characteristics, sociableness, and experimentation

2) Above average range of intellectual functioning

3) Perceive people more positively than college males or ministers

These studies often have focused on personnel in their initial training periods. As pointed out by Boyd, Davis, and Prytula, it is possible that differences exist between entry-level personnel and those who have been working for a period of time. Boyd, et al, collected data from three law enforcement agencies of active police personnel including a military police unit.[25]

The results indicated that active law enforcement personnel are similar to the trainees in the prior study with the restriction that more variability from average was found in the second study.

As relates to military policemen, the study reported that military policemen were not significant or different in terms of personality characteristics from other law enforcement personnel. In general, military police appeared to be more tough-minded and realistic while displaying a high positive attitude toward people in law enforcement settings.

In terms of values and value systems police are more concerned with personal values than other Americans,

> They care more about *a sense of accomplishment* and about being *capable, intellectual,* and *logical.* These findings suggest an image of the policeman as a person who, contrary to popular conception, sees himself as striving to perform his occupational functions in a professionally competent and responsible manner . . . police place a relatively high value on self-fulfillment, but one that exists within the framework provided by an authority-dominated and rule-oriented social organization.[26]

Based on the preceding information that law enforcement personnel are basically similar to the general population, it seems the interpersonal stress situations in which law enforcement personnel engage in daily have the same pitfalls as those faced by ordinary citizens. In particular these interpersonal encounters are by their very nature ones in which aggressive behavior is more likely to occur. The policeman's ability to respond in a responsibly assertive manner could reduce the incidents of aggressive behavior both on his/her own part and on the part of the individual. The ability to gauge the degree of assertiveness needed would prevent overreaction and diffuse potentially explosive situations. Finally, the ability to maintain assertion in the face of aggression would keep the officer in control of the situation. The officer would be able to carry out duties in a highly professional manner.

In addition, it would appear that the approach toward police personnel should be presented as a personal challenge to grow and become more professional. The material presented needs to contain both a challenge in terms of behavior change and a challenge in terms of development of an intellectual framework for a rationale of assertive behavior. The material is then seen as enhancing personal development while also making one more competent within the organization. As pointed out by Goldstein, Monti, Sardino and Green, the endorsement and active involvement of significant figures within the organizational structure defines the program as within the accepted approved rule/behavior structures.[27]

Psychological Intervention In Law Enforcement Settings

It seems appropriate at this time to talk concerning the application of psychological techniques in law enforcement settings. One important factor for the intervening professional to realize in terms of operations and planning the number one priority is the performance of law enforcement duties, i.e., shifting to man patrols and extended shifts under heavy demand periods. Therefore, a training program needs to be adaptable to changing needs and changing availability of personnel.

Second, mental health professionals working in this area should be sensitive to their own attitudes toward law enforcement personnel. That is, the presence or absence of positive attitudes toward the value of the police job and respect for those persons performing the job spells the difference in the success or failure of an intervention strategy.

Finally, a mental health professional needs to spend time in a police setting. Such experience should range from line duty to administrative affairs to the local police bar. Such experience allows one to observe the job requirements, both technical and interpersonal. Some of the stresses unique to this particular vocation become apparent, i.e., tolerance for boredom. In addition, the police subculture makes explicit demands upon the individual. The use of a technical advisor from within the particular department with which you are working is helpful. She/He can serve as a valuable source of both official procedural matter and unofficial "house" rules.

Response Maintenance

The problem of response maintenance constitutes the greatest challenge in any applied setting. Behavioral interventions into ongoing systems tend to be just that, intervention which fails to incorporate the means of follow-through and continuity. Part of this result may arise from our concept of training and possibly from funding patterns. The fatal key may tend to be in the elaborateness and sophistication of our intervention strategy. That is, whatever impact is made by mental health professionals will be carried on by personnel whose main concern lies elsewhere. It seems the role of the consultant is to reduce the complexity of applying psychosocial techniques and knowledge so that it is not only utilizable but also attractive to the consumer. Essentially, what one teaches are tools for each individual to continue developing skills in his/her own best interest. Behavioral interventions can then serve as growth tools.[28]

Another means of response maintenance lies in the concept of a naturalistic test probe. Such a procedure involves the programming of a situation which offers an opportunity to test assertive skills in real life situations. Such a test program requires certain controls. All the individuals involved should be informed that periodically unannounced test probes will occur. These tests are for the purpose of evaluating the individual's ability to handle difficult situations. Second, control must be maintained at all times so that the officer's safety is insured.

A test probe might be arranged in the following manner. Individuals are trained to portray roles which might stress the officer's ability to remain assertive, i.e., a woman who becomes very angry when issued a speeding ticket. The situation would then be arranged such that the partner in the vehicle is aware of the test set-up and sees that the car is positioned at the appropriate location to see the speeding violation. The unaware officer would then apprehend and proceed to deal with the situation. The other officer would assert control to maintain the situation. The participating officer then would be rated by the confederate, the supervising officer, and by himself. These data could then be used to evaluate the officer's ability.

REFERENCES

1. Alberti, R.E., and Emmons, M.L. *Your perfect right*. San Luis Obispo, California: Impact, 1974.

2. Blanchard, E.B., Turner, J., Eschette, N., and Coury, V.M. Assertiveness training for dental students. *Journal of Dental Education*. 1977, 41, pp. 206-208.

3. Fensterheim, H., and Baer, J. *Don't say yes when you want to say no*. New York: Dell, 1975.

4. Lange, A.J. and Jakubowski, P. *Responsible assertive behavior*. Champaign, Illinois: Research Press, 1976.

5. Goldstein, A.P., Monti, P.J., Sardino, T.J. and Green, D.J. *Police crisis intervention*. Kalamazoo, Michigan: Behaviordelia, 1977.

6. Curran, J.P. Social skills training and systematic desensitization. *Behavior Research and Therapy*, 1975, 13, 65-68.

7. Rimm, D.C., Snyder, J.J., Depue, R.A., Haanstad, M.J., and Armstrong, D.P. Assertive training versus rehearsal, and the importance of making an assertive response. *Behavior Research and Therapy*, 1976, 14, 315-321.

8. Blanchard, et al, 1977.

9. Ibid.

10. Alberti and Emmons, 1974.

11. McFall, R.M. and Marston, A.R. An experimental investigation of behavior rehearsal in assertive training. *Journal of Abnormal Psychology*, 1970, 75, pp. 295-303.

12. Hersen, M., Eisler, R.M., Miller, P.M., Johnson, M.B., and Pinkston, S.S. Effects of practice, instructions, and modeling on components of assertive behavior. *Behavior Research and Therapy*, 1973, 11, pp. 443-451.

13. Fensterheim and Baer, 1975.

14. Lange and Jakubowski, 1976.

15. Ibid.

16. Ellis, A. and Harper, R.A. *A guide to rational living.* Englewood Cliffs, New Jersey: Prentice-Hall, 1961.

17. Rogers, C.R. *On becoming a person.* Boston: Houghton Mifflin, 1961.

18. Goldstein, et al, 1977.

19. Turner, J.T. *The development of assertive skills in law enforcement personnel: A program report.* Paper presented at the annual meeting of the Southeastern Psychological Association, Hollywood, Florida, May, 1977.

20. Hollandsworth, J.G., Jr. Differentiating assertion and aggression: Some behavioral guidelines. *Behavior Therapy,* 1977, 8, pp. 347-352.

21. Rubin, J. Personality of police recruits. In R.F. Steadman (Ed.), *The Police and the Community.* Baltimore: John Hopkins University Press, 1972.

22. Prytula, R., Champagne, J.J., Grigsby, C.F., and Soltys, A.J. The personality and characteristics of police officers and their attitudes toward others. *The Police Chief,* 1972, 12, 54.

23. Boyd, P.W., Davis, S.F. and Prytula, R.E. *Personality characteristics of civilian and military policemen.* Manuscript submitted for publication, 1977.

24. Prytula, et al, 1972.

25. Boyd, et al, 1977.

26. Rokeach, Milton. *The nature of human values.* New York: The Free Press, 1976.

27. Goldstein, et al, 1977

28. Turner, J.T. *Radical behaviorism: A growth approach to clinical practice.* Paper presented at the Midwestern Association of Behavior Analysis, Chicago, May, 1976.

ATTITUDE CHANGE AMONG POLICE
John R. Milligan

There has been an extensive amount of literature concerning profession-
alization of police through increasing levels of educational attainment. The
literature contains evidence that increased education for police results in
(a) greater job satisfaction,[1] (b) better job performance,[2] and (c) more open-
minded, less authoritarian or punitive attitudes.[3] Education also is hypothe-
sized as preparing professionals who will be able to exercise discretion in
highly charged political environments and leading to criminal justice practitioners who appreciate the "why" of human behavior and thus less likely to respond in a cavalier fashion in domestic disputes or an abrasive manner toward
minority groups.[4] These college educated practitioners will also be better
able to cope with conflicting role demands and insitutionalized limitations on
societal responses to criminal behavior.

Social scientists have advocated, more by logical deduction than by empirical research, that it is best to select democratic non-authoritarian police
to perform police functions in a democratic, heterogenous society such as ours.
We lack empirical evidence as to both the desirability of different personality
types in police work and the criteria on which to measure performance related
to such personality types. In the unlikely event that democratic non-authoritarian personnel should survive the current police selection processes; there
is a high probability they will either leave police service due to the frustrations and limitations of paramilitary organizations[5] which have changed neither
their essential organizational structure nor managerial methods since 1829; or
they will simply allow situational job related pressures to suppress and eventually change democratic attitudes.

The differences in attitude between college educated and non-college educated police are often cited as the justification of encouraging higher levels of
education for police. There are very few psychologists, criminal justice educators and researchers who would disagree that the police and society need such
characteristics as open-mindedness in the police which seems so often associated
with college education. Implied in all such arguments favoring college education for police is the concept that the observed differences in attitudes are
the result of college education and not some other variable which could account
for the observed differences. In the criminal justice field we do not have any
scientific evidence to support the conjecture that college education is the
variable which accounts for the observed differences in attitudes. Essentially,

what we have been presented by advocates of college education is post-test differences which could just as logically be explained by socio-economic variables or possibly a wide variety of experiences other than education.

Although, college is important to police; its influence on changing attitudes in a socially desirable direction is highly suspect. Specifically, we may be observing differences which have little, if anything, to do with college education itself. Criminal justice personnel who chose to further their education and college educated people who enter police work may already have general personality traits which are favorable to democratic ideas. Those who have not received college education or chose not to further their education when there is opportunity to do so may have personality characteristics such as authoritarianism which are resistive to democratic ideas. Lefkowitz has indicated in his review of this subject that police as a group prefer the paramilitary structure of police organizations.[6]

Indeed, the overwhelming weight of evidence gathered since World War II in the area of authoritarianism supports the concept that such attitudes are enduring psychological traits acquired over a lifetime and subject to little manipulation. The fact that most police personnel tend to come from blue-collar families and the lower-middle class could just as well account for the observed differences in both educational level and attitudes of police. Exposure to college and differences between groups of police may simply reflect changing recruitment and economic conditions in which more middle-class college graduates are entering the job market and specifically the law enforcement job market.

There has been an extensive amount of research directed to attitude and opinion research in social psychology. Relatively little of this research has been directed toward the experimental manipulation of attitudes and opinions among such specialized groups as policemen. Previous research has centered around personality variables such as authoritarianism as related to expressed opinions among such groups as the police, however, there have been few studies which have actually attempted the manipulation of police attitudes and opinions.

The ability to modify attitudes and opinions within a police department is seen by this researcher as a major unrecognized problem both for the police administrator and the college level educator of police in the classroom. University level education for criminal justice personnel may be largely ineffective if the presentation of innovative ideas, concepts and theories are met with indifference or attitudinal sets which prevent the student from understanding or appreciating the idea being communicated. Dr. Larry Hoover in his 1975 Mono-

graph on Police Educational Characteristics and Curricula points to a prepon-
derence of studies which emphasized the purpose of college education as being
in the understanding and appreciation of theory relating to the control of
criminal behavior by structured societal response to such behavior. Attitudinal
sets which interfere with effective learning must be identified and changed,
before any benefit can be derived from college level education.

Police administrators who have devoted substantial time and energy to implementing new ideas and concepts developed by researchers in the criminal justice field often are surprised by the resistance new programs receive from the
rank and file in their departments. In some cases the tenure of police chiefs
has been determined by the ability or lack of ability to overcome resistive
attitudes toward change by the rank and file policemen.

The study reported here addresses only one small issue within one of the
two major areas previously mentioned. That issue is the effect on attitude of
police toward controversial issues such as victimless crimes and formal college
instruction emphasizing those issues. This study attempts to detect differences
in attitudes as a result of college instruction on various issues in criminal
justice.

METHODOLOGY

The methodology for this study involved the use of a control and experimental group in a college classroom setting with pre and post measures of expressed attitudes. The control group (n=23) for this study was a class of
policemen attending a college level course on physical science while the experimental group (n=23) was a criminology class composed of all policemen. As
with similar educational studies using naturally occurring groups, such as
classrooms of students, randomization of subjects between control and experimental groups was not possible. Statistical control by use of analysis of covariance was used to control for pre existing differences within the two groups
in the absence of randomization.

Both groups were administered pre and post attitude questionnaires asking
the subjects the strength and direction of their attitudes using a Likert-
type scale on ten issues in criminal justice. These issues ranged from legalization of abortion to limiting police searches for evidence (See Appendix A).
Two hours per week over a three month period were devoted to instruction and
discussion over the ten issues.

At the conclusion of the course, students evaluated the instructor on
various personality and educational items such as perceived expertise on the

subjects and manner of presentation. These student ratings gave the instructor overall above average ratings with individual ratings ranging from average to excellent.

RESULTS

Analysis of covariance results obtained significant levels of statistical differences beyond the .05 level on two of the ten questions between the experimental and control groups. Significant differences were found in the experimental group (post) on the legalization of marijuana beyond the .01 level. A summary of these results are presented in Table 1. (See Table 1.)

Significant differences in the experimental group were also found on the variable of legalization of prostitution at the .02 level. These results are shown by Table 2. (See Table 2.)

The questions which had the least amount of change in the experimental group dealt with (1) limitations on the search for evidence, (2) limitations on the legal use of wiretaps and, (3) the prosecution of police for illegal actions.

Analysis was also made as to the reliability of the questionnaire used in this study. Reliability estimates, (coefficient alpha) were at the .62 level. Although these are not high reliability estimates they are viewed by the researcher as useful since reliability is effected by both sample size and number of items on the instrument. The results of the reliability study are presented in Table 3. (See Table 3.)

DISCUSSION

The results are suggestive as to the effect of college instruction on attitudes. Previous research has been consistent in noting that attitudes are resistant to manipulation. This study, finding significant change on two of ten items tends to confirm such studies. The fact that any change whatsoever occured in such a relatively short period of time and on topics which tend to be controversial is of value. The effect of college instruction on attitudes is difficult to measure and requires more varied methodologies which can control or investigate other important variables. From this study we may tentatively conclude that relatively little attitude change can be expected as a result of college instruction and even this change may not endure over long periods of time; nor may it be independent of situational variables.

Previously reported studies which report differences in attitude between college educated and non-college educated policemen may be making unwarranted conclusions that such differences are the result of college education and not some other uncontrolled variable. This study has highlighted the need for further study as to the value of college education in police selection and its functionality in police departments. Another area, only briefly mentioned in this paper in which research is lacking is the area of attitude change within the police department and resistance to change within departments by the rank and file.

REFERENCES

1. Lefkowitz, J., Psychological attributes of policemen: A review of research and opinion. *Journal of Social Issues*, 1975, 31(1), 3-26.

2. Cohen, R. and Chaiken, J.M. *Police background characteristics and performance*. Lexington, Massachusetts: Lexington Books, 1973.

3. Culler, I.B., Higher education and policemen: Attitudinal differences between freshman and senior police college students. *Journal of Criminal Law, Criminology and Police Science*, 1972, 63, 396-401.

4. Hoover, L.T., Police educational characteristics and curricula (Law Enforcement Assistance Administration, U.S. Department of Justice). Washington, D.C.: U.S. Government Printing Office, July, 1975.

5. Lefkowitz, J. Industrial-organization psychology and the police, *American Psychologist*, May, 1977, 32(5), 346-364.

6. Ibid.

TABLE 1

ANALYSIS OF COVARIANCE
(LEGALIZED MARIJUANA)

Source of Variation	Sum of Squares	df	Mean Square	F	Sig of F
Covariates	132.98	5	26.60	5.45	0.00
6. Insanity Defense (Pre)	0.16	1	0.16	0.03	0.86
7. Prosecution of Illegal Police Actions (Pre)	23.97	1	23.97	4.92	0.03
8. Legalized Pornography (Pre)	108.20	1	108.20	22.18	0.00
9. Limit on Wiretaps (Pre)	12.88	1	12.88	2.64	0.11
10. Limit on Searches (Pre)	0.02	1	0.02	0.00	0.96
Main Effects	39.22	1	39.22	8.04	0.01
Control and Experimental Groups	39.22	1	39.22	8.04	0.01
Explained	172.20	6	28.70	5.88	0.00
Residual	190.24	39	4.88		
Total	362.43	45	8.05		

TABLE 2

ANALYSIS OF COVARIANCE
(LEGALIZED PROSTITUTION)

Sources of Variation	Sum of Squares	df	Mean Square	F	Sig of F
Covariates	384.71	5	76.94	26.98	0.00
1. Legalized Abortions (Pre)	10.99	1	10.99	3.85	0.06
2. Legalized Marijuana (Pre)	0.98	1	0.98	0.34	0.56
3. Capitol Punishment (Pre)	0.32	1	0.32	0.11	0.74
4. Legalized Prostitution (Pre)	170.18	1	170.18	59.68	0.00
5. Legalized Gambling (Pre)	0.01	1	0.01	0.00	0.95
Main Effects	16.54	1	16.54	5.80	0.02
Control and Experimental Group	16.54	1	16.54	5.80	0.02
Explained	401.25	6	66.87	23.45	0.00
Residual	111.20	39	2.85		
Total	512.45	45	11.39		

TABLE 3

RELIABILITY ANALYSIS FOR POLICE ATTITUDE STUDY

VARIABLES	ALPHA IF ITEM DELETED
Question 1 (Abortion)	0.57
Question 2 (Marijuana)	0.66
Question 3 (Capital Punishment)	0.62
Question 4 (Prostitution)	0.58
Question 5 (Gambling)	0.56
Question 6 (Insanity)	0.60
Question 7 (Prosecution of Police)	0.60
Question 8 (Pornography)	0.55
Question 9 (Wire Tap)	0.62
Question 10 (Search)	0.56
Reliability Coefficients	10 Items
Alpha = 0.62	Standardized Item Alpha = 0.60

APPENDIX A

ATTITUDE SURVEY

This survey provides an opportunity for you to express your feelings toward various issues in the area of criminal justice. You are asked to indicate the strength of your belief toward each statement by circling the number from strongly agree to strongly disagree. This is a voluntary survey and you are not required to participate. In the upper right section of this survey you are asked to give the last four numbers of your social security account number so that the results of this survey may be compared with a follow-up survey to be given at a latter date.

1. Legalized abortion

   11   10   9   8   7   6   5   4   3   2   1

Strongly agree   Strongly disagree

2. Legalization of marijuana

   11   10   9   8   7   6   5   4   3   2   1

Strongly agree   Strongly disagree

3. Capital Punishment

   11   10   9   8   7   6   5   4   3   2   1

Strongly agree   Strongly disagree

4. Legalization of prostitution

   11   10   9   8   7   6   5   4   3   2   1

Strongly agree   Strongly disagree

5. Legalization of gambling

   11   10   9   8   7   6   5   4   3   2   1

Strongly agree   Strongly disagree

6. Insanity as a defense to criminal responsibility

   11   10   9   8   7   6   5   4   3   2   1

Strongly agree   Strongly disagree

7. Criminal prosecution of policemen who illegally gather evidence by violating the law

   11   10   9   8   7   6   5   4   3   2   1

Strongly agree   Strongly disagree

APPENDIX A (Con't)

8. Legalization of pornographic literature or materials

    11   10   9   8   7   6   5   4   3   2   1
Strongly agree   Strongly disagree

9. Limitations on use of wire-taps by police

    11   10   9   8   7   6   5   4   3   2   1
Strongly agree   Strongly disagree

10. Limitations on right to search by police

    11   10   9   8   7   6   5   4   3   2   1
Strongly agree   Strongly disagree

THE USE OF BIOFEEDBACK TRAINING IN
ALLEVIATION OF STRESS IN THE POLICE OFFICER
Noel H. Thomas

INTRODUCTION

Comprehensive studies done by the Los Angeles County Sheriff's Department and the United States Department of Health, Education and Welfare indicate that Police Officers suffer one of the highest incidences of stress related diseases when compared to other occupational groups of similar age. The Los Angeles Study listed the three leading causes of non-accidental disability retirement among Policemen as cardio-vascular pulmonary disease, back disorders, and peptic ulceration.

Physical and psychological demands placed upon Police Officers are unique because of the nature of the job. Dr. Kroes in his book *Society's Victim - the Policeman* focuses on the true nature of what it means to be a Policeman. He identified the stressors that are unique to the Policeman and those that are common with other occupations. What the stressors are is important, but even more important is "HOW DO YOU REDUCE STRESS".

Traditionally, Police Officers - Agencies dealt with the effects of stress by placing the relief of tension on attempting to better train the Police Officers. As agencies grew the disparity between capability and community needs, behavioral demands - and changes in the criminal systems increased the stress placed on Officers increased to the point that adequate training no longer aided the Officers in reducing stress. The need for better utilization of man-power required the Police Agencies go outside their agencies for assistance to aid in controlling stress. Los Angeles was among the first to engage a full-time Psychologist followed by San Jose, California, and Dallas, Texas. Other agencies have contracted with psychologists to perform specific studies, Bard with New York Police Department. Within each of the agencies are a group of psychologists that provides a wide range of psychological services for the individual. Until late 1976, these agencies, while aware of the psychological and physiological effects of stress, offered only assistance in the area of psychological help.

In November, 1976, the Dallas Police Department began a study in the use of Biofeedback Training as a means of controlling the physiological results of stress. Using biofeedback equipment an Officer is able to monitor a particular body function and with the information given by the equipment, slowly learn to control that function. Within every individual is a unique method of coping with stress and a unique result of stress when it exceeds the tolerance level for that individual. For some the stress may manifest as a headache, upset stomach, pain in the back of the neck or in the lower back. While these pains only last for an hour, several hours, or a day, they are indications of the underlying stress building.

These outward signs of stress are the result of the autonomic nervous system reacting to perceived dangers the body may be facing. Police Officers are constantly aware of the fact that they may be called upon to protect themselves or another person from immediate physical harm. During training the Officer is trained in how to approach a car, how to knock on a door, and how to search a building or failure to will result in injury. Always the underlying message is the same - be prepared, ready to fight or you will die.

Officers are aware of this state but say they adjust to this attitude and it becomes habituation and it does not harm them. However, the autonomic nervous system reacts each time the individual prepares to start a shift. His heart rate, blood pressure, and certain gland activities increase because subconsciously the Officer is preparing to fight. Blood and glandular activity to the stomach, intestines, and interior of the body slow, permitting more energy for muscular activity of the legs, arms, and upper torso. As the shifts go by, the Officer does adjust but the results are increased muscle tension, high blood pressure, digestive problems, and cardiovascular diseases. Unchecked the Officer slowly adjusts to the point that he destroys himself.

INSTRUMENTATION

Biofeedback is a training program using biomedical instruments to monitor specific body processes permitting an individual to learn to control that specific process. The technique is basically one in which a physiological response is monitored and the response is modified, amplified and then displayed in modes that reflect changes in the physiological activity.

The monitoring of specific physiological response is accomplished by using the skin potential response (SPR), electromyogram (EMG), electroencephlograph (EEG), thermometer or any combination. In skin potential response are thought to indicate the degree of autonomic arousal of an individual. Using the SPR permits the direct training of the autonomic nervous system and is a general indicator of relaxation.

Electromyographs monitor the electrical impulses present in a specific muscle group. The number of impulses present in a muscle group indicates the stress present in that muscle; the increased numbers of impulses - the greater the muscular stress. The EMG is used in training programs for general relax-ation, migraine headaches, lower back pains and digestive system disorders.

While the EMG is an indicator of muscular tension, the electroencephlogram (EEG) is an indicator of brain wave patterns. The human brain produces elec-trical waves that vary with changes in emotion, feeling and sensory stimulation. During normal waking hours the brain is producing high-frequency and low amp-titude waves called 'beta'. In relaxation the brain will produce bursts of high amptitude, low frequency waves, or 'alpha' waves. The absense of alpha waves is an indication of anxiety or stress.

Temperature biofeedback is used to measure change in skin temperatures at a specific location or two specific locations. Changes in temperature of skin are determined by vascular constriction or dialation and can aid in relief of headaches and muscular tension.

METHODOLOGY

A biofeedback training program begins with an interview to determine the individual's specific reaction to stress and to determine if there is a medical reason for the specific stress reaction. Having found no medical problem, the individual is then **started** in a training program. During the first several sessions the consideration is on determining the specific level of muscular tension and in determining a relaxation technique that is best suited for the individual. The specific relaxation technique and instrumentation used to re-duce the stress depends on the specific nature of the physiological reaction to stress.

If the specific reaction to stress by the individual is a headache, or mi-graine headache, a training program would be established using the EMG and ther-mal instrumentation. The EMG would be used to train the individual to reduce muscular tension while the thermal training would permit the individual to alter or reduce the flow of blood to the head which is connected with the throbbing sensation of a headache.

Hypertension is also a physiological reaction to stress that can be con-trolled through biofeedback training. Overall high levels of muscular tension cause the blood vessels to constrict resulting in increased blood pressure. As an individual adapts to higher and higher levels of stress the blood pressure also increases. Using the general stress reduction techniques in learning to reduce muscular tension, the blood pressure will slowly begin to return to normal levels.

Regardless of the specific problem a training program follows a general basic procedure. This procedure begins with identifying a specific goal for the individual, followed by establishing a training program best suited for that particular problem, and then continuing the training program until the established goal is obtained.

The benefits of the biofeedback training and its acceptance is in the fact that the individual is training himself to maintain his particular reaction to stress.' The technician aiding the individual in his training program only aids the individual by giving him the information and expertise on the most appropriate training method. Actual training to reduce stress is done by the individual with the aid of the biofeedback instrumentation.

RESULTS

The use of biofeedback training in the reduction of hypertension among law enforcement individuals is significant. Members of the original hypertension study had an average blood pressure of 143/83 with one individual having blood pressure of 160/90. This one individual was under medical care, taking medication, and entered the program with his doctor's approval. After the training program, the average blood pressure of the group was 126/76 which represents an eleven (11%) percent drop in systolic reading and a seven (7%) percent drop in the diastolic pressure.

Additionally, the one individual under the doctor's care was able to reduce his medication and stabilize his blood pressure at 138/72. This individual had been unable to stabilize his blood pressure using the conventional medication approach to hypertension. It should also be added that the training program in this case was conducted with the aid of his personal physician.

In the group were several individuals who were having tension or migraine headaches. While the results of this training program can not be objectively established, these individuals did report a decrease in both intensity and frequency of the headaches. Several members of the training group reported being able to detect the beginning of a headache and reduce the tension causing the headache thereby eliminating the headache before it caused any pain.

Of the original group, one individual had lower back pains that were the results of an early back injury but was complicated by muscle tension. During the training program, this individual was able to reduce the level of tension in his back giving him greater mobility. In one training session this individual was having muscle spasms at the beginning of the training. Not only was this individual able to reduce his muscle tension but he was also able to eliminate the spasms.

While these results show that biofeedback can reduce or eliminate the physiological reaction to stress, a secondary psychological benefit was reported by the majority of individuals in the training program. These psychological benefits were increased awareness of occurrences around them, increased control of their reaction to stress, and an increased ability to maintain a calm, less hostile and more professional mannerism. The increased ability to control his own body functions appears to increase the individual's self-worth and generalized to his work.

While the sample group was not large enough to be statistically reliable, the results indicate that Biofeedback training can reduce or eliminate the major stress reaction present in law enforcement officers.

SUMMARY

During Biofeedback training an individual can teach himself to remain calm, reduce anxiety, and be more objective in appraising his psychological and physiological behavior. Based on the preliminary finds, the biofeedback training has substantial potentials in law enforcement. Biofeedback can reduce muscle tension, not only in headaches, but lower back pain syndrome as well. Peptic ulcerations can be reduced by lowering levels of accumulated stress in the Officer. Research has shown that blood pressure can be reduced by as much as 25% using biofeedback therapy. Additionally, the problems of Officers being able to sleep immediately after duty hours, which represents an indication of high stress, can be eliminated.

The effects of stress can, to some extent, be found in every individual. However, when these conditions can be attributed to stresses that can be seen as a necessary part of Police work, it seems inevitable that these physiological and psychological conditions will have to be controlled and/or eliminated. Law enforcement is becoming more demanding, thereby indicating more stress and more problems. Biofeedback training can effectively combat both the physiological and psychological conditions that accompany stress.

AN ACADEMIC COURSE ON ALCOHOL ABUSE FOR POLICE OFFICERS:
SOME DANGERS OF INTERVENTION BY PROFESSIONALS
P. Clayton Rivers and James Pipher

A study made by Lundman, Fox, Sykes, and Clark indicated that in 1969, "slightly over 20% of all F.B.I. reported arrests were for the offense of drunkenness.[1] If alcohol related offenses are also considered (i.e., liquor law violations, driving while intoxicated, disorderly conduct, vagrancy), then 46% of the more than five million arrests in 1969 were alcohol related." Despite the major role the alcohol abuser plays in American criminality, there are few published reports of professionals intervening to aid the police officer in understanding alcoholism and the alcoholic. There is currently a trend toward decriminalizing public intoxication and the police are being asked to play new roles. In view of this trend it is important to develop strategies and teaching methods to help police better understand alcoholics and to change attitudes of police officers from a purely legalistic approach to that of a helping and referral source for alcohol treatment agencies. For these reasons the authors have developed a college-level course designed to provide understanding of alcohol problems for police and to change their attitudes and behavior toward the alcohol abuser.

While a more complete description of the course is provided in another article, this article briefly describes the activities undertaken in that course, entitled "A Police Course on Alcohol Abuse and Alcoholism".[2] The class was structured around twelve lectures and small group activities which followed the lectures. The twenty-five participants all employed by the Lincoln, Nebraska Police Department, were further randomly subdivided into the small groups so that one half attended review sessions which discussed the lecture from a given night. The second subgroup of police officers participated in a "rap" group where the focus was on the officers' own feelings and attitudes toward alcohol, how they felt about dealing with alcoholics, and how they as police officers could change their roles in relation to alcoholics. All participants were also required to visit five local alcohol agencies and write a paper describing how they as police officers could more effectively use these agencies as a support source in their work as police officers.

The evaluation of the effects of the course on class members was primarily based on comparisons of pre- and post-class questionnaires designed to measure attitude changes and certain behavioral changes such as number of referrals to alcohol agencies. To aid in the evaluation, a roughly equivalent comparison group composed of officers not taking the course was established. This was accomplished by asking class officers to choose a brother officer who had similar rank, duties, and outlook on life. Fortunately, there were no statistically significant differences between class members and brother officer controls on pre-class measures.

In summary, the findings identified significant changes in participants' attitudes toward alcoholics. For example, participants (as compared to brother officer controls) saw the alcoholic as less to blame and more likely to improve, and they thought the alcoholic should be dealt with less severely. The class members also showed a significant increase in referrals to alcohol treatment agencies when pre-and post-class measures were compared. This seemed to accomplish the goal of changing police attitudes and behavior.

However, the authors were suspicious that there were hidden agendas which the data analysis did not uncover when simple group comparisons were made. For example, in the "rap" groups, a split between the more experienced and less experienced officers concerning their values and attitudes toward the policeman's role was noted. A measure of job satisfaction had been included in the questionnaire and it was decided to effect a median split of the officers in terms of experience as policemen. This tactic revealed that the younger, less experienced officers showed a significant decrease in job satisfaction while the older officers failed to show any change on this measure. There were no differences of this type in the control group.[3]

The conclusion that the course had possibly contributed to lowered morale of the young officers raised a number of questions. Did it function to highlight the frustrations of the younger officers? This is an important question if the younger officers are, as the authors judge, an important source of new ideas and potential for a successful, progressive police force. More importantly, the authors were forced to consider whether their intervention had done more harm than good. This last question gained added relevance when it was learned that several of the class participants had left the force.

There are grounds to suspect that the differential effect is a result of a number of factors. The particular police department within which this study was conducted adheres to a legalistic model, and this stance determines the type of intervention that the police make into the life of the problem drinker.[4] The reward system is geared towards arrest and conviction (i.e., "getting a good bust"). In contrast to the police department's stance, the course had taken a position more in line with the Uniform Alcoholism and Intoxication Treatment Act which maintained that public intoxication and alcoholism should not be dealt with as crimes but rather as problems that can be prevented and controlled through a broad range of health and social services. Thus, the course had possibly encouraged class participants to do things, such as referring problem drinkers, that were, in some cases, contrary to departmental policy.

At this point one might raise questions and speculate--even with little or no empirical data--on what *might have happened* in this particular intervention before going on to broader issues.

Speculation I--*The intervention highlighted difficulties that the younger officers were already experiencing in their police work.* Clearly, the younger officers were already more committed to "serving people" than to enforcing the law, and the intervention helped further emphasize for them the discrepancy between their goal of "helping people" and the demands and limitations placed on them by the department in which they worked. While empirical support for this speculative hypothesis is limited, the younger officers did seem to differ from the older officers in their "rap" group comments about the department's policies. One of the most important aspects of job satisfaction is that the worker must believe that what he is doing is important and that he or she is fulfilling a valuable function. The younger officers did not seem to place great emphasis on the legalistic position of the department. They saw their roles as being "helpers", "educators", and in general, public servants. They also objected more strenuously to the bureaucratic requirements of the department, particularly its para-military organization. On the other hand, the older officers seemed to value their law enforcement role more highly and were more attuned to a public safety approach (i.e., protecting the city against crime). Obviously, in a situation where young officers already feel frustrated, advocacy of a position that supports the younger officers' frustrations as legitimate exacerbates the existing conflict. Indeed, there are indications that conditions of conflict already existed between younger officers and departmental policy before we arrived on the scene. Recent debate and controversy surrounding the issue of choosing a new police chief highlighted a division of philosophy within this department. Apparently, intervention which is inconsistent with departmental goals, may indeed, contribute to lowering officer morale.

In Lincoln, as in many other police departments, the emphasis on education as a route to merit pay increases has encouraged many officers to return to school. Most of the police officers in the class had at least a sophomore standing in college while some were close to graduation. What effect this may have in other parts of the country is open to question, but the younger, college-educated officers in our course reflected a "social science" approach to their work. Older officers seemed to value classwork more as a means to an end (i.e., an increase in pay) and were less affected by the values and judgments presented in these courses. The question to be asked, very tentatively, is whether teaching officers liberal positions and values toward law enforcement and life is often in conflict with their role as police officers in the more conservative atmosphere of the average police department? Another question concerns whether intervention should be made by social scientists without participation by all levels of the organization, including the police chief? This is a sticky question when one considers that most opportunities to consult do not involve the total organization. For example, one is more apt to receive a request to teach a course on alcohol for 25 officers than to construct a total agency program to deal with community alcohol use. Of course, we are aware that there are many other frustrations for younger officers (e.g., the enduring of a long apprenticeship as patrolman before he can assume a job with primary decision-making power).

Speculation II--*Interactions between criminal justice personnel and social scientists are many times hampered by a lack of understanding or inadequate appreciation of each other's philosophies, goals, training, experiences, roles, and abilities.* Ignorance and an accompanying fear of the unknown by police officials poses a great threat to the social scientist. In addition, criminal justice personnel often have unrealistic expectations, both positive and negative, about what the social scientist can and cannot do to help or hinder their task of enforcing the law and serving the public's needs. Ignorance of each other's roles has no terrible consequence if there is a minimum need to interact or if goals never overlap. However, social scientists and criminal justice personnel have been brought together by a combination of governmental fiat, interest, social pressure, and, interestingly enough, complementary needs. For the mental health professional interested in prevention, early detection and treatment, and community action and research, the policeman is a front-line resource person who is out "where the action is". For the policeman dealing with alcoholism, family disturbance, juvenile delinquency, and community apathy, the social scientist is a valuable resource with skills in a variety of areas (e.g., public relations, psychopathology, program evaluation, and staff relations).

At present what is the status of the police-social scientist relationship and what are some factors influencing this relationship? First of all, there are a number of differences between the criminal justice system and the mental health system in terms of such things as philosophy, training, and goals. Monahan presents a number of contrasts between the two systems.[5] For example, he de-

cribes the criminal justice system as viewing each individual as exercising
free will (i.e., each person must be considered responsible for his or her
actions). In contrast, the mental health system perceives a person as more
determined (i.e., such factors as heredity and environment lead to whatever
behavior an individual displays). If criminal justice personnel and social
scientists are to work together effectively, they must be aware of their differences. As professionals, we must recognize the biases we bring into any
situation and where these biases come from. For example, one can speculate
that a significant factor involved in the differences in philosophy and goals
is the different contexts in which police and social scientists operate. To
illustrate this point, let us consider the area of alcoholism. The policeman
deals with the problem drinker on the street, usually in an arrest situation.
The problem drinker may be drunk and, perhaps, verbally or physically abusive.
He may have caused a serious accident. He will probably lie about how much
he has had to drink. He may get sick; in fact, he may get sick in the officer's car. These types of behaviors (all of which were described by class,
participants) are hardly conducive to humanistic compassion or benevolent
understanding. The social scientist, on the other hand, typically sees the
alcoholic in a treatment setting. The alcoholic is a very difficult client,
but the behavior of an alcoholic in treatment and the treatment context are
more favorable for attitudes of concern, caring, and understanding. Perhaps
most importantly, treatment personnel have the opportunity to see those people
for whom treatment has worked. On the other hand, the police for the most
part, see only the failures. When a policeman refers an alcohol-related offender to treatment and the treatment succeeds, the offender's drinking days
are over and the officer never sees him again. If treatment fails, the policeman, in all probability, will be involved in future alcohol-related arrests
with that individual.

There is another important area of misunderstanding. As criminal justice
personnel and social scientists work together, they must communicate their
expectations and also tell each other what they can and cannot do. Clearly at
this stage of the game, there exists a great deal of misunderstanding about
what resources and abilities each group has to offer. Again, an example may
serve to clarify this point. While working in a mental health center the junior
author of this article received a court referral to test a habitual shoplifter
with the request to predict on the basis of the test results whether the subject would shoplift in the future. The court had expectations for social
science (in this example, psychology) that could not be met. In this instance,

it is probably social science that is most blameworthy for perpetuating the "psychological mystique". Social scientists need to strike down the myth of their being able to predict the future and make it clear that they can only speak in terms of probability.

In summary, social scientists and criminal justice personnel need to communicate effectively with each other. The alcohol course for police officers described in this article suggests that opening communication between police and alcohol agencies can be helpful to both. At the end of the class policemen were asked to rank activities in the course in terms of the degree they thought these activities influenced a change in their attitudes toward alcoholics. The visits to alcohol agencies and discussions with alcohol professionals in those agencies were ranked highest by the class police officers. Many agencies also indicated that the visits helped change their impressions of officers, although information here was purely anecdotal in nature. Officers indicated surprise at the dedication of alcohol treatment personnel and the alcohol treatment personnel found the policemen more concerned and caring than they had anticipated. Some police officers visited agencies several times to give talks after the course was completed.

Speculation III--*The project presented in the first part of this paper could have been more effective had some simple planning been done in advance.* This police course, like most projects, developed rather rapidly and allowed little time for planning. In addition, the authors were quite naive about police officers and police departments and generally unequipped to deal with the appearance of many related issues. With these factors in mind, one might speculate in retrospect on what should have gone into a course on alcoholism for police officers.

1. Most basic to this planning should be the establishing of a planning committee composed of both social scientists and police officers. Great care and considerable thoughtfulness should go into the establishing of this committee. For example, criminal justice personnel typically operate within a line organization format. For this reason, personnel representing a cross-section of the organization should be included. Also, it is necessary to begin with the approval of the higher echelon staff and to confer with them as to how the committee will operate. In the case of the alcohol class, the authors were asked to present the course at the Police Department by an Inspector (i.e., an individual just below the police chief). Since the Inspector had taken the alcohol course on campus prior to requesting the course for his personnel, we were assured of support. This support could have opened the door to the

creation of a social scientist-police officer committee with police drawn from throughout the hierarchy of the police department, which could have alleviated any number of difficulties. The police members of the committee may have seen the issues differently than the social scientists and might have suggested a different training format than the one chosen. The authors might also have learned earlier about the differences between younger and older officers and the realistic issues surrounding the referral of an alcoholic to treatment by police officers. With this information the authors could have sought support from the upper echelon of the department. Working within departmental regulations, the police officer, particularly the younger officer, would have had less frustration and ambiguity in dealing with the alcoholic.

2. The higher echelon of the department should have been kept involved and informed about the project as it proceeded. Unfortunately, the higher echelon did not understand the format of the alcohol class; nobody told them that a detailed evaluation of the impact of the class would be made. This communication was not carried out because the certainty of the course being offered was not assured until shortly before it was to begin and because the evaluation was not planned until just before the class started. Had early communication developed, the course could have been more in line with departmental policy.

3. Suggestions concerning such things as course content should have been sought from police officers. The course could have easily been more closely adopted to the policemen's needs through better communication prior to classes. While every attempt was made to meet these needs, it was frequently on an improvised basis and frequently lacked the coherence needed to teach a college level course.

In conclusion, the authors accept full responsibility for the weaknesses of their program. Discussion has focused on the alcohol course, but one might suspect that the "lessons" of this experience apply to most social scientist-criminal justice interactions. Most social scientists have good intentions in their attempts to work within the criminal justice system; however, it is our contention they fail to check their notions against reality. More effort needs to be put forth by both the social scientists and criminal justice personnel to reduce misunderstanding and to assure they are working toward common goals.

REFERENCES

1. Lundman, R.J., Fox, J.C., Sykes, R.E. and Clark, John P. Drunkenness in police citizen encounters. Unpublished manuscript, Observational Research, University of Minnesota, 1971.

2. Pipher, J. and Rivers, P.C. A course on alcohol abuse and alcoholism for police: A descriptive summary. *Journal of Alcohol and Drug Education*, 20(2), 1975, pp. 18-26.

3. Rivers, P.C. and Pipher, J. Job satisfaction as a function of policeman attitudes and role requirements. Paper presented as part of a symposium: "Job Satisfaction Measures as Indicators of Change in Human Service Organizations", American Psychological Association Convention, New Orleans, September, 1974.

4. Wilson, J.Q. *Varieties of Police Behavior*. Cambridge, Massachusetts: Harvard University Press, 1968.

5. Monahan, John. Social accountability: Legal justification for imprisonment and civil commitment. Paper presented at Law-Psychology Research Conference, Lincoln, Nebraska, 1975.

THE OFFICE OF PROFESSIONAL STANDARDS:
A NEW CONCEPT IN POLICE DISCIPLINE
Sloan T. Letman

On August 16, 1974, James M. Rochford, Superintendent of Police for the City of Chicago, issued a general order establishing the Office of Professional Standards (OPS) "as a component of the personal staff of the Superintendent to investigate complaints of excessive force and other complaints as directed by the Superintendent."[1] The administrators of the Office of Professional Standards were to report directly to the Superintendent, and the office was given the following responsibilities:

1. to receive and register all complaints against Department members,

2. to coordinate all resources of the Department and the total effort of the Office of Professional Standards towards the investigation of excessive force complaints and other complaints as directed by the Superintendent,

3. to refer to the Commander of the Internal Affairs Division (IAD), or his designate, any and all complaints against Department members which were not to be investigated by the Office of Professional Standards,

4. to conduct a comprehensive investigation into the circumstances of each complaint which required an investigation,

5. to review instances of injury or death involving alleged action of a Department member and conduct an independent investigation, when warranted,

6. to establish and maintain liaison with the State's Attorney, the Chicago Commission on Human Relations, the Office of the United States' Attorney, the courts, bar associations, other law enforcement agencies, and community groups, for the Superintendent in matters concerning excessive force or corruption, and

7. to review all cases wherein a member was recommended for separation and, upon approval of the recommendation by the Superintendent, be responsible for the thorough and legal preparation of the cases for presentation to the Chicago Police Board.[2]

In a press conference of August 1, 1974, Superintendent Rochford announced that thirty civilian investigators, who would be the backbone of the office, would be hired, and that the hiring process was nearly completed.[3]

Three administrators, highest rank in the Office of Professional Standards, had been hired months earlier and were already at work. The three--James Casey, Robert Wooldridge, Richard Salas--were all lawyers and Casey and Salas had been Assistant United States Attorneys. Significantly, Rochford chose one white, one black, and one Latino for the three positions.

On August 6, 1974, Rochford announced that thirty investigators and four supervisors had been hired. The staff included men, women, whites, blacks, Latinos, former government investigators, and ex-military personnel. Rochford stated that this group would handle complaints, not only involving the use of force, but later, after acquiring experience, accusations of corruption and official misconduct.[4]

The office began functioning on August 19, 1974, after the newly hired investigators had completed two weeks of training in investigative and administrative procedures and constitutional rights at the Chicago Police Academy.

According to the *Chicago Tribune,* credit for the establishment of the office was due to its eight-part series on police abuse of innocent persons published in November of 1973. The series had won national acclaim. After the series appeared, political figures had joined others in charging that policemen used excessive force in carrying out their duties.

Perhaps the *Chicago Tribune* series provoked the action of Superintendent Rochford in August of 1974 but the origins of the police brutality complaints went back to *The Metcalf Report on the Misuse of Police Authority in Chicago,* published in the *Chicago Defender* in July, 1973. This had been a report and recommendations based on testimony before a Blue Ribbon Panel convened by the Honorable Ralph Metcalf, Representative, First Congressional District of Illinois, on June 26, July 17, July 24, and July 31, 1972. At a meeting of community leaders on March 20, 1972, Metcalf had told the then Superintendent of Police, James B. Conlisk, that he would be "hard pressed to go into any home in the black community and not find at least one member of that family who either feels that they have been abused verbally and physically by some member of the police force, or has first hand information of such an incident."[5] And, in his introduction to the report, Metcalf had pointed out that while abusive police treatment had been a major issue for years, the community outcry against abuse of authority by Chicago policemen had increased sharply in 1972.[6]

Numerous complaints of mistreatment by police had been received from citizens across the city, and community groups had sought, without success, to obtain a meaningful response from responsible public officials concerning abusive police conduct. Further, there had been a growing concern about the high crime rate in inner-city communities.

During the four-day hearings, the Blue Ribbon Panel heard testimony from persons claiming to be witnesses or victims of police brutality. The panel also considered evidence submitted by experts on police administration and experts on the psychological and legal aspects of police problems.[7]

The hearings had indicated that the police department's own internal investigation mechanism, the Internal Affairs Divison, was not working. IAD had two duties: first, to investigate allegations of police brutality, misconduct, and corruption; and second, to assist the Corporation Counsel and the Superintendent of Police in the defense of officers alleged to have violated an individual's rights. Congressman Metcalf concluded "that the conflicting roles of the police discipline system and the Corporation Counsel must be accomodated somehow, and it seems obvious that the accomodation is to favor policemen and to disfavor complaining citizens."[8]

Other reasons cited for the failure of IAD to properly investigate abusive actions were the amount of "clout" certain police officers had, the effects of cronyism (many of the officers of IAD knew department members under investigation), and the amount of comradeship that existed among all department members. For whatever reasons, the statistics indicated IAD was not working. (See Table 1.)

The recommendations of the Blue Ribbon Panel specifically called for the creation of an independent investigation agency designed to handle the most serious allegations of misconduct by police toward the public--those involving escessive force, violations of civil rights, and criminal activity of any sort. These recommendations were remarkably similar to what eventually became the Office of Professional Standards.

The Office of Professional Standards is closer to the police department than other civilian review boards. Although it is administered from outside the department, it reports directly to the superintendent, operates from the police headquarters, and is funded from the police budget. This system has its critics, although it was defended editorially by the *Chicago Tribune*.[9]

Statistics from the office's first year in operation show that OPS sustained nearly eight times more complaints than did IAD the previous year. (See Table 2.)

OPS procedures reflect a deep concern for the rights of the accused officer and for a thorough professional investigation. A review of these procedures based on my own experiences as an investigator and as Supervisor of Investigations is in order.

Initial Complaint

A. Walk-in Complaint

Upon personal notification that a citizen has a complaint falling within the scope of OPS's responsibility, complaint desk personnel complete all required forms and give the case a complaint register number (C.R.). An OPS supervisor then assigns an investigator to take the walk-in complainant's statement and to complete other initial investigative work.

B. Telephone Complaint

If the call originates from an alleged victim or other complainant and the victim is injured, the complaint desk takes all relevant information and notifies the OPS supervisor, who ascertains the present location of the victim and determines whether the immediate dispatch of an investigator is warranted. The decision is based on the elapsed time since the alleged incident occured, the availability of on-duty personnel, and the amount of information supplied by the victim/complainant.

C. Write-in Complaint

When OPS receives a letter of complaint that falls within its jurisdiction, desk personnel record all pertinent information, time stamp the letter and envelope, make sufficient copies of the letter and transmit all materials to the OPS supervisor for assignment.

Assignment of Investigation

OPS supervisors assign cases to investigators by the rotation system. However, supervisors must be sensitive to the caseload of each investigator, the duty schedule, vacation periods, and prolonged illnesses. As a result, the rotation system is not rigid, and, in addition, supervisors occasionally make assignments to groups or teams of investigators so that the investigation will not be prolonged or delayed by one of the above factors.

The Investigation

Above all else, all cases must be investigated in an objective manner. The investigation must also be thorough and timely. Investigators are required to (1) contact all complainants and witnesses as soon as possible; and, (2) take written statements from complainants and witnesses when such statements will assist the investigator in reaching a sound conclusion in the case.[10] If the allegation is such that a recommendation for separation is unlikely, the statement need not be the formal question and answer type but may be narrative style. However, if the allegation is such that the case may result in a recommendation for separation, the statement must be in question and answer form.

The investigator must also interrogate the accused officer and other officers who have knowledge of the alleged misconduct, taking written statements when necessary. If the allegation is such that a recommendation for separation is unlikely, the statement may be in the form of reports from the accused officer.

If the allegation is such that the case may result in a recommendation for separation, the statement of the accused officer must be in question and answer form. The accused officer may be required to submit a written report when so ordered by his commanding officer and to answer questions which specifically, directly, and narrowly relate to the alleged misconduct or to the performance of his official duties.[11]

During the investigation, the investigator may uncover evidence of violations that do not pertain to the allegation of excessive force, and, when applicable, a related original charge. When this occurs, the violations are noted in a separate report and reference is made to where evidence of the particular violation can be found in the file.[12] Investigators are expected to follow rigid guidelines and then evaluate their work with a printed check list.

Investigation Closing

When the investigators are satisfied that their investigation is complete, they complete a summary report containing a heading, a list of attachments, investigative facts, an analysis of facts (aggravation and mitigation), and a finding. The investigator neither makes a recommendation for disciplinary action in sustained cases, nor obtains a copy of the accused officer's previous disciplinary history. The findings are made solely on the facts and evidence at hand. After the summary report is completed, the total case file is submitted to the OPS supervisor for evaluation.

Supervisory Evaluation

When supervisors receive a completed case from investigators, they read the entire case file (they have knowledge of the cases and contents prior to receiving the completed files). They evaluate the file for thoroughness, neatness, and completeness of statements and interviews. If the supervisor is not satisfied with the case file or if questions arise relative to any facets of it, a consultation with the investigator is the next action. If satisfactory answers cannot be given or if the supervisor still thinks the case is incomplete, the case file is returned to the investigators for completion or a new investigator is assigned.[13]

When the supervisor is satisfied with the investigation and the investigative process, he attaches a cover report containing a heading and a statement of concurrence or non-concurrence with the findings. If there is non-concurrence, explicit reasons are given and a separate finding is made.

If a report of secondary violations is submitted with the case file, the supervisor does not make a recommendation for disciplinary action in sustained cases, but merely requests from the Internal Affairs Division Record Section a copy of the accused officer's previous disciplinary history. The supervisor then submits to the OPS Administrators the case file, the evaluation report, and, where applicable, the copy of the previous disciplinary history.

Administrative Review

The OPS Administrators personally review each completed case and if satisfied with the investigation and the investigative process, send a cover report to the Superintendent of Police. The report states their findings and gives their recommendations relative to disciplinary action in sustained cases.

External Review

After the Administrators have made their decision, the case is sent to the Chicago Commission on Human Relations, the Cook County State's Attorney, and the accused officer's chain of command. These agencies review the case and return it to OPS with recommendations.

After the case has been sent back to OPS, the Administrators review the recommendations of the aforementioned agencies. At this point either the case is permanently closed, or additional investigation is initiated, or the case is sent to the IAD for either acceptance or rejection of the recommended disciplinary action for the accused officer.

Under certain circumstances, the Administrators authorize review of cases by other individuals, groups, organizations, and agencies. The release of a case for review is made only upon the written order of the Administrators or the Superintendent of Police. No criteria has yet been established for determining the circumstances that dictate such release.

The complainant and/or the accused officer may consult with one or more of the Administrators. This consultation usually includes a review of the case and an explanation of the findings and consequent disciplinary action.

Administrative Recommendation

In sustained cases, the accused officer has the right to either accept the recommendation for disciplinary action or reject it and ask for a Complaint Review Panel hearing.

When the Administrators have recommended that disciplinary action be taken and after their perusal of the external reviews, the case is sent to the IAD Records Section for the obtaining of acceptance or rejection. If the accused officer elects to accept the recommendations, the case file is returned to OPS by IAD. The case is then forwarded to the Superintendent of Police with a suspension order, if required, for approval. If the Superintendent approves the action, the case is returned to OPS. Upon receipt of an approval case, OPS gathers all copies of the file and forwards them to IAD for final disposition and filing.

If the accused officer elects to reject the recommendation, IAD informs OPS of this fact and follows whatever procedure is established by the Commander of IAD for the obtaining of a Complaint Review Panel hearing. Upon conclusion of the hearing, the case is submitted to the Superintendent of Police through the Administrators of OPS. The Superintendent then makes his decision relative to the accused officer and returns the case to OPS. The files are gathered and forwarded to IAD for implementation of the Superintendent's decision and final closing and filing.

If the OPS Administrators recommend separation but the Superintendent rejects the recommendation, the case is returned to the OPS Administrators with his decision, and, if they do not decide to request a conference with the Superintendent to discuss the case, the completed case is sent to IAD for implementation of the decision. If the OPS Administrators elect to discuss the case with the Superintendent, his dictate will be followed after the conference.

If the final recommendation of the OPS Administrators is separation, the case is submitted to the Superintendent of Police for perusal and decision. If the Superintendent approves the recommendation, the case is returned directly to OPS for Police Board action. The Police Board is the official body of the Chicago Police Department charged with determining whether a police officer should be discharged from his employment. The board is composed of six civilian community and civic leaders and chaired by a lawyer. The board is an administrative body and falls under the purview of administrative law and procedure. The Superintendent of Police can not discharge any police officer. He may only suspend the officer for a time period of no more than 30 days.

The Ops Administrators prepare the proper charges for the board, listing the main items of evidence. The case is then given to the OPS Police Board Officer who forwards it to the Corporation Counsel of the City of Chicago for approval. After approval, the OPS Police Board Officer arranges for the hearing and becomes responsible for assisting in scheduling dates, subpeona of witnesses, serving charges on the accused officer, responding to questions from involved parties, maintaining contact with witnesses, recording, security of files, notification of continuance dates, and liaison with the Corporation Counsel for prosecution.

When a decision has been reached by the Police Board, the OPS Police Board
Officer notifies the OPS Administrators and closes the case.

Constitutional Limitations

One of the most important issues in an investigation of police brutality
is the rights of all parties involved. The rights of the complainant are not
in controversy. Under the due process clause of the 14th Amendment and the
principle of fundamental fairness, all citizens are guaranteed fair treatment
by any law enforcement officer. Tangential upon this is the right of all
citizens to a fair and impartial investigation of any phase of police misconduct.

However, more controversy has surrounded the rights of the accused police
officer in a civilian brutality investigation. The protection of the individual
under the 14th Amendment against coerced statements prohibits the use of statements obtained under threat of removal from office in subsequent criminal proceedings. This right extends to all. However, such statements can be used
at a Police Board hearing provided the accused was given his rights. Illinois
follows the leading case of *Garrity v. State of New Jersey* which held that a
statement given by a police officer under direct order can not be used against
him in a criminal trial.[14]

The OPS has taken elaborate provisions to safeguard the rights of the accused officer. When the possibility of criminal charges exists, the Illinois
Revised Statutes must be strictly followed. The accused officer must be warned
in writing of the specific improper or illegal act. He also has the right to
have a lawyer present during the course of the investigation.[15] It must also
be kept in mind that when the possibility of criminal charges exists, the
possibility of Police Board trial also exists and proper warnings must therefore be given for both possibilities.

Two types of forms are prepared prior to the initiation of any interrogation in this instance, the Criminal Rights Form, the accused is notified in
writing of the allegations. Also entered on this form are the name of the
complainant, the date and time of the incident, and the location of the incident. The form is prepared in duplicate with the accused signing it, acknow-
ledging receipt. Each time the accused is interrogated, he must be re-issued
this form. The form indicates that the accused has the right to remain silent.
Because of this right, the accused cannot be ordered to give answers to the
questions asked.[16]

In the Waiver of Counsel Form, the accused either waives his right to having a lawyer present or asks for a continuance to obtain a lawyer. Under no circumstances does this continuance time exceed 72 hours. The police department does not furnish lawyers for accused officers.[17]

Conclusion

This paper has examined the creation and procedural aspects of the Office of Professional Standards. Several facts must be noted. First, no agency has concentrated so much effort in protecting the rights of the accused officer. Second, the office has procedurally constructed enough checks and balances so that a thorough and honest investigation is assured.

The concept of civilians investigating the police is a relatively new thrust in police discipline and in the criminal justice system. An office of the type outlined in this paper will not only provide a feasible alternative to civilian review but will also strengthen police/community relations. Citizens will more readily voice their complaints regarding the police if they can see members of their own community doing the investigations. The image of the police department will be improved simply because through the hiring of civilians, the police have shown their willingness to accept community input. And this type of civilian review *works*--certainly better than internal review. Clearly, the Office of Professional Standards is the future direction of police discipline in this country.

REFERENCES

1. James M. Rochford, "General Order 75-22," Unpublished Chicago Police Department Rules and Regulations, (1975), pp. 1-2.

2. Ibid.

3. *The Chicago Tribune,* August 1, 1974, Section 1, p. 3.

4. *The Chicago Tribune,* August 7, 1974, Section 1A, p. 13.

5. *The Chicago Defender* "The Metcalf Report on the Misuse of Police Authority in Chicago", (July, 1973), pp. 1 - 5.

6. Ibid.

7. Ibid.

8. Ibid.

9. *The Chicago Tribune,* p. 13.

10. Sloan T. Letman, "The OPS Investigators Manual," unpublished Chicago Police Department Investigative Guidelines, (1974), pp. 86-94.

11. Ibid.

12. Ibid.

13. Ibid.

14. 385 U.S. 493. (1971).

15. Letman, The OPS Investigators Manual, p. 140.

16. Ibid.

17. Ibid.

TABLE 1

DISPOSITION OF COMPLAINTS AGAINST PERSONNEL OF THE

CHICAGO POLICE DEPARTMENT FOR THE YEAR 1973

TYPES OF COMPLAINTS	INVESTIGATIONS COMPLETED	COMPLAINTS SUSTAINED
Excessive force and Civil Rights Violations	1,156	16
Interdepartmental Violations	3,938	1,073

SOURCE: The Metcalf Report on the Misuse of Police Authority in Chicago.

TABLE 2

DISPOSITION OF COMPLAINTS AGAINST PERSONNEL OF THE

CHICAGO POLICE DEPARTMENT FOR THE YEAR 1973

DISPOSITION OF CASES

Unfounded[a]	632
Exonerated[b]	247
Not sustained[c]	899
Sustained[d]	123
Cases Completed	1901

[a]Unfounded--the complaint was not based on facts as shown by the investigation, or the reported incident did not occur.

[b]Exonerated--the incident occured but the action taken by the officer was deemed lawful, reasonable and proper.

[c]Not sustained--the allegation is supported by insufficient evidence which could not be used to prove or disprove the allegation.

[d]Sustained--the allegation is supported by sufficient evidence to justify disciplinary action.

SOURCE: Chicago Police Department Statistical Report for 1976.

PERSPECTIVE ON POLICE CORRUPTION:
RESEARCH AND EXPOSURE
Thomas Barker

Within the past few years there has been a great deal of interest in police
corruption. A number of journalistic accounts of corrupt police behavior have
appeared in the popular press.[1] One of these works, *Serpico*, became a best-
seller and was made into a major motion picture which received several Academy
Award nominations. Several ex-officers have authored or co-authored accounts
of their deviant exploits.[2] The Journal *Crime and Delinquency*, the official
publication of the National Council on Crime and Delinquency, has begun to report instances of police corruption in its section of News and Notes. Police
journals, such as *The Police Chief: The Professional Voice of Law Enforcement*,
are now beginning to publish articles on police corruption. In a recent five-
month period of *The Police Chief* there were eight articles on police corruption
(See Table 1). The first annual symposium of the American Academy for Professional Law Enforcement was devoted to "Corruption and Its Management."[3] Following in line with this concern has been an "urgent" call for research on the
causes and prevention of corruption.[4] Unfortunately, little empirical research
has been conducted on this subject. There has been no nationwide research, and
there is no organization which collects and disseminates information about
police corruption investigations.

BACKSTAGE ACCESS

The bureaucratic structure of police departments, per se, creates problems
for any would-be researcher. Police organizations, as well as all formal organizations, maintain "front" and "backstage" regions.[5] Police departments as formal
agents of local governments and representatives of the larger criminal justice
system must present an acceptable "front" of efficiency and honesty. It is
in their best interest to manage and resist the corruption label. Consequently,
the backstage arena is where one finds instances of corruption, and access to
this arena is usually denied to any would-be researcher.

Arthur Niederhoffer, Professor of Sociology and Anthropology at John Jay
College of Criminal Justice, and a twenty-one year veteran of the New York City
Police Department, writes that sociologists have shown little interest in the
police because a "blue curtain of secrecy" screens most police organizations
and prevents the researcher from gaining entree into the life and world of the
police.[6]

The researcher's personal appearance as well as his attitudes toward the organization will be carefully scrutinized by the "gate keepers" of the police department before access is granted.[7] Blumberg[8] extends this fear of outsiders to all the subsystems of the criminal justice system--police, prosecution, courts, and corrections. He states that each of these subsystems functions as a closed community with a defensive and paranoid attitude toward "outsiders" and "critics." These subsystems deny backstage access to any non-member whenever possible.

It may be argued that all formal organizations, to some extent, resist inquiries by outsiders; but the police appear to be far more resistant to outside investigations. James Q. Wilson, reporting from personal experience, states that it is "far easier to do research on almost any other kind of organization including those which--like big city political machines and Negro protest associations--might rightfully be as suspicious of outsiders as the police."[9]

One can identify several reasons why the police have cause to fear research in the area of police deviance. The publication of research findings could damage the department's reputation and lead to a "shakeup" of the entire organization and dismissal of those who cooperated with the researcher as well as those exposed as corrupt. Research by an outside agent could possibly alert corrupt officers and drive their activities underground, thereby disrupting any on-going anticorruption efforts. Any exposure of corruption, even to a lone researcher, may inpugn the integrity and reputation of honest police personnel. The whole organization may be labeled deviant because of the deviance of some of its members.[10] The police organization and its members have ample justification to fear the repercussions of damaging information in the hands of an unethical researcher more interested in sensationalism and muckraking than in the advancement of scientific knowledge.

EXPOSURE OF CORRUPTION

The public exposure of corrupt police behavior has usually occurred when the blatant act or acts of some member or members of the organization has exceeded the tolerance limits of an outside agency or group and has created a scandal. In rare cases uncorrupted or reform minded members of the police organization have brought evidence of widespread corruption to the attention of these outside agencies and groups, e.g., the recent investigation of police corruption in New York City.[11]

It is unlikely that reform minded officers will "spill the beans" when one considers the institutionalized evasions of the law which exist in many, if not all, police departments, e.g., illegal harassment arrests, allowing certain fences and bootleggers to operate for informational purposes, payoffs to informers, reduction of charges, and the underenforcement or nonenforcement of certain laws. The "honest" police officer who attempts to expose corruption is in a very precarious situation because there are many departmental rules that are routinely overlooked but can be invoked at a particular time to punish an over-zealous or reform minded officer. All police officers violate departmental rules and regulations and sometimes criminal statutes; it is inherent in their discretionary powers.[12]

In addition to rule violations which probably exist in all police departments, there are many departments where few members have not engaged in some form or forms of corrupt practices. They become co-opted by their involvement, and this precludes their reporting corrupt members of the organization. Most members of "corrupt" departments possess some knowledge which could expose the deviant members, but as an ex-police informant claimed:

> It all depends upon how deeply you are involved. If you've been a guy who has gone along with a free cup of coffee, the gratuities, the real petty things and you'd happen to drive up on a major theft, drive up on another policeman with his shoulder against the door, then you might take action. However, if you had gone a little farther, say you had done some shopping (picking up items at the scene of a burglary or an open door) then you're forced to look the other way. It's like a spider spinning a web, you're drawn in toward the center.[13]

The "pure" cop may not exist in a number of police organizations. Police corrupt behavior is not a dichotomous attribute for most individual police officers; one is usually not either corrupt or honest, nor are any departments free of all corrupt practices. Corruption is "a more or less thing" distributed along a continuum of possible corrupt behaviors.[14] Rubinstein reports that the only way for an officer in the Philadelphia Police Department to resist engagement in any corrupt practices was to resign:

> . . . the only way a policeman can be honest in the exacting sense required by his oath of office is to resign. The policeman does not want to quit, so he makes little compromises, which bring him a few dollars and *more importantly, solidify his relationship with his colleagues,* and he continues to do his job. He knows he does things that are illegal, but he has no choice.[15]

The Knapp Commission also reported that it was easier for an honest rookie coming into the New York City Police Department to become corrupt than to remain honest. A police sergeant, with fifteen years experience, told this writer that the best course of action for an honest policeman in his departmnet was to resign from the force: "If they can't stand the heat, they should get out of the kitchen."

"HONEST" OFFICER'S ALTERNATIVES

Actually an "honest" policeman in a department where corrupt practices exist has a limited number of alternatives. He can look the other way and ignore the corrupt practices; however, in these instances he becomes implicated through his own complacency. Under these circumstances, should it be shown that he has not reported a fellow officer's transgressions, he may also be subject to disciplinary action. He can request a transfer to units within the department where there are little or no opportunities for corruption, e.g., tactical units, fixed-point traffic assignments, training or planning bureaus, police community relations units.

The "uncorrupted" officer can report practices to his superiors and hope that they are not involved or fearful of the repercussions of reform actions, an unlikely event if corrupt practices are widespread or of long duration in the organization. The reform minded officer can also report the existence of corruption to an outside agency, anonymously if he fears reprisals; however, outside agencies are not likely to act on unsubstantiated, anonymous tips.

The officer who reports corruption may place himself in a very untenable position no matter how true his allegations. He has broken the cardinal rule of policeman secrecy,[16] and the consequences for him will probably be bad no matter what the outcome.

> Well, I think policemen have been aware of some horrible examples of other police officers who have come forward, with all good intentions, to uncover a corrupted situation.
>
> I remember in Denver, I think 1961, the Police Department was relatively free of corruption. It developed a burglary ring amongst some of the patrolmen there, and another patrolman became aware of it, reported his findings to the chief, and the chief sent him to a psychiatrist for examination.
>
> When the psychiatrist sent him back to the chief, saying he was perfectly sane and telling the truth, the chief acted on the accusation. There were indictments and a substantial portion of the department was found to be involved. But the chief had to leave, had to resign, and the officer who uncovered it had to resign and leave the city.[17]

The man who turns in another officer becomes a virtual outcast among his fellow officers.

Man, I've seen some men in this department do some things
you wouldn't believe. But, I'm not about to turn them in.
If you turn a man in you're dead as far as the other men
are concerned. You're lower than whale shit on the bottom
of the ocean. Police have to stick together, everyone else
is against them (South City Sergeant).

Finally, the officer has two remaining alternatives; he can become involved
in corrupt practices, some or all; or he can quit the force and "get out of the
kitchen."

It is paradoxical that the largest body of formal "labellers" in our society--
the police--have gone to such lengths to resist the labelling of their own members as deviant.[18] Most of what we know about the phenomenon of police corruption
has come from the popular press and public scandals.

Although there has been little research, police corruption promises to be
a fertile yet problematic area of research in the sociology of deviant behavior.
This field is fertile in the sense that little research has been conducted, and
also because such research promises to provide insights into occupational or
work-related deviance. Research in this area is problematic in view of the potential hazards--physical and mental--difficulties, and time-consuming nature
of such research.[19]

Research on deviant behavior is often difficult under ideal conditions,
but when the "deviant" group is also suspicious of interlopers, powerful, and
has a vested interest in maintaining the "proper" organizational front, research
problems are compounded.

REFERENCES

1. Ahern, J.F. *Police in Trouble*. New York: Hawthorn Press, 1972. Mass,
    P. *Serpico*. New York: Viking Press, 1973. Williams, R.H. *Vice Squad*.
    New York: Thomas Y. Crowell, 1973.

2. Schecter, L. and W. Phillips. *On the Pad*. New York: G.P. Putnam, 1973.
    Barrett, J.K. "Inside the Mob's Smut Racket." *Readers Digest*. (Novem-
    ber, 1973, 128-133.)

3. American Academy for Professional Law Enforcement. "Corruption and Its
    Management." National Symposium. Washington, D.C. Program Outline. Jan-
    uary 8-10, 1975.

4. Top Administrators Cite Urgent Need for Research on Causes of Police Cor-
    ruption. *Criminal Justice Newsletter*. (December, 1972), 19, 193-194.
    National Advisory Commission on Criminal Justice Standards and Goals.
    Police. Washington, D.C.: G.P.O., 1974. Law Enforcement Council. "Of-
    ficial Corruption." *Crime and Delinquency*. (January, 1974), 15-19.

5. Coffman, E. *The Presentation of Self in Everyday Life*. Garden City, New York: Doubleday.

6. Niederhoffer, A. *Behind the Shield*. Garden City, New York: Anchor Books: Doubleday.

7. Fox, J.C. and R.J. Lundman. "Problems and Strategies in Gaining Research Access in Police Organizations." *Criminology*. (May, 1974), 52-69.

8. Blumberg, A.S. *Criminal Justice*. Chicago: Quadrangle, 1970.

9. Wilson, J.Q. "The Police and Their Problems: A Theory: In The Ambivalent Force: Perspectives on the Police." Edited by A. Niederhoffer and A.S. Blumberg. Waltham, Massachusetts, Xerox College Publishing Co., 1970, pp. 293-307.

10. Barker, T. and J. Roebuck. *An Empirical Typology of Police Corruption*. Springfield, Illinois: Charles C. Thomas, 1973.

11. Knapp Commission. The Knapp Commission Report on Police Corruption. New York: George Braziller, 1973.

12. Doublas, J.D. *Research on Deviance*. New York: Random House, 1972.

13. Stoddard, E.R. "The 'Informal Code' of Police Deviancy: A Group Approach to a 'Blue-Coat Crime'." *Journal of Criminal Law, Criminology and Police Science*. (June, 1968), p. 208.

14. Barker, T. and Julian Roebuck. *An Empirical Typology of Police Corruption*.

15. Rubinstein, J., Jr. *City Police,* New York: Farrac, Straus and Giroux, 1973, pp. 400-401. Italics added.

16. For a general discussion of secrecy and the police, see Westley, W.E. *Violence and the Police*. Cambridge, Massachusetts: M.I.T. Press, 1971.

17. Testimony from Captain Daniel McGowan of the N.Y.P.D. to the Knapp Commission. Knapp Commission, 1973, pp. 181-182.

18. For a general discussion of the use of "cover-up" tactics used by police organizations, see Barker and Roebuck, 1973.

19. Manning relates the case of a police researcher who developed a severe psychosomatic problem during his research. This same researcher was later thrown out of the department for his probing. Manning, P.K. *The Police: Mandate, Strategies, and Appearances*. In *Criminal Justice in America: A Critical Understanding*. Edited by R. Quinney. Boston: Little, Brown and Co., 1974.

TABLE 1

POLICE CORRUPTION ARTICLES IN *THE POLICE CHIEF*

JANUARY 1973 - MAY 1974

ISSUE	TITLE	AUTHOR	PROFESSIONAL AFFILIATION
January 1973	The Knapp Commission and You	Dempsey, L.J.	Lieutenant, New York City Police Department
March 1973	A Candid Analysis of Police Corruption	Parsons, J.C.	Chief of Police, Birmingham, Alabama, Police Department
July 1973	Police Professionalization and Internal Controls	Goforth, B.R.	Captain, Birmingham, Alabama, Police Department
August 1973	A Descriptive Study of Police Corruption	Meyer, J.C., Jr.	Assistant Professor of Criminal Justice, University of New Haven
September 1973	Deceit in Uniform	Smith, W.H.T.	First Deputy Commissioner, New York City Police
December 1973	Police Corruption	Murphy, P.V.	President, Police Foundation, Washington, D.C. (Former Police Commissioner New York City)
December 1973	Police Integrity: Accent on the Positive	Anderson, R.E.	Director, Field Operations Division, International Association of Chiefs of Police
April 1974	Police Discretion v. Plea Bargaining	Archueta, A.O.	Chief of Police, Clearfield, Utah

EVALUATION OF LAW ENFORCEMENT INNOVATIONS
Glenn E. Littlepage and John F. Schnelle

Each year billions of dollars are spent to enforce laws.[1] In the process, millions of criminals are apprehended.[2] However, all is not well with the law enforcement process. For example, there has been highly publicized data which revealed that large percentages of serious crime are not reported.[3] Furthermore, police offices have been criticized for being highly unreliable in reports of how many criminal incidents are cleared.[4] Finally, the entire prosecution and punishment process has been characterized as being inconsistent and subjective.[5] Thus, there is much room for improvement in police procedures. This chapter deals with the prospect of evaluation of police programs. Evaluation is seen as a necessary step for improving policework over the current state of the art. In many ways, policework is highly scientific. For example, ballistics, fingerprint analysis, and forensic medicine are based on careful scientific procedures. However, all areas of policework are not as firmly grounded on careful analysis and standard procedures have typically evolved on the basis of habit or educated judgments. These procedures generally have not been evaluated thoroughly and it is uncertain how their effectiveness compares to other possible procedures. In order to determine the effectiveness of current police procedures and to develop more effective law enforcement procedures, careful evaluations are needed. This chapter surveys several innovative law enforcement projects which have involved careful evaluations of their effectiveness. The results are frequently not in line with prior expectations and demonstrate the necessity of careful evaluation. Because evaluation is necessary to determine the effectiveness of various programs, it is vital to the improvement of police procedures.

TRAFFIC SAFETY

Two large-scale changes in traffic laws and enforcement methods have been evaluated systematically. These can serve as models for other evaluations of social policy changes. The first of these, the Connecticut crackdown on speeding, occurred at the end of 1955.[6] The change called for much more severe penalties for speeding, including a mandatory 30-day license suspension for anyone convicted of speeding. In addition, the use of unmarked police cars and radar for traffic enforcement were increased.

Initial evaluation of this crackdown was highly favorable and indicated there had been a twelve and one-half percent decrease in traffic fatalities and a saving of forty lives. This conclusion came from a simple comparison of the 1955 and 1956 fatality rates. However, closer attention to the results have shown many deficiencies of this comparison. It appears that one reason for the large drop was that 1955 was a particularly bad year. Indeed, this was a primary reason for the crackdown on speeding. The problem is that because of a statistical principle called "regression to the mean" it was likely that traffic fatalities would have decreased EVEN WITHOUT THE CRACKDOWN. Regression means that when a measure (in this case the number of traffic fatalities) is unusually high or low, the next measure will generally be less extreme. Thus, Campbell and Ross examined the results of the Connecticut crackdown very carefully to determine if the reduction was greater than a simple return to normal. Similarly, they took steps to see that the decrease was actually caused by the crackdown and not by other factors such as safer cars, better winter weather, or less driving.

Campbell and Ross's careful analysis shows that the more severe laws were actually being enforced. This is apparent from a very large increase in the number of licenses suspended and also by a threefold increase in the percentage of licenses suspended that were suspended because of speeding. During the first six months of this strict enforcement, the number of licenses suspended had increased from two hundred and thirty-one during the same period of the preceding year to four thousand, five hundred and fifty-nine. It also appears clear that the more severe penalties reduced speeding since the number of speeding arrests dropped fifty-three percent and spot checks also revealed decreased speeding.

Campbell and Ross did two things to look at the effectiveness of the crackdown at saving lives; they compared the number of persons killed for several years before and several years after the crackdown. This latter analysis showed that fatalities had actually been reduced by the change in the law, but that the change was not as great as the comparison of only the deaths for the 1955 and 1956 would suggest. The second comparison was between the rate of fatalities in Connecticut and in neighboring states. Before the crackdown, there was a fairly stable fatality rate in Connecticut and in the neighboring states, but since the crackdown, Connecticut has shown a larger decrease than the other states. Thus, through the careful analyses of Campbell and Ross, it was possible to show that the change in the penalties for speeding caused a decrease in the number of traffic fatalities. The decrease was not as great as was initially believed, but nevertheless, the decrease seems to have clearly been the result of the changed law rather than the result of chance year to year variation, improved weather conditions, safer cars or other factors.

Another large-scale intervention into traffic safety, the breathalizer program, was instituted when the British Road Safety Act of 1967 was passed. The law provided for strict penalties for persons convicted of driving under the influence of alcohol. Penalties included a mandatory one-year suspension of the driver's license and a fine of one thousand pounds and/or up to four months imprisonment. Police were also authorized to give on-the-spot breath tests to anyone suspected of drinking and driving, anyone suspected of having alcohol in his body, anyone involved in an accident, or anyone suspected of committing a moving traffic violation.[7] Thus, the police were given wide license to apply the breathalizer tests. Persons failing the breathalizer test were taken to the police station for more accurate blood or urine tests. Thus, police had the authority and methods to enforce the law strictly and the penalties were quite severe.

The evaluation methods used by Ross, Campbell and Glass were quite sophisticated. First, they looked at monthly casualty rates (deaths and serious injuries). Then these monthly rates were adjusted to correct for large seasonal variations in these measures. Analysis of this seasonally adjusted accident rate revealed that the intervention immediately produced the largest monthly drop in the five-year comparison period preceding the intervention. This was a seasonally adjusted drop of one thousand, six hundred and fifty-four serious injuries and fatalities (and a drop of one thousand, one hundred and ninety-nine without the seasonal adjustment). The drop in injuries and fatalities is even more apparent when one looks at the specific times when fatalities attributable to alcohol are at their peak, weekend nights from ten o'clock p.m. until four o'clock a.m. the following morning. During this period there was an immediate forty to forty-five percent reduction in fatalities and serious injuries. In order to serve as a control for other factors such as a general increase in safety consciousness, or improved weather or road conditions, or less driving, accidents were monitored for a time period when pubs were closed. These "closed hours" were seven to ten o'clock a.m. and four to five o'clock p.m. daily. There was no reduction of injuries or fatalities during these closed hours, a time when driving while intoxicated was relatively infrequent even before the crackdown. This comparison of the changes in injury and fatality rates during closed hours and weekend nights provides a means of estimating whether the change had a continuing effect. For the year following the start of the breathalizer program and the stiff penalties, injuries and fatalities were relatively constant during the closed hours, but the initial reduction of injuries and fatalities during weekend nights was maintained. This analysis revealed that the crackdown had its maximum impact for the first three months, reducing serious injuries and fatalities by some forty to forty-five percent. In the year following initial change, there was a continued reduction of thirty percent in the number of deaths and serious injuries occurring on weekend nights. This careful evaluation not only showed that the breathalizer tests and stiff penalties reduced traffic casualties, but also showed that the greatest reduction was on weekend nights when drinking was heaviest.

These approaches to automobile safety rely heavily on enforcement and punishment in an attempt to maintain appropriate driving behavior. However, there have also been attempts to use non-coercive measures such as publicity or information compaigns to improve traffic safety. For example, in 1955, there was an intensive two month nationwide U.S. program on the general topic of traffic safety, using newspaper, radio, TV, posters, bumper stickers, buttons, and even balloons. The results failed to show any improvement; in fact, the number of fatalities was up ten to twelve percent from the same months in the preceding year.[8]

Publicity approaches which focus on a specific violation have yielded mixed results. For example, a British publicity campaign against drunk driving failed to reduce accidents due to drunk driving,[9] while a Danish publicity campaign was successful in increasing the frequency with which drivers placed small children in the back seat.[10] Perhaps the difference in effectiveness is related to ease of compliance, or perhaps parents' high level of concern for their children. Thus, publicity campaigns have not been shown to produce consistent changes in most indices of traffic safety, but may work on some specialized driving practices.

A study conducted on a local level compared to the effects of newspaper publicity, increased enforcement, and publicized enforcement on residential speeding.[11] This study was designed to determine the effect of publicity alone, increased enforcement alone, and the combination of the two resulting in publicized enforcement. Speed was determined by measuring the time it took each vehicle to complete a one-eighth mile segment of selected streets.

Following an eight-day baseline period, a newspaper intervention was initiated to draw attention to speeding along a particular street (Street A). Two newspaper articles were used to publicize the high degree of speeding on street A; one was a feature article occupying five columns and containing two large pictures of observers timing cars. The second was a smaller follow-up article.

Analysis of speeding along Street A revealed that publicity alone had no effect on speeding. The average speed during the baseline period was 32.17 mph, and 32.58 mph during the newspaper intervention.

Both the enforcement and publicized enforcement interventions were initiated concurrently with a large article stressing that speeding had not been reduced along Street A and increased enforcement along that street would necessarily follow. The article was accompanied by a picture of the local safety commissioner reviewing the data for Street A. During the enforcement intervention, an officer was assigned to divide his time in a marked police car conducting radar enforcement along Street A and another street (Street B). Thus during the third time period, Street A received a publicized enforcement intervention, while Street B received unpublicized enforcement. This intervention lasted three days. The police officer was *not* conducting radar enforcement at the time observations were made, thus changes resulting from this intervention were not simply the results of speeders slowing down in the immediate presence of a police officer. Area B, which received only unpublicized enforcement during the third time period showed no change from baseline during either intervention period. This suggests that unpublicized enforcement did not result in reduced speeds. Note that there was intermittent enforcement for three days; it is likely that given a longer period of consistent enforcement, drivers may have learned to regard the area as one with a high incidence of enforcement and, therefore, reduced their speeds. However, during the publicized enforcement along Street A, there was a significant decrease in speeding. The mean was 30.73 mph, a relatively small but statistically reliable decrease.

It seems clear that the newspaper intervention used in that study did not reduce speeding. Similarly, it does not appear that the level of increased, but unpublicized, enforcement utilized in the study produced a significant reduction in speeding at times when police were not actually present.

It does, however, appear that newspaper publicity serves to increase the effectiveness of enforcement procedures. Publicized enforcement does result in a reduction in speeding that generalizes to times when police were not actually present. Thus, publicizing enforcement on a particularly dangerous street should produce more dramatic and more general speed reductions than unpublicized enforcement.

Before concluding that, by themselves, noncoercive measures which call for cooperation on the part of the citizens are generally not successful, it is worthwhile to look at an innovative program which produced substantial reductions in traffic violations.

A very personalized and perhaps the most successful non-coercive approach to traffic safety was conducted in Israel by Ben-David and his colleagues.[12] They showed that calling drivers' attention to their offenses produced large improvements in driving behavior. In their study, warning letters were sent to drivers who failed to stop at a stop sign and also to drivers who failed to follow the arrows indicating proper lane usage. These letters, which were sent by the Israeli National Council for the Prevention of Accidents, detailed the location, date, time, and nature of the offense. These letters resulted in substantial reductions in the driver's designated violation (up to thirty to forty percent). Furthermore, these reductions lasted from three to six months and generalized to other locations near the site of the offense. Three levels of threat were implied in the letters and since all were effective, the authors concluded that the improved driving was not the result of an implied threat, but rather the result of persons being made aware of their violations.

Thus, this sampling of studies has shown how careful evaluation of programs designed to promote traffic safety can provide guidelines for improvement of police traffic safety measures. For example, it was found that increased enforcement in Connecticut reduced traffic violations and also reduced fatalities. Another study suggests that publicizing the location of enforcement activities will produce even greater changes in driving. The British breathalizer study showed that very substantial changes in casualty rates resulted from strict penalties and more effective enforcement methods. Finally, these studies suggest that traditional media campaigns, by themselves are relatively ineffective, but personal reminders noting that the message applies to you personally may reduce violations

PATROL EVALUATION

Patrol activities represent a major expenditure of police time and money. However, until recently the effectiveness of police patrols have not been evaluated. The evaluations that have recently been accomplished have produced surprising results and some practical suggestions about the nature of effective police patrols.

One of the oldest and presumably most important activities of police officers is patrol. Patroling refers to officers moving through various areas and making checks based on their discretion and their judgments of suspicious behavior or circumstances. In the past few years there have been several studies of the effectiveness of patrolling and comparisons of various patrol strategies. As with the evaluations of traffic programs, the results have shown some attempts to be effective, others less effective. The results of these evaluations are not always consistent with the prior expectations of the police and community.

One of the largest and perhaps most surprising evaluations of patrol was the Kansas City Preventive Patrol Experiment.[13] This study manipulated the degree to which various areas of the south side of Kansas City were patrolled. Fifteen areas were chosen for study. Five were given increased patrol emphasis to the extent that patrols were at least doubled in these areas (proactive zones). Five were given reduced patrol emphasis (reactive zones) and were generally not patrolled, although police officers answered calls for help, served warrants, and provided other necessary police services. Five additional areas served as controls and no change was made in the patrol procedures used in these areas. These conditions of increased, decreased or unchanged level of patrol were maintained for one year.

Evaluation was based on a variety of measures, including overall and specific crime rates, victimization surveys which indicate the extent to which persons have experienced crime (which may or may not have been reported), citizen fear of crime, business attitudes toward crime and police services. Use of such diverse data sources should strengthen conclusions.

As far as the police were concerned, the results of this large scale study were far from heartening. Although there were some scattered differences between the various experimental areas, differences in patrol generally did *not* produce measurable effects upon the various measures of crime. Thus, it appeared that a high level of police patrol had no more of a deterrent effect upon crime than the strategy in which police merely responded to calls and followed up reports of crime.

Although the Kansas City study is impressive in many ways, two major criticisms of the study seem appropriate.[14] One problem was that some of the areas were quite narrow and bordered on areas with a different patrol strategy. Thus, persons might not notice differences in the visibility of police if there were fewer police in a reactive zone, but a greater number of police in a proactive zone only a few blocks away. A second criticism of the study is that the actual behavior of the police officers assigned to patrol was not monitored. It is not clear exactly how the additional officers spent their time. This limitation is corrected in a study by Schnelle, Kirchner, Casey, Uselton and McNees in Nashville.[15]

This latter study differed from the Kansas City study in several important respects. First, the increase from the normal patrol to the saturation patrol was from one car per beat to five cars per beat. This is a slightly larger increase than in the Kansas City Study. Secondly, in a particular zone, patrol strength was increased during daytime or nighttime hours separately allowing a comparison of saturation patrols during the two times. Third, the four additional cars were instructed not to interrupt patrol activities for routine matters. The four additional cars did not respond to calls except for emergencies and crimes in progress. A final difference is that the Nashville study instructed officers to patrol at low speeds (below 20 mph) and used tachographs (an instrument which objectively records car performance) to monitor the amoount of time moving and the amount of time spent in low-speed patrol. These procedures increased the total number of cars in the zone to five times the normal level, increased the overall patrol movement to four times normal levels, and increased slow patrol to around thirty times normal levels. Thus, this study provided a marked change in the level of patrol.

Results of the study showed that saturation patrols did *not* decrease daytime crimes. The high level of patrol did result in a decrease in the number of serious nighttime crimes, particularly crimes against persons (i.e., assaults, rape, armed robbery). However, the high costs of the additional patrol may make the procedure economically unfeasible. Thus, these results provide additional refinement of the Kansas City findings.

A relatively new concept of police patrol which is currently being evaluated in Cincinnati and Rochester is team policing. Team policing involves assigning multiple police responsibilities of a team of officers who become responsible for all police services in a specific location. The team policing concept is most obviously manifested by the fact that team officers perform both patrol and investigative functions within their areas of responsibility in lieu of reliance on a centralized detective bureau. Block and Bell have reported preliminary data from Rochester which indicates that team policing does lead to an increase in clearance rates of crimes and to an increase in the "on scene" robbery arrests but not necessarily to a decrease in crime rate.[16]

Thus, these studies show that higher levels of patrol may lead to reductions of nighttime crime and that team policing procedures may result in more efficient apprehension of robbery suspects. However, to date the major evaluations of patrol procedures have suggested that traditional routine patrol procedures have a relatively small impact on crime.

BURGLARY PREVENTION PROGRAMS

Burglaries are one of the most frequent of the serious crimes. A statewide survey in Maryland indicated that burglary was the second most feared crime.

Burglary rates have increased dramatically, doubling since 1960.[17] This section describes evaluations of several attempts to prevent burglaries.

The Kansas City Patrol procedure described earlier, showed that saturation patrols did not reduce various types of crimes including burglaries. In view of these findings, Schnelle and his colleagues instituted a specialized burglary patrol in Nashville.[18] This study which emphasized prevention or residential burglaries differed from the previously described Kansas City program in the following ways. First, patrol strength was increased to a level much higher than the Kansas City study (up to fifteen officers patrolling); patrols were increased only on the day shift (most home burglaries occur during the day); the additional patrolmen were in unmarked cars and were dressed in plain clothes; they were given a book containing identity, pictures, and information on individuals previously arrested for burglary. This intervention procedure was successful in that burglary arrests increased from 1.7 per week before the intervention to 4.2 per week during the specialized program. However, with respect to reducing the number of burglaries, the program was unsuccessful. There was no change in the number of burglaries.

A series of studies were next conducted by Schnelle and his colleagues utilizing helicopter patrols to reduce the incidence of burglaries.[19,20]

The first study examined the effectiveness of helicopter patrol in one highly populated area of Nashville. Baseline rates of home burglaries in the area were noted and compared to rates during two separate helicopter interventions. Prior to helicopter patrol, the average number of burglaries was .89 per day. Helicopter patrol reduced the rate by almost two-thirds to .33 per day. The helicopter patrol was temporarily discontinued and reinstated to provide a more convincing demonstration of its effectiveness. After removal of the helicopter patrol, burglaries increased to 1.22 per day and following reinstatement of helicopter patrols, the level of burglaries again dropped to .33 per day. Thus, it is clear that within this zone, helicopter patrol decreased burglaries. However, the reduction lasted only as long as the helicopter patrol continued. Thus, burglary rates increased once again following removal of the helicopter. Crime rates for other types of crimes within the area as well as burglary rates in other areas were monitored to determine if reductions in burglaries in the area receiving helicopter patrol resulted in increased burglaries in other areas or increases in other types of crimes. No such displacement was found.

The helicopter patrol next was instituted in four additional areas. This time two areas were much larger and less densely populated than the target area of the first evaluation. The remaining two areas were highly populated and similar to the other areas observed in the first evaluation. In the highly populated area, the helicopter was almost continuously visible to all parts of the small area. In the low density areas, the helicopter was only occasionally visible. The effects of the helicopter were replicated in the high density areas but helicopter patrol produced no burglary deterrent effects in the low population density area. Thus, the helicopter patrol provides a useful tool for the prevention of burglaries, but it is effective only in densely populated areas.

The helicopter patrol procedure is of course a very expensive procedure costing approximately $30 per hour in fuel and maintenance costs alone. Nevertheless, when used in the densely populated areas, the dollar savings to citizens resulting from the decreased number of burglaries more than offset this expense.

Other approaches to burglary prevention have been attempted. For instance, an investigation of silent burglar alarms were installed in 350 locations and connected directly to the police station. Comparison of the burglary rates of these locations with 350 control locations not receiving the alarms over a two-year period showed no differences in the burglary rates. However, burglary apprehensions were higher in locations with silent alarms.

A recent study by the San Diego Police Department evaluated their use of frequent field interrogations. A field interrogation involves contact between a police officer and a citizen when there is no probable cause for arrest but when there is "reasonable suspicion".[21] San Diego has traditionally emphasized field interrogations in all of their patrol operations but wanted to experimentally document the effectiveness of the field interrogation procedure. To accomplish the evaluation, researchers compared field interrogation techniques in three separate conditions. In one area, police officers were given intense specialized training in field interrogation. This latter training was supplementary to the training provided all other officers. In a reversal area, all field interrogations were suspended for a nine month period and then reinstated. Thus, crime rates and citizen opinion of police could be compared in the latter area during three conditions: a period when normal field investigation procedures were used, a reversal period when no field interrogations were conducted, and a third period when normal field interrogations were resumed. Finally, both of the latter two areas (special training area and reversal area) were compared to the third experimental area in which field interrogation procedures as executed by non-specially trained police officers were maintained according to normal departmental procedures.

Results suggest that field interrogations, when suspended in one zone, resulted in an increase in crimes normally committed by juveniles (i.e., home burglaries and malicious mischief). Alternatively, when field interrogations were reinstated, these juvenile related crimes decreased. There were no significant differences between the areas patrolled by the specially trained officers and the area patrolled by normally trained officers. There was also no difference between the three areas as to citizen opinion of police officer efficiency or citizen complaints about police officers' behavior. Thus, field interrogation procedures seem to be useful techniques for burglary prevention.

In summary, the presence of a technology through which police officers can more efficiently perform their duties is slowly being realized. Much of this technological development has occurred in the past few years and dates to the time that police officials started to ask evaluative questions about traditional police procedures. These recent empirical evaluations generally have led to surprising outcomes which have primarily documented the limitations of police procedures. Furthermore, this latter evaluative research has directly stimulated to conceptualization of new police techniques which are in turn being empirically evaluated and revised based on their outcome.

Thus, the development of more efficient law enforcement techniques is largely due to the development of an evaluation research methodology which permits police departments to abandon ineffective procedures and to progressively adopt and refine new procedures. This latter reliance on empirical evaluation promises to promote police skills to a new level of professionalism which is based not on tradition or folklore but on scientifically validated knowledge.

REFERENCES

1. Kelling, G., Pate, T., Dieckman, D., and Brown C. *The Kansas City preventive patrol experiment: A technical report.* Washington, D.C.: Police Foundation, 1975.

2. Wilson, J. Do police prevent crime? in S. Halleck, P. Lerman, S. Messinger, N. Morris, P. Murphy and M. Wolfgang (eds.) *The Aldine Crime and Justice Annual, 1974.* Chicago: Aldine, 1974.

3. Law enforcement assistance administration, trust and the police. Time, 1974, 103, 124.

4. Greenwood, P.W., Chaiken, J.M., Peterslio, J. and Prusoff, L. The criminal investigation process, Volume III: Observations and analysis. Rand, Santa Monica, California, 1975.

5. Wilson, J.O. *Thinking About Crime*. Vintage Books, New York. 1977.

6. Campbell, D.T. and Ross, H.L. The Connecticut crackdown on speeding: Time-series data in quasi-experimental analysis, *Law and Society Review*, 1968, 3(1), pp. 33-53.

7. Ross, H.L., Campbell, D.T. and Glass, G.V. Determining the social effect of a legal reform: The British "Breathalyzer" crackdown of 1967. *American Behavioral Scientist*, 1970, 13(4), pp. 493-509.

8. Griep, D.J. Propaganda and alternative countermeasures for road safety. *Accident Analysis and Prevention*, 1970, 2, pp. 127-140.

9. Griep, 1970.

10. Jorgensen, N.O. and Steen-Peterson, K. The effect of a Danish propaganda campaign for children to be placed in the back seat of cars. *Accident Analysis and Prevention*, 1972, 5, pp. 77-79.

11. Littlepage, G. and Kosloski, K. Comparison of newspaper publicity, enforcement, and publicized enforcement for the reduction of residential speeding. Paper presented at Southwestern Psychological Association Convention, 1976.

12. Ben-David, G., Lewin, I., Haliva, Y. and Tel-Nir. Influence of advisory letters in changing the driving behavior of private motorists in Israel. *Accident Analysis and Prevention*, 1970, 2, pp. 189-200   and Ben-David, G., Lewin, I., Haliva, Y. and Tel-Nir. Influence of personal communication on the driving behavior of private motorists in Israel. *Accident Analysis and Prevention*, 1972, 4, pp. 269-301.

13. Kelling, et. al., 1975.

14. Davis, E.M. and Knowles, L. A critique of the report: An evaluation of the Kansas City preventive patrol experiment. *Police Chief*, 1976, 6.

15. Schnelle, J.F., Kirchner, R.E., Casey, J.D., Uselton, P.H. and McNees, M.P. Patrol evaluation research: A multiple-baseline analysis of saturation police patrolling during day and night hours. *Journal of Applied Behavior Analysis*, 1977, 10, pp. 33-40.

16. Block, P. and Bell, J. Managing investigations: The Rochester system. Washington, D.C.: Police Foundation, 1975.

17. White, T., Regan, K., Waller, J. and Whaley, J. Police burglary prevention programs. Washington, D.C.: U.S. Government Printing Office, 1975.

18. Schnelle, J.F., Kirchner, R.E., Lawler, J.R. and McNees, M.P. Social evaluation research: the evaluation of two police patrol strategies. *Journal of Applied Behavior Analysis*, 1975, 8, pp. 232-240.

19. Schnelle, J., Kirchner, R., Macrae, J., McNees, P., Eck, R., Snodgrass, S., Casey, J., and Uselton, P. Police evaluation research: An experimental and cost-benefit analysis of a helicopter patrol in a high crime area. Unpublished, Middle Tennessee State University.

20. Schnelle, et. al., 1977.

21. Boydston, J. San Diego field interrogation: Final report. Washington, D.C.: Police Foundation, 1975.

PART III: THE TREATMENT OF OFFENDERS

MAKING TIME FIT THE CRIME
Sen. Edward M. Kennedy

During the past few months, a bill I introduced in the Senate calling for the imposition of mandatory minimum sentences in cases of violent street crime (S. 2698 11/20/75) has received extensive publicity. The bill is grounded in the theory that certainty of punishment, if coupled with swift justice, can be an effective deterrent to the type of violent crime that most troubles our citizens. It was introduced as the first part of a larger legislative crime package designed to deal with our nation's soaring crime rate.

The bill provides that in certain cases of violent street crime - the type of crime that most troubles the nation's citizens - a two-year minimum sentence of imprisonment would be imposed. An important feature of the bill is the "mitigating" circumstance provision which would permit the sentencing judge to forego imposing the mandatory minimum if the court found that the convicted offender was under 17 years of age, was mentally unstable, acted under duress, or was merely an accomplice and not the principal. Thus the charge may not be made that the bill completely ignores the history and characteristics of the individual offender.

Though mandatory minimum sentencing is not the magic cure-all to crime, it is one important step in the right direction. In addition, the publicity surrounding introduction of the bill has served the valuable function of awakening the public not only to the need for providing certainty of punishment to the violent offender but also to the critical need for relieving trial court congestion and backlog, especially in our large metropolitan courts.

I have consistently stated that mandatory minimum sentencing would be self-defeating if it were not coupled with congressional action to relieve our courts of the backlogs and delays which threaten to inundate our entire judicial system. Civil delay in the Massachusetts Superior Court is as long as 66 months; in some New York City courts criminal offenders must wait over one year to be tried. The situation throughout the country is scandalous. I have recently introduced legislation in the Senate designed to combat the problem of court congestion and backlog.

The public's concern with the pros and cons of mandatory minimum sentencing and trial delay must not obscure and undercut the importance of a second companion bill which I introduced at the same time as the mandatory minimum sentencing bill (S. 2699 11/20/75). Entitled the "Sentencing Guidelines Bill" and cosponsored by a bipartisan group of seven senators, this legislation makes long overdue reforms in the federal criminal sentencing process.

The bill is designed to deal with two major problems which plague the Federal Court system and the administration of criminal justice - the total absence of any legislatively prescribed guidelines to aid judges during the sentencing process and the wide disparity in the sentences actually imposed in criminal cases. The two problems are, of course, inextricably related.

Sentencing disparity - in which, all too often, two convicted defendants with similar backgrounds convicted of the same crime receive widely differing sentences - has become a national scandal and can be traced directly to the unbridled, unreviewable discretion we give our federal judges in imposing sentences. The "quidelines" bill brings some welcome uniformity to the sentencing process by articulating for the first time the general purposes and goals of sentencing to be considered by the judge prior to imposing a sentence of imprisonment.

In addition, the bill provides for appellate review of sentences and establishes a United States Commission on Sentencing whose function it will be to promulgate a specific fixed sentencing range for similar defendants who commit similar crimes. The sentencing court will be required by statute to impose a sentence within the guidelines established by the Commission unless it can demonstrate in writing a justification to sentence outside of such guidelines.

For example, the Commission might establish a guideline which states that in cases of armed bank robbery, in which the defendant was a first offender and no injury resulted, a sentence of imprisonment of between 4.5 years and 5.8 years be imposed. The sentencing judge could not sentence outside such guideline a guideline absent the existence of a mitigating circumstance, e.g., the offender robbed in order to feed his starving children. Even then the reason justifying the sentence variation must be in writing and is subject to appellate review.

The guidelines bill also serves two other vital purposes which tend to be overlooked during a first casual reading. It eliminates indeterminate or open-ended sentencing by requiring judges to sentence a convicted offender to a fixed period of imprisonment. In articulating the general purposes and goals underlying a sentence of imprisonment, it helps the sentencing judge decide not only how long an offender should be imprisoned, but, more importantly, aids the court in determining whether the offender should be imprisoned at all. In effect, the bill establishes for the first time a federal sentencing philosophy designed to answer the questions of who should be imprisoned and for what purpose.

Deciding whether a convicted offender should be incarcerated, placed in some type of diversionary program, or released on probation is the critical issue which determines the success or failure of our correctional system. But this fact is all too often lost today in discussions about prison reform and alternatives to incarceration. Although widespread criticism of our correctional system is justified - our prisons are overcrowded and understaffed, few prisons seem to "cure" criminals of crime, and grim statistics document the failures of various "halfway houses," "furlough release," and other diversionary programs - such criticism is misdirected.

The underlying reason for the lack of success in our correctional system is the absence of principled sentencing practices. The issue is not whether more offenders should be sentenced to prison (they should not), nor is it that prisons should be abolished and replaced with a wide variety of diversionary programs (we will always need prisons for certain offenders). The real issue is determining - with some degree of fairness and uniformity - which offender belongs in prison and which does not. We must direct our immediate attention away from the ideological argument of incarceration versus diversion and debate the need for improving our sentencing practices.

S. 2699 is a step in that direction.

What are the general purposes and goals underlying a sentence of imprisonment which are mentioned in the bill? Four are listed:

(1) "the nature and circumstances of the offense and the history and characteristics of the defendant;

(2) the need for the sentence imposed (A) to reflect the seriousness of the offense and promote respect for law by providing just punishment for the offense, and (B) to afford adequate deterrence to criminal conduct;

(3) whether other less restrictive sanctions have been applied to the defendant frequently or recently; and

(4) any sentencing guidelines established by the United States Commission on Sentencing."

One immediately notices that although there are references to the traditional sentencing goals of retribution and deterrence there is no reference whatever to the time-honored concept of "rehabilitation." Why? Has rehabilitation of the offender ceased to be a valid purpose for imposing a prison sentence? The answer is yes and for the same reason that indeterminate sentencing is no longer permitted under the bill.

The simple fact is that prison rehabilitation programs have not been successful - at least in those cases where such programs are compulsory in nature and forced on the prisoner. This should not be surprising. Coercive rehabilitation programs too often force the prisoner to make a Hobson's choice - either reject the programs offered, in which case such apparent lack of cooperation with the prison authorities assures the prisoner a longer indeterminate sentence, less likelihood of parole, and less opportunity for participating in early release or other diversionary programs, or, on the other hand, "go along with the game plan" and pretend to respond to prison training programs which are forced upon him. In the latter case, "rehabilitation" is little more than a sham used to ingratiate the prisoner to his parole board.

I am not, of course, advocating the abolition of prison rehabilitation programs. Indeed, such programs should be expanded, especially in the areas of vocational and educational training. What I am advocating is the abolition of compulsory rehabilitation as a justification for imprisonment. Forced rehabilitation does not work and can be used by the parole board as a justification for retaining custody of a prisoner until it determines that he is sufficiently rehabilitated to become a peaceful member of society.

The failure of compulsory rehabilitation also highlights the failure of the indeterminate sentencing concept. The latter means that the prisoner's actual term of imprisonment is set, not by the legislature or the sentencing judge, but by an agency such as the parole board. The board decides - while the prisoner is serving his unlimited, open-ended sentence - when the prisoners is sufficiently rehabilitated and poses no future criminal threat to society.

But indeterminate sentencing is grounded on the faulty premise that a prisoner's behavior while in a prison rehabilitation program is an accurate predictor of how such prisoner will behave in the community once he is released. As already indicated, however, compulsory rehabilitation does not provide such an accurate prediction. Indeterminate sentencing is a failure, therefore, because we simply cannot predict the likelihood of a prisoner's criminal conduct in the community by observing how such prisoner responds to coercive prison rehabilitation programs.

Thus, there is no justification for rehabilitation being a purpose of imprisonment; a benefit, yes, a purpose, no. The guidelines bill makes no reference to rehabilitation as a purpose or goal of imprisonment. Nor does the bill permit the imposition of an indeterminate sentence; all sentences are for a fixed period, according to guidelines established by the Commission.

The bill does direct the attention of the sentencing judge to the concepts of retribution and deterrence. But these concepts deal with society's concern with punishing, not rehabilitating the offender - a concern obviously more attuned to imprisonment. No arbitrary prediction of the offender's future criminal behavior enters into considerations of retribution or deterrence. Even that part of the bill which requires the court to consider whether "less restrictive sanctions" had previously been imposed on the offender refers to the offender's correctional history and the need for the court to impose harsher punishment in light of it. Thus, under the guidelines bill, a convicted offender is sentenced for what he did in the past, not for what he might do in the future. And imprisonment is imposed only to punish, not to rehabilitate.

An interesting question raised by the sentencing guidelines concept concerns the future of the parole board. In a sentencing system in which the indeterminate sentence is abolished and guidelines assure uniform sentences for similar offenders convicted of similar crimes, the traditional role of the parole board becomes obsolete. No longer would a prisoner be eligible for parole after 1/3 or 1/4 of his sentence; the parole board's current function of determining when a prisoner should be released would be incorporated into the sentencing guidelines themselves. (It is ironic that under our present federal sentencing and correctional systems - in which judicial sentencing guidelines are unfortunately absent - the federal parole board itself has acted to bring some element of uniformity and fairness into the sentencing process. The board promulgated objective parole guidelines which give the prisoner reasonably accurate notice of his release date. In addition, such parole guidelines helped to soften the arbitrariness of sentencing disparity by setting uniform parole release dates for similar defendants convicted of similar crimes.)

The parole board might, however, play a new innovative role in a modified correctional system. Along with its traditional functions of extending the release dates of prisoners who commit disciplinary offenses while in prison and of computing so-called "good time," the board might marshall its energies in the direction of voluntary rehabilitation programs.

"Early release" and "community based" diversionary programs, which are now beginning to receive the concentrated attention they deserve, might be administered by the parole board, which would determine qualifications and preconditions for participation. (All community based diversionary programs rest on the basic premise that community influences, pressures, and responsibilities are necessary if the offender is to be successfully rehabilitated. In light of this it is not surprising that prisons - which serve to isolate and socially ostracize the prisoner - usually fail to rehabilitate. In cases where rehabilitation succeeds, it is usually the result of the prisoner succeeding in spite of his environment.) No longer burdened with the responsibility of determining a prisoner's "proper" release date, the board could turn its undivided attention to the successful implementation of alternatives to imprisonment.

The lingering myths of our criminal justice system - that sentencing is fair and objective, that rehabilitation is a goal of imprisonment and can be forced on the offender, that parole boards and prison officials can "predict" the offender's future behavior in the community - must yield to a more practical corrections policy. It is time to recognize that the key problem confronting our criminal justice system lies in our unprincipled, arbitrary sentencing practices compounded by an overburdened judicial system. The nation's crime rate is continuing to soar. Action is needed now; the place to start is with our courts and how they sentence the convicted offender.

COMMUNITY EDUCATION: A POSITIVE PROGRAM
FOR MEETING THE JUVENILE DELINQUENCY CHALLENGE?
Robert Gaunt

Problems caused by a rising tide of juvenile delinquency seem to be con-
founding law enforcement agencies in most parts of our nation today. As Jensen
states, "Our country has never experienced a revolt by young people on such a
massive scale, nor on so many diverse fronts."[1] Society, of course, reacts by
attempting to counter the trend through "the juvenile delinquency industry."
Haney and Gold have concluded that "current treatment and prevention programs
are, in a word, misdirected,"[2] and much of the available evidence suggests that
their observations have substance and validity. Clearly, there is a challenge
to seek new programs and methods of improving existing activities. The task
is complicated when one considers that problems of financing, lack of community
involvement, and misunderstanding of the true nature of the problem are all
working to create additional complexities. During recent years, however, an
increasing number of communities have sought to deal with local problems by
adopting a plan which stresses citizen involvement and cooperation between citizens and the formal agencies of the social structure. That plan is called
community education.

Community education has experienced a rather rapid growth during recent
years. Much of the growth has been inspired by the spectacular successes of
the pioneering efforts begun in Flint, Michigan in 1936. While the Flint program is generally assumed to have been the original community education effort,
Olsen points to such early educational philosophers as Comenius, Spencer,
Rousseau, and Dewey, claiming that these persons were stressing similar concepts at much earlier dates.[3] The community education idea rests upon several
simple premises which, when judged collectively, may be said to add up to "nothing new." Perhaps the reality is that the ideas of community action and
citizen participation have been temporarily forgotten in too many places.

Community schools are facilities which are open day and night, usually
twelve months of the year, with programs chosen by local advisory committees
designed to meet the needs of the total communities which they serve. The community school recognizes that learning and self improvement are a life-long
process, and it directs its activities to all ages--boys and girls, men and
women. School buildings thus become community centers after school and during
evening hours for tutoring, recreation, adult education, vocational training,
counseling, community forums, etc.[4] Typically, the community school employs a

professional staff member who coordinates the activities which are planned by
the local advisory council. Actual programs are conducted by a combination of
part-time employees, volunteers, and representatives of local agencies.

A powerful factor which lies at the heart of community education, and which
sets it apart from programs which are externally planned, is the inclusion of
citizen involvement. As Minzey observed, "In essence, those of us who believe
in community education believe that it provides a technique for returning to
a participatory democracy."[5] Efforts to resolve problems through governmental
actions have, perhaps, created a new set of problems. As Hetrick noted, "The
institutions of society, including the schools, have lost touch with the individual citizens which they were designed to serve. As the bureaucratic
maze and the impersonal nature of the organization has grown, the result has
been public apathy and disenchantment."[6] Community education is an attempt to
get people back into a "partnership" relationship with the community. In other
words, the individual citizen moves back into the decision-making process.

A local community education program operates through direction provided
by its community council. The typical community council consists of from ten
to twenty local persons chosen on a cross-sectional basis by the local citizenry. The council meets periodically to identify local priorities, to locate and
mobilize resources, and to develop programs calculated to deal with the needs
of the community. A well organized and responsive council can produce these
results:

1. A program which is in perfect harmony with local needs--the
    chief reason being that the program design is developed by
    persons who have day-to-day contact with problem areas.

2. The opening of lines of communication. If sound two-way
    communication flows between individuals and agencies, be-
    tween agencies and other agencies, and between people who
    are hampered by misinformation, prejudice, and misconceptions,
    then the community can become a better place.

3. A more effective use of available resources. Duplication,
    overlapping, inter-agency competition, and under-use of
    available resources can be replaced by united efforts.

4. Participation by local citizens in the planning and problem
    solving processes tends to create a much needed base of
    local support. Instead of recreation being regarded as "the
    city recreation program, it is more likely to be regarded
    as "our recreation program".

According to Karensky and Melby, "The total community becomes involved in
identifying problems, established practices, and mobilizing and allocating resources towards the solution of identified problems and needs. The genius of

community education is found in the process--a process of doing and becoming; it is a process whereby communities discover themselves and each other."[7]

Because communities are not identical, and because they have varied needs, actual programming will differ from place to place. For example, one community might decide to emphasize recreation and formal classroom instruction. At the same time, another town might determine that it must address goals calculated to reduce local unemployment and improve health services. In either case, the same process of planning, program development, and cooperative action would serve as the base for positive action.

To illustrate the potential of community education as a system which can help to deal with a juvenile delinquency problem, let us consider a hypothetical case. In our imaginary program, a council is being organized. In order to insure a broad base of input, the membership includes the young and the elderly. Also, there are parents and non-parents, businessmen and housewives. A representative of the mayor's office is there, as is a clergyman, a middle school principal, and a labor union stewart. Each racial group in the community is represented. The members are persons who have a close contact and vested interest in the community. Suppose the council, at an early meeting, determines that juvenile delinquency problems are of sufficient community concern, and the matter is chosen as a priority for action. The moment delinquency becomes a council priority, it no longer is a concern which is considered to be appropriate for "the police to take care of;" rather, it becomes a community project.

A moment of thoughtful reflection on the matter may cause the observer to conclude that the juvenile delinquency matter is one which is very appropriate for full community involvement. Anyone who has ever participated in the process of "fixing the blame" for the juvenile problems has probably noted an inevitable amount of accusations and counter-accusations. Typically, the homes, the police, the schools, the courts, and the effects of television programming are alternately accused and become accusers. In the end, wrath is provoked, nothing of a positive nature seems to result, and no one emerges as being willing to assume guilt for the situation. How logical it seems to suggest that the same elements might join forces to develop solutions to the problems. Community education facilitates such give-and-take interaction.

In a typical community, the council might identify and enlist the support and cooperation of a number of agencies and community elements including (but not limited to) school counselors, child welfare workers, drug specialists, police authorities, probation personnel, recreation planners, parents, teachers, and certainly students as well. The product of the interaction created at such sessions could be a joint and cooperative plan.

It has been this writer's experience as a school administrator to note that contact between schools and law enforcement personnel (two local agencies) tends, all too often, to develop only when some hapless student has engaged in a delinquent act. How much better the situation might have been, in hundreds of American schools, had police and school personnel been engaged in a positive program designed to create conditions where the act would not have happened. Community schools are trying to promote such programming today through community education.

Hopefully, when enlightened perspectives are brought into general acceptance through the interaction process, there will emerge a new concept of the true nature of the delinquent. If attention can be shifted from the American juvenile delinquency stereotype, and toward more realistic understanding, then great strides shall have been made. As Hany and Gold point out, "The image of the stereotype juvenile delinquent leaning on a lamppost, cigarette in hand, a leer on his face, free to create crime, for kicks, because his gang controls this part of the black ghetto, is not only wrong, but is also dangerous."[8]

Because of false assumptions about who commits delinquent acts, the wrong programs are aimed at the wrong groups. The first step in improving the system which, despite good intentions, serves so inadequately is to put myths to rest.[9]

If the juvenile delinquent does not fit the stereotype image, then what do we know that can be relied upon? First of all, if there is such a creature as a "typical juvenile delinquent", he (or she) certainly defies description. They tend to come in all sizes, shapes, racial-ethnic backgrounds, and from "good" homes as well as "bad" homes. Research does reveal some characteristics which concerned persons can use as a beginning point when new programming is contemplated. Torrence, for instance, maintains that the deviant act is but an expression of the individual's desire for recognition--an enhancement of the self concept.[10] Jensen adds, "When an individual possesses a stable self concept, he is on the threshold of learning and fulfilling his potential."[11] Given an atmosphere consisting of concerned people pledging a concerted effort, community education can identify and provide multitudes of activities which can help stimulate creativity, and which will markedly promote the growth of self concepts in the process.

Rogers, Kell, and McNeil[12] provided strong support for community-education-type programming when they reported the conclusions of a two-year study which examined the behavioral tendencies of a group of delinquent children. Of six factors considered, the best predictor of behavior was the individual's concept of himself. The researchers concluded that efforts should be directed toward revising the child's attitude toward himself and changing the child's social adjustment. The primary aim, they recommend, would be to provide opportunities for social release, insightful acceptance of self, and a positive reorientation of self.

With the evidence available, it would seem reasonable to wonder why the schools have not taken appropriate steps to meet the challenge through curriculum revision and changed perspectives. The entire matter of the ability of public schools to act responsively to needs of communities which they serve is one which deserves separate consideration in itself. For the moment, however, may we suggest that the task of resolving juvenile delinquency problems does not lend itself to the schools *alone* assuming full responsibility and authority. First of all, the vast majority of professional school employees are not trained to deal with the unique nature of the deviant individual. In a word, expertise is lacking. At the same time, there are simply not sufficient additional resources within the schools to permit such an undertaking. Within the community, however, there are agencies, organizations, and many individuals who can potentially make a contribution--should someone recognize possibilities and take the initiative to organize for action. Community educators are organizing for action today in many parts of the country; yet, at the same time in many areas that cry out for such leadership, fragmental and ineffective programming prevails.

Lest we lose some potential adherents to the community education cause, it ought to be made clear that the concept is not one which envisions the "schools" assuming a role as grand overseer, with all other elements of the community relegated to subordinate positions. The community education plan is not a "school" program. Nor is it a "police", "recreation department", or "senior citizen" program. All of these, and more, are important to the programming in community education, but in final analysis, the success which it may enjoy is generated through people. Emphasis, therefore, ought to be on the "community" aspect of the topic. When community education is successful, it is not a "victory for the school" nearly so much as it represents proof that faith in the people is indeed justified.

Because community education is a relatively new concept, it is being subjected to much research study (including the dissertation being produced by this writer). At this moment, however, there has not been large-scale attention focused upon the relationship between community education and the reduction of delinquency. To date, in fact, research projects examining these relationships have numbered two.

Ellison considered programs operating in the San Francisco area and concluded that they "did not have the expected impact on reduction of vandalism."[13]
Still, the program (which was funded by a Criminal Justice Act Appropriation)
seemed to reduce school vandalism, both in terms of number of incidents and
dollar cost of destruction. Palmer, who centered his study in a small Michigan
city, stated that "as citizen participation in community education programs increased, the overall mean score for vandalism incidents decreased."[14] Palmer
categorized sixteen crime areas which were watched for increases or decreases.
Disappointingly, increases were noted in nine of the sixteen areas, while activity decreased in only four of the categories. It may be observed, then, that
each study produced mixed results which is a basis for qualified enthusiasm,
at best.

In final analysis, therefore, it is perhaps too early to regard community
education as an ultimate weapon in the hands of law-abiding society. At the
same time, however, there does not seem to be any abundance of positive programming which establishes clearly superior options and alternatives. Perhaps
the matter all boils down to this question: If you are satisfied with the
current state of affairs, then it may be that the concept is not for you. If
you are among those who envision a need for new approaches and positive action,
then you may want to take a closer look at community education.

REFERENCES

1. Eric Jensen, "Juvenile Delinquency--Deprived Creativity," *Community Education Journal*, September/October, 1975.

2. Bill Haney and Margin Gold, "The Hardnose Case for Community Education,"
   Community Education Journal, March/April, 1975.

3. Edward G. Olsen, "Standing on the Shoulders of Pioneers," *Community
   Education Journal*, November/December, 1975.

4. W.P. Metzner, "The Role of Community Schools in Combating Juvenile Delinquency," *Community Education Journal*, March/April, 1974.

5. Jack Minzey, Center for Community Education *Bulletin*, Florida Atlanta
   University, June, 1976.

6. William M. Hetrick, "Community Process: Community Education's Promise,"
   Center for Community Education *Bulletin*, June, 1976.

7. William Karensky and Ernest Melby, *Education II Revisited: A Social Imperative* (Midland: Pendell Publishing, 1971).

8. Bill Hany and Martin Gold, "The Hardnose Case for Community Education," *Community Education Journal*, March/April, 1974.

9. Ibid.

10. E.P. Torrence, *Guiding Creative Talent* (Englewood Cliffs: Prentice Hall, Inc., 1962).

11. Eric Jensen, "Juvenile Delinquency--Deprived Creativity," *Community Education Journal*, September/October, 1975.

12. Carl R. Rogers, Bill L. Kell, and Helen McNeil, "The Role of Self Understanding in the Prediction of Behavior," *Journal of Consulting Psychology*, Vol. 12, 1948.

13. Willie S. Ellison, "The Impact of Community Schools on the Reduction of School Vandalism" (unpublished Ph.D. dissertation, The University of Michigan, 1974).

14. John L. Palmer, "A Study of the Community Education Program as a Deterrent of Violence and Vandalism in a Small Rural Michigan Community" (unpublished Ph.D. dissertation, The University of Michigan, 1975).

THE AMERICANIZATION OF <u>PARENS</u> <u>PATRIAE</u>:
A RIGHT TO TREATMENT FOR JUVENILE OFFENDERS?
William B. Taylor, Lewis Slay and Nicholas Carimi

A great deal has been said and written about the enormous debt which the United States owes to England's common law and legal practice. "It is an historical fact," write Professors Alonzo and Fletcher, "that the overwhelming majority of American jurisprudence is a direct outgrowth of and adjunct to English Common Law."[1] This view of affairs cannot be disputed; it is clear that the legal anchor of the American Republic was built by English labor.

One must suspect, however, that the precedent-seeking legal mind has stretched this "hands across the sea" argument to its breaking point all too often. English law evolved on a small island; it reflected the economic and social realities of a feudal system; and it was advanced in the political context of monarchy from first to last. Conversely, the United States was launched on social and economic principles diametrically opposed to feudalism, on political principles characterized by reaction against monarchy, and on a large, untamed continent. In light of these basic differences, one must be aware that there was often considerable difference between *de jure* and *de facto* application of English legal precedent in the United States. Clearly, in the formative years of the republic, high-sounding Latin rubrics with impeccable English credentials were sometimes applied most dubiously to justify distinctly functional practices demanded by conditions peculiar to the New World. This gap between legal theory and legal practice has proved vexatious and embarrassing in several cases, especially with regard to the doctrine of *parens patriae*.

Juvenile vagrancy and delinquency are prices which modern man has paid for the attainment of his notions of economic and social progress. This painful fact became increasingly clear as the nineteenth century unfolded,[2] and the state responded in a practical manner. In dealing with both delinquents and abandoned children, the American courts continued to follow the traditional guidelines of English poor law administration: apprenticeship, institutional commitment, and later adoption were used to confront a pressing social problem.[3]

From the beginning, a certain amount of legal haze surrounded the handling of juveniles. Precedent was clear in cases involving abandoned children. Here, custody was uncontested and the state acted in *loco parentis,* or in place of the parent. While this rubric clearly expressed the power of the state to control a child once it had obtained custody by default, legal precedent did not clearly establish the power of the state to gain custody of urchins whose parents were alive and desirous of maintaining custody of their children. English procedure on this point was at best unclear, at worst legally objectionable. The poor laws, which dated from Elizabethan times, served to control the labor of the lower classes. Under them, children could be taken from pauper parents at the discretion of an overseer.[4] The rich, according to Blackstone, were "left at their option, whether they will breed up their children to be ornaments or disgraces to their family."[5] This class-oriented double standard was altogether inconsistent with the spirit and perhaps the latter of American constitutional law. Juvenile proceedings, therefore, posed a potentially serious problem for American jurists dating from the inception of the Republic.

It was not until 1839, however, that an American court felt obliged to give legal justification to the operation of poor law principles in juvenile matters. In the case of *Ex Parte Crouse*,[6] the Pennsylvania Supreme Court asserted a state interest which was over and above the interest of a parent:

> It is to be remembered that the public has a paramount interest in the virtue and knowledge of its members, and that of strict right, the business of education belongs to it. That parents are ordinarily intrusted with it is because it can seldom be put into better hands; but where they are incompetent or corrupt, what is there to prevent the public from withdrawing their faculties, held, as they obviously are, at its sufferance? The right of paternal control is a natural, but not an unalienable one. It is not excepted by the declaration of rights out of the subjects of ordinary legislation; and it consequently remains subject to the ordinary legislative power . . . .

This construction was perfectly logical but, divorced from English poor law, it was legally unprecedented. Moreover, while citing absolutely no authority, the court attempted to justify its opinion by pointing to the doctrine of *parens patriae* which, it ruled, rendered the state the "common guardian of the community. . . ."

Seldom has a court of law more completely misinterpreted a legal doctrine. The doctrine of *parens patriae* touched the very heart of the theory of Divine Right of Kings, and it had served for centuries as a bulwark of English feudalism. It expressed both the power and the obligation of the English monarch, posing as the father or parent of his country, to act on behalf of those who were incapable of identifying and acting on their own interests. Standing as part of the legal justification for parental government, it was an all-encompassing doctrine, and only in English Chancery had it touched on the affairs of minors. There it had been applied to assure the orderly transfer of feudal duties from one generation to another, to insure that there would be someone to perform those duties, and to prevent the victimization of vulnerable parties. Chancery, as an agent of the monarchy, acted as *parens patriae* to harmonize testimentary and guardianship problems in the interest of order and hierarchy.[7] Now, however, the *Crouse* case took this phrase, subverted its meaning, and transplanted it into a branch of the poor law where it was used to justify state statutory schemes to part poor or incompetent parents from their children. Dating from 1839, therefore, two Latin rubrics combined to form the foundation of American juvenile law: *parens patriae* awarded the state custody of the child; *in loco parentis* gave the state the power to control the child once it had obtained custody.[8]

This practical arrangement was constitutionally dubious but, at the same time, morally justifiable. On the one hand, it was impossible to separate *parens patriae* from either the power of the English Crown or the legal structure of English feudalism. This, in itself, raised serious questions regarding its applicability in the United States. Then, too, the *Crouse* interpretation of the doctrine took a narrowly defined obligation of English Chancery and applied it broadly as a thinly veiled agent of social control. This legal endorsement of English poor law raised serious questions regarding the entire structure of due process. On the other hand, however, much could be said for applying the principle of *parens patriae* as acted upon in English Chancery. There the doctrine was grounded on clear, long-standing feudal duties. The power of the state was justified only when it accepted responsibility for the defenseless party's interests; it assumed the power to act *in loco parentis*, but obligation was the price of that power.

The power of the state to gain custody of children and act as "the common guardian of the community" under the doctrine of *parens patriae* was asserted repeatedly in the case which followed *Crouse*. For example, in 1881, a benevolent state acting through the Kansas Supreme Court upheld a lower court ruling that the superintendent of a poor farm had every right to apprentice the children of parents on the farm without either notice or consent.[9] And as late as 1899, the Connecticut Supreme Court upheld a lower court adjudication which uprooted and separated the members of a pauper family. "No constitutional right was violated," ruled the Court. "Town paupers belong to a dependent class. The law assigns them a certain status. This entitled them to public aid, and subjects them, in a corresponding degree, to public control."[10]

Unfortunately, the willingness of the state to control the lives of the children of "undeserving" parents was not complemented by a willingness to assume the obligations inherent in the doctrine of *parens patriae*. This reluctance stemmed from the economic, social, and political. mentality of the nineteenth century. Poverty was regarded as a crime by the American bourgeois. In their eyes, public relief could be justified only when it was balanced by measures which promised to eradicate the causes of poverty. Hence a pauper child or a delinquent could be "saved" only if it were removed from the baneful influence of its parents. Paradoxical, however, was the closely-guarded idea that the state had no direct social obligation to the people it served. This opinion, which was the essence of the nineteenth century god of *laissez faire*, rendered the state a mediator - not an active participant - in economic and social affairs. In juvenile matters, therefore, the state gained custody of children on the basis of *parens patriae*, disposed of its wards on the basis of *in loco parentis*, but generally refused to concern itself with the welfare of its wards once they were institutionalized, apprenticed, or adopted.

The net result of this arrangement was a state of human degradation and exploitation which was riddled by hypocrisy from beginning to end. Existing with neither clear-cut legal precedent nor established procedural guidelines, the doctrine of *parens patriae* was applied vaguely to justify statutes which tore both good and bad children from the arms of sometimes irresponsible, but always poor parents.[11] After gaining custody by posing as a benevolent and enlightened foster parent, the state, acting *in loco parentis*, promptly renounced the obligations inherent in *parens patriae* and followed the guidelines of English poor law administration in disposing of children. Consequently, the few juvenile institutions which were founded during the first three quarters of the nineteenth century were poorly conceived, miserably financed, and generally productive of more harm than good. Monitored by no agent of the state, apprenticeship was often tantamount to slavery. And adoption, though sound in theory, was questionable in practice so long as the state refused to assume a truly parental role in the disposal of wayward and abandoned children.

Possibly most disconcerting, however, was the refusal of the courts to redress the grievances of those who questioned the manner in which the state as *parens patriae* met its obligations. In 1876, the Wisconsin Supreme Court reviewed legal precedent and summed up the consensus opinion of both jurists and the American middle class:

> . . . when a parent is unable or unwilling to provide for his child, and leaves the child dependent on the charity of the state, we are at a loss to comprehend the right of the parent to object to the form which the state gives to its charity, with intelligent regard for the welfare of the child.[12]

On the basis of *parens patriae*, however, this seductive argument was no more valid than the state's ability and willingness to act more intelligently for the welfare of the child than the child's biological parents. This point rendered the American bastardization of *parens patriae* extremely vulnerable, and the last three decades of the nineteenth century produced currents which led to a crucial alteration in the legal application of the doctrine.

These currents were set in motion by a number of related developments. Of primary importance was the rapid growth of the American bourgeois class during the second half of the nineteenth century. The War Between the States signalled the triumph of industrial capitalism, and in its wake came unprecedented prosperity. Economic expansion quite naturally broadened the middle class and this, in turn, fostered an explosion of charitable feelings and religious optimism, both of which were implicit components of the Protestant ethic.

Increasing prosperity also brought better developed educational facilities, and the American reading public grew enormously in a very short period of time. Meeting the demands of this new literary market was a mountain of prose which both appealed to and promoted charitable feelings and religious optimism. Fortunes were made through the publication of soppy Victorian novels, and narratives concerning underprivileged children abounded. Pathetic little characters like Charles Dickens' "Tiny Tim" and "Oliver Twist" brought tears to the eyes of a greatly enlarged segment of the population, and the "rags to riches" theme of Horatio Alger came to be synonomous with the American ethic.

On the reading lists of a smaller but still important group of Americans were the writings of Karl Marx, Emile Durkheim, Enrico Ferri, and other social scientists. Their theories qualified the hopelessness inherent in the biological determinism of Charles Darwin and Cesare Lombroso by equating criminality with the economic and social fabric of society. Whereas earlier generations had spoken authoritatively of a "criminal class" fed by genetic inferiority, the environmental determinists pointed to poverty, mobility of population, urban disenchantment, and a weakened family unit as the keys to crime. Marx laid the blame on the heartlessness of the capitalist system; Ferri spoke of "penal substitutes" in shifting responsibility from the criminal to the state. A popular proposal resulting from this meeting of biological and environmental determinism was the "methodized registration and training" of *potential* criminals, "or these failing, their early and entire withdrawal from the community."[13]

Emerging full-blown from these currents was the child-saving movement of the late nineteenth century, a movement which called for the extension of governmental control "over a whole range of youthful activities that had previously been handled on an informal basis." Actively involved in this crusade were feminist groups, who argued that it was a woman's business to be involved in regulating the welfare of children. These women established settlement houses for wayward and abandoned children, organized women's clubs to deal with juvenile problems, and lobbied for support from Bar Associations and penal organizations.[14]

Possibly more important to the child-saving movement was the late nineteenth century organization of penologists and correctional workers. International cooperation between penologists had increased steadily throughout the nineteenth century, but in 1870 this cooperation began to produce tangible results in the United States. In that year the first National Congress on Penitentiary and Reformatory Discipline was held in Cincinnati. Influenced by the religious optimism of the day, the numerous participants "stood at the crossroads" with the "winds of change" blowing in their faces determined to "toil in the vineyards" in order to head off the post-Civil War "crime wave". They were, moreover, determined to head it off not by "punishing" offenders, but by "treating", "reforming", "regenerating", "correcting", and "rehabilitating" them.[15]

Occupying a prominent role in their deliberations was the juvenile offender, who, in one speaker's opinion, was "hedged round with principles of an inviolable liberty, and rights of *habeas corpus*", and yet "treated like a dog at a fair . . . ." "I do not say that it can be done", he continued, "but in order to transform the next generation, what we should aim at is to provide substitutes for bad homes, evil training, unhealthy air and food, dullness and terrible ignorance, in happier scenes, better teaching, proper conditions of physical life, sane amusements, and a higher cultivation."[16] This opinion dominated the deliberations of the Congress, and the participants agreed that "if criminals . . ., instead of being cast off, were rather made objects of a generous parental care", the interests of the state would be better served.[17]

From the meeting in Cincinnati came the incorporation of the American Prison Association, the reformatory movement, and a subsequent revolution in juvenile corrections which elevated their adult counterparts. The reformatory movement combined with the other components of the child-saving crusade to produce America's first juvenile courts, and for the first time a juvenile justice system based on both the powers and obligations inherent in the doctrine of *parens patriae* began to emerge.

This movement spawned two crucial questions. First, did the state as *parens patriae* possess the power to deny wayward and delinquent children equal protection under the Due Process Clause of the Fourteenth Amendment? Second, if the state as *parens patriae* possessed this power, what obligations were incurred by the state?

There were those who questioned the state's right to remove juveniles from the protection of the Constitution. Among them was a majority of the Illinois Supreme Court who, in 1870, while the National Congress on Penitentiary and Reformatory Discipline was in session, rendered an opinion which struck at the foundation of American juvenile law. In the case of *O'Connell v. Turner*,[18] the Court struck down a typically vague statute which mandated the institutional-ization of a child who "is a vagrant, or is destitute of proper parental care, or is growing up in ignorance, idleness, or vice." Since this description could be construed to include the bulk of the population at all times, and all children at specific times, the Court was not unrealistic in challenging the statute's "general grant of power, to arrest and confine for misfortune." The Court found the statutory definitions and procedural safeguards lacking; it ruled that vague promises of benefits for the child did not make a reform school any less a prison; and it found that children, too, were protected by the Con-stitution.

Though the *O'Connell* decision found support in important circles, its challenge to the state's hitherto unqualified power to gain custody of wayward children had very little impact. This was owing largely to two facts. First, the child-saving movement was greatly improving juvenile institutions, and middle-class opinion held that children would be infinitely better off in the newly-conceived reformatory than in the hands of "underserving" parents.[19] Second, the bench, noting striking improvements in juvenile institutions, saw little reason to champion constitutional safeguards when it was apparent that the reformatory movement was bringing the realization of the state obligations inherent in *parens patriae*.

However, while refusing to require the application of constitutional safe-guards in juvenile proceedings, the American bench made it clear that a new day had dawned. For example, in 1899, the Wisconsin Supreme Court, while ruling on the constitutionality of statutes which created the state's first juvenile court, suggested that children in the custody of the state had a *right* to pro-tection and care:

> Now the persons liable to be placed under guardianship under the statutes in question belong to the classes of help-less unfortunates that the state *is in duty bound,* through some proper agency, to protect and care, primarily for the benefit of the children, but for the common good as well.[20]

Similarly, in 1908, the Idaho Supreme Court could justify the denial of due process rights only in cases in which the state assumed specific responsibilities in improving children:

> For the state to thus take charge, care and custody of a minor, *for the purpose of protecting, educating, and training him,* is not depriving him of his liberty without due process of law. . . .[21]

Such language was a world apart from that expounded in *Crouse* and the other cases which had preceeded the child-saving movement, and it represented a revolution in juvenile law. This revolution brought the *de facto* application of the English doctrine of *parens patriae* to American juvenile proceedings: the power of the state to circumvent constitutional safeguards in gaining custody of minors came to be justifiable only when the state accepted responsibility for the child's interests and acted to protect, educate, train, and generally improve him.

The implications of this triumph of *parens patriae* have begun to be appreciated only during the past eleven years. During this period a considerable amount of case law, apparently molded by both advances in behavioral science and changing morality, has placed unprecedented but justifiable emphasis on the obligations of the state as *parens patriae.*

In the famous *Kent* decision of 1966,[22] the United States Supreme Court questioned whether the state as *parens patriae* was fulfilling its obligations well enough to justify the traditional circumvention of constitutional safeguards. Justice Fortas wrote:

> There is evidence, in fact, that there may be grounds for concern that the child receives the worst of both worlds; that he gets neither the protection accorded to adults nor the solicitous care and treatment postulated for children.

Later, Justice Fortas, *In re Gault,*[23] penned the majority opinion which curtailed state powers and reemphasized state obligations:

> The early reformers were appalled by adult procedures and penalties, and by the fact that children could be given long prison sentences and mixed in jails with hardened criminals . . . . The child was to be 'treated' and 'rehabilitated', and the procedures, from apprehension through institutionalization, were to be clinical - not punitive.

Justice Fortas' choice of the word "clinical" apparently has had a great impact on the contemporary construction of *parens patriae*, for a great deal of recent litigation has involved the juvenile offender's right to treatment.

In 1967, the United States Court of Appeals, District of Columbia, heard a contention by appellant Enock Creek that his confinement in a receiving home pending final disposition had been without psychiatric treatment and was therefore in violation of a section of the D.C. Code which bound the state to secure for a minor custody, care, and discipline reasonably equivalent to that which a parent should provide. The Court ruled:

> But the purpose stated in 16 D.C. Code, Section 2316, is to give the juvenile the care 'as nearly as possible' equivalent to that which should have been given by his parents, (and this) established not only an important policy objective, but, in an appropriate case, a legal right to a custody that is not . . . inconsistent with the *parens patriae* premise of the law.[24]

In *Martella v. Kelley*[25] the United States District Court of New York also addressed the existence of a right to treatment. Plaintiffs claimed that their detention in a juvenile facility without either treatment or effective programs or rehabilitation constituted cruel and unusual punishment. This unique contention led the Court to trace the historical development of state obligations under the doctrine of *parens patriae* and to conclude that

> . . . the law has developed to a point which justifies the assertion that: 'A new concept of substantive due process is evolving in the therapeutic realm.' This concept is founded upon recognition of the concurrency between the state's exercise of sanctioning powers and its assumption of the duties of social responsibility. Its implication is that effective treatment must be the *quid pro quo* for society's right to exercise its *parens patriae* control, whether specifically recognized by statutory enactment or implicity derived from the constitutional requirement of due process, the right to treatment does exist.

A similar opinion was rendered in *Morales v. Turman*.[26] In this case a Federal District Court heard allegations that children in Texas' six juvenile institutions were forced to endure an alarming number of physical abuses and, in some cases, were denied educational instruction. The Court, after carefully obtaining complaints and expert testimony, ruled that the exposure of juveniles to such conditions not only violated their right to be free from cruel and unusual punishment, but also violated their right to due process of law, which guaranteed juvenile offenders a constitutional right to "treatment".

Judicial review has also challenged the philosophical basis of rehabilitative programs where the improvement of a minor is questioned. In *Nelson v. Hyne*[27] the court examined the adequacy of the Indiana State juvenile facility's rehabilitation program. The program, which was adopted in 1971, was labeled the Quay System. Upon admission to the facility, juveniles were classified on the basis of standardized personality tests and labeled either "inadequate", "neurotic", "aggressive", or "subcultural". They were then housed with fellow inmates who had similar test results. Each cottage staff consisted of a counselor, an educator, and a consulting psychologist. The cottage staff met weekly for an evaluation of each child's progress. Each child was evaluated in four aspects of institutional life: cottage, school, recreation, and treatment response. The juvenile earned privileges by excelling in these four areas. Yet, notwithstanding the existence of a logical rehabilitation program geared to "treat" juveniles, the United States Court of Appeals, Seventh District, passed the buck when faced with the question of what constituted *effective* treatment under the *parens patriae* premise of the law:

> We conclude that the district court could properly infer the Quay System as used in the school failed to provide adequate rehabilitative treatment. We leave to the competent district court the decision: What is the minimal treatment required to provide constitutional due process, having in mind that the juvenile process has elements of both the Criminal and Mental Health processes?

This is no mean question.

A great deal of irony permeates the evolution of *parens patriae* in the United States. The legal definition of the doctrine has come full circle - from social control to social welfare to a blossoming right to treatment - and at each stage of its development judicial review has qualified state powers and extended state responsibilities. Whereas in 1966, Justice Fortas suggested that children were receiving "the worst of both worlds", there is ample reason to suggest that minors soon will receive the best of both worlds: that they will get the legal protection accorded to adults as well as an absolute right to effective treatment. The wisdom of such a decision is questionable; the ability of the state to meet such a responsibility is doubtful; and it is clear that this construction of *parens patriae* is as alien to the doctrine's English roots as was the construction established by the *Crouse* case. To be sure, however, this dilemma is the price we are paying for the legal pragmatism of nineteenth century jurists.

REFERENCES

1. *Cases and Materials on the Juvenile Justice System,* (1975), p. 2.

2. See generally Tobias, *Urban Crime in Victorian England,* (1972); and *Nineteenth-Century Crime: Prevention and Punishment,* (1972).

3. Risenfield, "The Formative Era of American Public Assistance Law", 43 *California Law Review* 175 (1955).

4. See generally 5 Eliz. c. 4 (1562), and 43 Eliz. c. 2 (1601).

5. Blackstone, 1 *Commentar on the Laws of England,* (18th ed. 1821), pp. 451, 513-14.

6. 4 Whart, 9, 11 (Penn. 1839).

7. Cogan, "Juvenile Law Before and After the Entrance of 'Parens Patriae'", 22 *South Carolina Law Review* 147 (1970).

8. Rendleman, "Parens Patriae: From Chancery to the Juvenile Court", in Faust and Brantingham (eds.), *Juvenile Justice Philosophy: Readings, Cases and Comments* (1974), pp. 72-118.

9. *Ackley v. Tinker,* 26 Kan. 485 (1881).

10. *Harrison v, Gilbert,* 71 Conn. 724, 43A, 190 (1899).

11. Rendleman, pp. 81-82.

12. *Milwaukee Industrial School v. Supervisors of Milwaukee County,* 40 Wis. 328, 337 (1876).

13. Platt, "The Rise of the Child-Saving Movement . . .", in Faust and Brantingham (eds.), *Juvenile Justice Philosophy,* pp. 119-124.

14. *Ibid.,* pp. 126-128.

15. Mitford, *Kind and Usual Punishment: The Prison Business* (1973), p. 33.

16. Pierce, "General View of Preventive and Reformatory Institutions in the United States", in Wines (ed.), *Transactions of the National Congress on Penitentiary and Reformatory Discipline Held at Cincinnati, Ohio, October 12-18, 1870,* (1871), pp. 21-22.

17. "Principles of Penitentiary and Reformatory Discipline Suggested for Consideration by the National Congress", XV, *Ibid.,* p. 553.

18. *People ex rel. O'Connell v. Turner,* 55 Ill. 280 (1870). For comment, see Rendleman, pp. 95-98.

19. For general comment, see Chute, "Fifty Years of the Juvenile Court", *National Probation and Parole Association Yearbook,* (1949).

20. *Wisconsin Industrial School for Girls v. Clark County,* 79 N.W. 422 (1899).

21. *Ex Parte Sharp,* 96 P. 563 (1908).

22. *Kent v. U.S.,* 541, 86 S. Ct. 1045 (1966).

23. 387 U.S. 1, 87 S. Ct. 1428 (1967).

24. *Creek v. Stone,* 379 F. 2 d. 106, 111 (1967).

25. 349 F. Supp. 575 (1972).
26. 364 F. Supp. 166 (1974).
27. 491 F. 2d. 352 (1974).

SUGGESTIONS FOR RELEASING PUBLIC OFFENDERS:
AN AFFIRMATION OF HISTORICAL APPROACHES

Charles J. Eckenrode, J. Eugene Waters and Arthur B. Gavin, Jr.

Much criticism is being directed at the American criminal justice system. The public calls for action when the press bombards its readers with reports that crime is increasing. Often the publicized failure of the criminal justice system or the demand for crime prevention is directed at the corrections field. Part of the public's concern may exist in the failure of the correctional component of the criminal justice system to clearly define its basic purpose and to delineate how that purpose is to be obtained.

Ambivalence does seem to exist over the basic purpose of the prison. Theorists suggest that prisons provide punishment, retribution, deterrence, societal protection, or a combination of these variables.[1,2,3] More recently, correctional personnel have directed their efforts at rehabilitation. However, the continued existence of high recidivism rates and the growth in prison disturbances, such as Attica,[4] have brought about an increased awareness of a problem situation facing many penal institutions.

Prisons are criticized for their failure to prevent crime[5] and their failure to rehabilitate.[6,7] It has been suggested that prisons are one of the least successful social institutions in existence[8] while the very existence of prisons has been challenged.[9] In response to the criticisms, suggestions for a reversal or adaptation of the rehabilitation model have evolved.

Again, corrections faces a time for decision. Even though statements criticizing the "treatment model" are popular,[10,11] the public is reminded of the proposals for a model suggesting the correction of the offender.[12,13,14] Carlson suggests a balance between corrective programs and the deterrence-retribution purpose of prisons. In searching for an approach as to what avenue to pursue, a re-examination of previously used concepts is suggested.[15]

This article will describe a concept for releasing the incarcerated offender after he completes a prescribed program of remediation that is based on predetermined needs. Thus, further development of a "correcting model" for prisons is recommended. The abandonment of previous approaches is not suggested. Instead, this proposal suggests the integration of concepts that were previously used.

Historical antecedents for such a model do exist.

HISTORICAL PERSPECTIVE

The growth of Diagnostic and Reception Centers is indicative of the importance of the classification of offenders. As reported by Yepsen,[16] the idea of classification evolved in the state of New Jersey in 1918 while Giardini[17] discussed the use of a 1933 classification project in Pennsylvania. Classification as an important concept to the prison setting is reflected in the publication of the *Handbook on Classification in Correctional Institutions* by the American Prison Association.[18] The evolutionary process denoting the utility of the classification concept continued with the topic still being included in the American Correctional Association's *Manual of Correctional Standards*.[19]

Usually traditional classification centers provide diagnostic information after sentencing. Some have suggested that the needs of the offender be determined prior to sentencing.[20,21] Sweat[22] recommends that all judges have access to diagnostic facilities, presentence investigative reports and indeterminate sentencing in all felony cases.

Historically, the importance of the classification idea is reflected in the literature. Likewise, the ingredients for the development of the indeterminate sentence can be traced to earlier times in our history. The writings of Archbishop Whaley and the ideas of Sir Walter Crofton and Alexander Maconochie provided the early formulation for an indeterminate sentence.[23,24] The ideas of these men from the mid 1800's era were refined and adapted by Zebulon R. Brockway.

Brockway, Superintendent of the Detroit House of Correction, was instrumental in Michigan's 1867 enactment of the first indeterminate sentence in the United States. Applying only to prostitutes, this provision was limited. Responding to the Declarations of Principles of the National Congress on Penitentiary and Reformatory Discipline, the reform era of corrections evolved. One of the major principles adopted at that 1870 Congress stated, "Preemptory sentences ought to be replaced by those of indeterminate length."[25] The concept was embodied in Brockway's draft of an act governing conduct at the Elmira Reformatory in Elmira, New York. According to Lindsey modifications resulted in the following act:[26]

> Every sentence to the reformatory of a person hereafter convicted of a felony or other crime shall be a general sentence to imprisonment in the New York State reformatory at Elmira and the courts of this state imposing such sentence shall not fix or limit the duration thereof. The term of such imprisonment of any person so convicted and sentenced shall be terminated by the managers

> of the reformatory, as authorized by this act; but such im-
> prisonment shall not exceed the maximum term provided by
> law . . . .

These early ideas led to the development and implementation of various forms of indeterminate sentencing. By 1922, thirty seven states had some form of indeterminate sentencing.[27]

Various types of indeterminate sentencing exist. A description of these can be found in Kadish and Paulsen,[28] Miller, et al.,[29] and Spaeth.[30] Basically, these types can be listed as follows: (1) a maximum and minimum sentence is imposed by the court as required by statute; (2) a maximum and minimum sentence is imposed by the court; however, the minimum can not exceed a fraction of the maximum sentence; (3) the court sets a maximum sentence with a minimum established by laws governing parole; (4) maximum sentence set by statute with the minimum sentence determined by the court; and (5) court sets a maximum and minimum sentence within statutory limits.

Much of the criticism directed at the indeterminate sentence focuses on the discretionary power of the parole boards and the uncertainty of a release date for the offender. Sometimes this uncertainty of a release date is purported to be a source of prison violence. In the absence of convicting research establishing a causal relationship between prison violence and the use of indeterminate sentencing, the authors suggest restraint in lieu of hasty and drastic change. Furthermore, the so-called "problem" - if in fact it is a problem - of discretion merely reflects our society. Discretion and uncertainty affects all aspects of our society. It is certainly inappropriate to argue for the continued utilization of an incorrect concept or behavior because of its existence elsewhere. However, the authors question the suggestion that the uncertainty of a release date is necessarily bad. Uncertainty confronts people in various situations: work, school, therapy, hospitalization, et cetera.

Often the indeterminate sentence is criticized because it reflects discretionary justice or perhaps, injustice. However, this is also a characteristic of our society and the various systems that comprise our society. Spaeth's review of Kenneth Culp Davis' examples of the types of discretion that citizens encounter daily confirms this point.[31]

It is beyond the scope of this paper to continue the current debate on indeterminate sentencing. Advocates and opponents have adequately discussed the issues involved in this approach to sentencing.[32-39]

The criticisms are recognized. Nevertheless, the proper utilization of some form of indeterminate sentencing is viewed as being a workable concept.

This paper supports the indeterminate sentence as posited by Brockway.[40]

Indeterminate sentencing and presence classification are available in some form today. For example, some jurisdictions have a presence investigation completed by court probation officers. Also, juvenile courts tend to rely heavily on background reports in determining the sentence disposition of young offenders. However, as noted by Chamelin, Fox, and Whisenand,[41]

> "Most states simply leave the order for the report to
> the discretion of the judge. The simple fact is that there
> are not enough probation officers to do the presence in-
> vestigation reports in any state, whether it is mandatory or
> not, so they generally get done only in cases designated
> by the judge."

Also, sentencing based on needs assessment is reflected in 18 U.S. C.A. § 4208(b)[42] in which the offender is given a sentence and is assigned to a facility for observation and diagnosis. That section states:

> If the court desires more detailed information as a basis
> for determining the sentence to be imposed, the court may
> commit the defendant to the custody of the Attorney General,
> which commitment shall be deemed to be for the maximum sentence
> of imprisonment prescribed by law, for a study . . . The re-
> sults of such study, together with any recommendation which
> the Director fo the Bureau of Prisons believes would be help-
> ful in determining the disposition of the case, shall be fur-
> nished to the court within three months unless the court
> grants time . . . for further study. After receiving such
> reports and recommendations, the court may at its discretion:
> (1) Place the prisoner on probation as authorized . . ., or
> (2) affirm the sentence of imprisonment originally imposed,
> or reduce the sentence of imprisonment, and commit the offender
> under any applicable provision of law.

Materials to be included in the study are described in section 4208(c) which states in part:

> This report may include but shall not be limited to
> data regarding the prisoner's previous delinquency or
> criminal experience, pertinent circumstances of his social
> background, his capabilities, his mental and physical
> health, and such other factors as may be considered perti-
> nent.

These innovations, as proposed by the Cellar-Hennings Act of 1958, coordinated judicial sentencing with correctional classification. According to Bennett,[43] this was a major gain within the Federal system. Basically this procedure enables the judge to adjust the sentence of the offender after reviewing diagnostic information. The sentence is coupled with the scientific information of a classification process so as to formulate the optimum sentence in terms of limitations discovered in the diagnostic evaluation.

This paper proposes that a similar approach be integrated with indeterminate sentencing. This approach is similar to the Georgia Youthful Offenders Act.[44] This act provides for the sentencing of offenders, ages 17 to 25 years, to an indeterminate sentence of zero to six years. The offender is released after completing a prescribed "treatment" program based on needs assessed during a diagnostic process. The offender enters into a "contract" to remove deficiencies/limitations as a pre-requisite to parole consideration. Contrary to criticisms usually registered against indeterminate sentencing, offenders are not serving unusually long sentences.

A limitation of the Georgia program is the misplaced utilization of the diagnostic and classification process. Diagnosis and classification occurs at a central reception center *after* the offender has been sentenced and, furthermore, after post conviction time in jail. Certainly, presentence investigations occur in some cases. However, as noted above, this is generally the exception and not the rule. The presentence investigation performed by court workers under the present system is generally repeated at a reception center. Such repetitious and disjointed activities need to be eliminated. The court should have access to a thorough and scientific diagnosis and classification process *prior* to sentencing. This information could then serve the correctional field. No need would exist for another costly evaluation at some later date. The diagnostic facility should serve the court as well as the correctional aspect of our criminal justice system.

With the importance of the classification process being reflected in the literature,[45,46] a more systematic utilization of diagnostic information is needed. Placement of the diagnostic and classification process at the presentencing stage would tend to make more efficient use of the data collected and legitimize its usage when made a part of the sentencing function.

Thus, the sentence would be of an indeterminate type and include the prescribed treatment or habilitation program as determined by the diagnostic process. At the completion of the prescribed program, the offender would be released.

In sum, historical antecedents exist for the concepts of classification and indeterminate sentencing. This paper suggests the coordinated use of the indeterminate sentence and presentence diagnosis and classification.

Contrary to popular belief, correctional treatment is not dead. While the "nothing works" proposal of Martinson[47] has gained some support, the responses of Palmer,[48] Adams,[49] and Glaser[50,51] clearly answers such a charge. Even the senior author of the study[52] on which Martinson's article is based questions the "nothing works" statement of Martinson.[53]

Correctional habilitation within the model proposed in this paper does not guarantee correction of all offenders. However, it does place responsibility for change on the offender and not society. Release should be earned by completing a prescribed program of work and "Correction". The indeterminate sentence, with its demonstrated efficacy,[54] provides the boundaries for offender change.

Exposure to correctional programs does not promise reform of offenders. Human behavior is not that simplistic. This proposal is not offered as the panacea for corrections. It can be no worse than other correctional efforts, especially the dangerous and hasty decision to follow the popular myth "nothing works".

REFERENCES

1. Cantor, N. *Crime and Society*.   New York: Henry Holt & Co., 1939.

2. Thomsen, R. "Sentencing the Dangerous Offender". *Federal Probation*, 1968, 32, pp. 3-4.

3. Burns, H. *Corrections: Organization and Administration*. St. Paul, Minn.: West Publishing Co., 1975.

4. McKay, R. *Attica: The Official Report of the New York State Special Commission on Attica*. New York: Bantam Books, 1972.

5. Brooker, F. "The Deterrent Effect of Punishment". *Criminology*, 1972, 9, pp. 469-490.

6. Martinson, R. "What Works? Questions and Answers about Prison Reform". *The Public Interest*, 1974, 35, pp. 22-54.

7. Conrad, J. "We Should Never Have Promised a Hospital". *Federal Probation*, 1975, 39, pp. 3-9.

8. Galtung, J. "Prison: The Organization of Dilemma". In *The Prison: Studies in Institutional Organization and Change*. Edited by D. Cressey. New York: Holt, Rinehart and Winston, Inc., 1961.

9. Jordan, V. "The System Propogates Crime". *Crime and Delinquency*, 1974, 20, pp. 233-240.

10. Martinson, reference note 6.

11. Wilks, J., and Martinson, R. "Is Treatment of Criminal Offenders Really Necessary?" *Federal Probation*, 1976, 40, pp. 3-9.

12. President's Commission on Law Enforcement and Administration of Justice. *The Challenge of Crime in a Free Society*. Washington, D.C.: U.S. Government Printing Office, 1967.

226

13. National Advisory Commission on Criminal Justice Standards and Goals. *Corrections*. Washington, D.C.: U.S. Government Printing Office, 1973.

14. Bennett, J. *I Chose Prison*. New York, Alfred A. Knopf, 1970.

15. Carlson, N. "The Federal Prison System: Forty-five Years of Change." *Federal Probation*, 1975, 39, pp. 37-42.

16. Yepsen, L. "Classification - The Basis for Modern Treatment of Offenders." *The Prison World*, May, 1940, pp. 12-14.

17. Giardini, G. "Preliminary Classification of Male Prisoners in Penal Institutions in Pennsylvania." *Proceedings of the American Prison Association*. New York: American Prison Association, 1934.

18. American Prison Association. *Handbook on Classification in Correctional Institutions*. New York: Author, 1947.

19. American Correctional Association. *Manual of Correctional Standards*. College Park, Md.: Author, 1965.

20. Menninger, K. *The Crime of Punishment*. New York: Viking Press, 1966.

21. Bennett, reference note 14.

22. Sweat, N. "How Do We Achieve More Consistent and Appropriate Sentencing?" *National Conference on Corrections*. Williamsburg, Virginia, 1971.

23. Lindsey, E. "Historical Sketch of the Indeterminate Sentence and Parole System. *Journal of Criminal Law and Police Science*, 1925-26, 16, pp. 9-69.

24. Bruce, A., Harno, A., Burgess, E. and Landesco, J. *The Workings of the Indeterminate-Sentence Law and the Parole System in Illinois*. Montclair, N.J.: Patterson Smith, 1968.

25. Mitford, J. *Kind and Usual Punishment: The Prison Business*. New York: Alfred A. Knopf, 1973, p. 80.

26. Lindsey, reference note 23.

27. Lindsey, reference note 23.

28. Kadish, S. and Paulsen, M. *Criminal Law and Its Processes*. Boston: Little Brown, 1975.

29. Miller, F. et al. *The Correctional Process*. New York: Foundation Press, 1971.

30. Spaeth, E. "A Response to *Struggle for Justice.*" *The Prison Journal*, 1972, 52, pp. 4-32.

31. Spaeth, reference note 30, pp. 15-16.

32. Miller, M. "The Indeterminate Sentence Paradigm: Resocialization or Social Control." *Issues in Criminology*, 1972, 7, pp. 101-124.

33. Rothman, D. "Lawful Sentences: If Prison, How Much?" *Justice in Sentencing: Papers and Proceedings of the Sentencing Institutes for the First and Second United States Judicial Circuits.* Edited by L. Orland and H. Tyler. Mineola, N.Y.: Foundation Press, 1974.

34. Cargan, L. and Coats, M. "The Indeterminate Sentence and Judicial Bias." *Crime and Delinquency,* 1974, 20, pp. 144-156.

35. Hodges, E. "Crime Prevention by the Indeterminate Sentence." *American Journal of Psychiatry,* 1971, 128, pp. 71-75.

36. Mitford, reference note 25.

37. Bruce, et al., reference note 24.

38. Bennett, reference note 21.

39. Sweat, reference note 22.

40. Brockway, Z. *Fifty Years of Prison Service.* London: Oxford University Press, 1912.

41. Chamelin, N., Fox, V., and Whisenand, P. *Introduction to Criminal Justice.* Englewood Cliffs, N.J.: Prentice-Hall, 1975.

42. Title 18 United States Code Annotated § 4208(b)(c), 1958, pp. 371-372.

43. Bennett, reference note 21.

44. *Georgia Laws,* 1972, pp. 592-599.

45. Wilks, R. *Correctional Psychology: Themes and Problems in Correcting the Offender.* San Francisco: Canfield Press, 1974.

46. National Advisory Commission, *Corrections,* reference note 13.

47. Martinson, reference note 6.

48. Palmer, T. "Martinson Revisited". *Journal of Research in Crime and Delinquency,* 1975, 12, pp. 133 152.

49. Adams, S. "Evaluation: A Way Out of Rhetoric." *Rehabilitation, Recidivism, and Research.* Hackensack, N.J.: National Council on Crime and Delinquency, 1976, pp. 75-91.

50. Glaser, D. "Review of *The Effectiveness of Correctional Treatment.*" *Journal of Research in Crime and Delinquency,* 1976, 13, pp. 179-182.

51. Glaser, D. "Concern with Theory in Correctional Evaluation Research." *Crime and Delinquency,* 1977, 23, p. 177.

52. Lipton, D., Martinson, R., and Wilks, J. *The Effectiveness of Correctional Treatment.* New York: Praeger, 1975.

53. "Profile of Douglas Lipton." *Quarterly Journal of Corrections,* 1977, 1, pp. 34-35.

54. Carney, F. "The Indeterminate Sentence at Patuxent." *Crime and Delinquency,* 1974, 20, pp. 135-143. Also, see Spaeth, note 30, and Hodges, note 35.

JAIL CRISES: CAUSES AND CONTROL
Laurence French and Janet B. Porter

Jails have always been a penal enigma posing the greatest hardships for their inmates and problems for their keepers. They have been condemned as dire failures yet they provide one of the most essential functions within our criminal justice system, that of detaining suspects for the various stages of adjudication. Part of the confusion associated with jails is their dualistic role. They are used as both "holding" and as "serving" facilities. And while serving jails have been justifiably criticized for their lack of treatment programs for their mostly misdemeanant wards, the more critical issue of psychological anomie is perhaps closer associated with holding jails.

In holding jails the uncertainty of one's fate is conducive to excessive stress and normlessness and more likely to result in rash behavior such as suicide, jailbreak, physical assault and sexual aggression. Our basic argument is that the transient nature of holding jail environments is likely to disrupt the stability of the inmate's assumptive world leading to psychological ambiguity and social anomie (normlessness). Cut off from supportive and meaningful primary relationships, the socially marginal as well as the suddenly shocked, otherwise highly integrated, inmate finds it difficult to adjust to the chaotic jail environment losing track of their familiar epistemological methodology or "world view." Thus once their traditional psycho-cultural dimensions and boundaries fail to operate, providing the necessary closure, their minds run rampant attempting to justify their anomic condition hence often resulting in rash behavior such as attempted and completed suicides and other forms of criminal and sexual assault, jailbreak, and the like.

The Nature of Jails

One of the more significant contributions of the Omnibus Crime Control and Safe Street Act was the LEAA Jail Study providing us with a comprehensive profile of jails not only in terms of numbers and programs but including an accurate indicator of the process of jail incarceration as well.[1] This study indicates that the vast majority (75%) of these local jails are small institutions accommodating 20 or fewer inmates. Moreover, jails seem to be more prevalent in the South where 16 Southern states account for 48 percent of all such facilities and 39 percent of the overall National jail population.[2]

Jails, then, are local correctional facilities utilized as either pretrial detention centers or as serving institutions for convicted misdemeanants, or both. They strongly reflect the concept of local judicial autonomy hence accounting for their popularity in the South and other regions where county government is still strong. The difficulty with most jails is not so much a political issue, that is county versus state and federal jurisdictions, as it is an economic one. An overtaxed public is hesitant to support additional fiscal allocations for jails thus these institutions often come to suffer from poor physical conditions, inept and undertrained staff and a total lack of social and even health programs. Jails in the United States, then, are primarily custodial and they are not intended to be anything else.

Nonetheless while the other two penal components, rehabilitation and punishment (official retribution), are seldom intended elements of most jail programs, the latter is certainly a latent, or unintended, consequence of the prevailing jail atmosphere. A common sentiment concerning jails in the United States has been made by McGee when he described them as being a scandal. Karl Menninger, in a 1977 interview at age 84, called for the end of jails indicating that they are instruments of a more barbaric and archaic era and should have been discontinued along with asylums, poor houses and debtors' prisons. He considered jails part of the "crime of punishment" hinting that they cause more problems than they solve. Lemert terms this process "secondary deviance"[3] while judge Jamieson postulated that jails have little to do with corrections per se and that people locked up in our Nation's jails are only made all the more anti-social.[4] Perhaps Jessica Mitford best explained the jail phenomenon when she stated that jails have no apologists since they are universally recognized as hellish places.[5]

Francis notes that pre-trial detainees can languish in jail anywhere from one day to two years awaiting trial and that this represents punishment prior to having the opportunity to be properly adjudicated. He contends that this amounts to punishment merely for being arrested, a violation of due process and equal protection guarantees.[6] In a similar vein, Goldfarb carries this argument a step further stating that jails reflect discriminatory justice with poor people greatly over-represented in our Nation's jail populations: "One stark fact of life is that generally people of means never see the inside of a jail. Wealthy people can make bail, get medical treatment, make restitution, pay fines, and generally find alternative techniques to resolve their problems."[7]

Jail Anomie

Marx,[8] Durkheim,[9] Freud[10] and Merton[11] all addressed themselves to the issue of psycho-cultural detachment accompanying social dishevelment. Marx spoke of "alienation," the psychological reaction to undesirable social conditions.

Fromm later more closely linked alienation with the functioning of the individual psyche.[12] A generation following Marx, Durkheim offered his concept of "anomie" or normlessness, realizing that both social and personal conditions could init- iate this psychological state. Later, Freud coined a similar term, "anxiety," used to explain psychological frustration. Clearly all three terms are closely interrelated attempting to explain the same phenomenon, that of psychological ambivalence resulting from cultural or personal chaos. Merton, like Fromm, at- tempted to better articulate the nature of this psycho-cultural phenomenon developing a paradigm reflecting probable psychological adaptations to cultural chaos and calling this system: "Social Structure and Anomie." Four deviant adaptations could result from disjunctive means/goals coordination, according to Merton, leading to either "ritualism," "innovation," "retreatism" or "re- bellion." The first two adaptations best illustrate a process of adjustment while retreatism and rebellion are more dire reactions to normlessness. More- over, while retreatism and rebellion can exist in subcultural environments, they most often reflect spontaneous reactions to crises situations. At their extremes, retreatism results in suicide while rebellion culminates in homicide.[13] Palmer was instrumental in distinguishing between excessive personal frustration and the direction of aggression linking the latter with the degree of socializa- tion.[14] In this study of murder, Palmer postulated that severe frustration ex- perienced in infancy and early childhood is a strong contributing factor in ex- plosive aggression during adolescence or adulthood. He then linked the degree of socialization with the direction of aggression through three statements:

1. An undersocialized person will most likely direct his ag- gression outwardly towards others in a more or less indis- criminate and unacceptable fashion.

2. An adequately socialized person will usually displace his aggression outwardly in an indirect and fairly acceptable manner usually through sports activity and the like.

3. An oversocialized person will presumably turn his aggres- sion inwardly upon himself.

The extreme aggression reactions to both (1) and (2) are death, the former re- sulting in homicide and the latter culminating in self-destruction, usually through suicide.

A more recent modification of this earlier theory is that homicide and suicide are opposite sides of the same coin and that while socialization may play an important role in cumulative frustration, the proscribed direction of aggression, as stated above, need not follow in spontaneous or unexpected situa-

tions of personal disorganization especially those associated with chaotic normlessness. Jails represent such a chaotic and anomic situation for many suspects
caught up in this situation regardless of their degree of socialization, class,
race, sex or the like. Nonetheless, Palmer's frustration and socialization
theory is a valuable indicator of expected jail behavior and could prove quite
useful in preventive programs.

Psychologically, "holding" jails are more disruptive than are serving
jails or any other penal facility for that fact, mainly because of the uncertainty associated with this ambivalent situation. Here the individual is
caught up in a crises situation without being quite sure of the consequences,
thus obviating the protective mechanism of psychological closure. Clearly this
situation is made worse by the absence of any viable inmate subcultural substitute for the inmate to identify with such as exists in most serving penal
facilities. This situation coupled with the negative and often aggressive
nature of jail environments culminates in "psychic loss." The magnitude of this
loss is determined by a number of factors, the most significant being the individual's ability to cope with a crises situation. If the suspect finds it difficult or even impossible to resolve his cognitive dissonance, notably that of
effectively anticipating the outcome of this personal crises, and maintain
order of his assumptive world, then one could expect a drastic reaction on his
part such as self or other-directed aggression.

Psychological loss is our term for serious disruptive life-events which
etch a lasting scar on the inmate's psyche, much like what Goffman termed as
a negative pro-active status.[15] Palmer cited disruptive life-events in the
lives of murderers, notably murderers who killed in the heat of passion. Correspondingly, Gibbs found the same true for suicide victims stating that:

1. The greater the incidence of disrupted social relations
   in a population, the higher the suicide rate of that
   population.

2. All suicide victims have experienced a set of disruptive
   social relations that is not found in the history of
   non-victims.[16]

Drawing on both Palmer and Gibbs' assertions, we might also add that action
short of self or other-directed destruction might well be considered to be a
"cry for help".[17] Included in this category are such personality traits as excessively quarrelsome or aggressive behavior, uncontrollable weeping, deep depression, manic/depressive cycles and attempted suicide.

Studies on psychological loss show that arrest and jail incarceration are
significant disruptive life-events, especially for males. Humphrey noted in his

study of 160 psychological autopsies of completed suicides that arrest and jail
incarceration were significant "loss" factors thus contributing to the victims'
ultimate demise.[18] Another study conducted by the United Southeastern Tribes
(USET) showed again that arrest and jail incarceration are significant stress-
factors affecting Native Americans.[19] This is all the more significant when
one realizes that cirrhosis of the liver, suicide and homicide are the three
leading causes of death among members of this racial group. This compares with
cardiovascular illnesses, cancer and accidents as the leading causes of death
among the general United States population.[20]

This brings to light yet another important factor affecting jailed Native
Americans or others like them who share a phenomenological, as against our existential, cultural life-style. Members of phenomenological, or "folk" cultures, usually are socialized so as to share their personal experiences with a
core of significant others, regardless if these experiences are positive or
negative. "Shame" is a shared negative experience often exacerbated by jail
anomie hence increasing the likelihood of suicide among Native American inmates.
"Guilt," on the other hand, is an existential phenomenon found in competitive
societies such as ours.[21,22] This signifies that considerable attention must
be given to the cultural orientation of jail inmates especially regarding their
expected reaction to jail anomie. Those from an existential orientation (Protestant ethic) will more than likely experience guilt while those from a phenomenological orientation (Harmony ethic) will presumably experience shame.
Again we must keep in mind both Palmer's "degrees of socialization" and Gibbs'
"disruptive social relations" whenever anticipating the actions of any victim
of jail anomie regardless of their cultural orientation.

Granted, solutions to jail anomie are neither easy nor simple, yet enough
information is available to warrant the implementation of realistic, tailor-
made crises intervention in our Nation's jails. This is especially crucial if
our ideals of justice are to remain valid and viable notably the idea of due
process and the presumption of innocence until proven guilty beyond a reasonable
doubt.

CONTROL

Jail incarceration is a disruptive life event for most prisoners. In a
small number of cases, this personal crisis leads to physical or sexual assault, jailbreak, or suicide. Esparz reports that the suicide rate is three
times higher among prisoners than the general population.[23] Whereas Rieger
found only 10.5 per 100,000 suicide rate in the federal prison system,[24] Esparz

reported 5 times that rate in county jails.

Suicide and self-destructive behavior* exacerbate the usual problems confronting jail administrators. The publicized suicide or suicide attempt often results in the accusing finger being pointed at the administrator or correctional worker. The question is asked, "why couldn't this have been prevented." Today this event may trigger a public investigation of the jail and the appointment of a blue-ribbon committee to study the problem.

Controlling or preventing suicidal behavior can be viewed conceptually in three ways: primary, secondary, or tertiary.[25] Primary prevention efforts attempt to change the inmates pre-prison environment known to be associated with suicidal behavior. Secondary prevention attempts to identify those individuals who are highly vulnerable in order that appropriate intervention can take place. Tertiary prevention involves some type of treatment for those who have already attempted suicide. The goal of the intervention is to prevent those high risk inmates from killing themselves or to prevent a recurrence of the suicidal behavior.

Primary suicide prevention looks at the pre-prison social environment which promotes or magnifies the forces leading to suicide in jail. Primary prophylaxis for jail suicide would require full employment, elimination of poverty, racism, parental neglect, poor schools, inadequate housing and medical care. At a meeting of correctional workers in 1972, Judge Bazelon expressed concern that instead of facing up to the true dimensions of the problem and admitting that crime is an inevitable by-product of our society's social, political, and economic structure, we focus on the individual and attempt to "cure" him. Because of the difficulty of considering fundamental political or social changes or massive income redistribution, we continue to use secondary or tertiary means to deal with the crisis-prone jail inmate.

Most of the research on self-destructive behavior has involved secondary prevention. This preoccupation is understandable because if we could develop demographic or clinical profiles of those persons who are high risks for self-destructive behavior, an effective intervention could be devised. Prediction, therefore, is the first step toward preventing or controlling self-destructive behavior.

Beck reviewed research models which have been used by researchers to predict self-destructive behavior and suicide.[26] The developmental model (Freudian)

---

*The term self-destructive behavior will be used interchangeably with suicidal behavior.

assesses the subject's life history to determine how the person underwent the critical stages of development. Learning theorists document retrospectively all the events which indicate intentionality to determine which of these reinforce suicidal behavior. They also observe individuals to determine which situations tend to reinforce and maintain suicidal ideation. The neurophysiological model focuses on information processing. If a person is subjected to unremitting stress, his inner or psychic resources are depleted and this leaves him less able to cope with subsequent environmental demands, particularly traumatic events such as jail incarceration. It is the ecological or demographic and clinical models which have been most extensively reported by researchers in suicide prediction. Demographic data ignores specific individual characteristics since it describes group suicidal behavior. The clinical approach (emphasizing holistic, intuitive judgment as well as psychological data) is more accurate in pinpointing those particular individuals who are high suicide risks. Both suicide intent scales and psychological tests have been developed to predict suicidal behavior. However, according to Beck there is currently no detection scheme which identifies the genuine suicide risk without erroneously identifying a lot of people who are not suicide risks.[27] The falsely labelled no-risk cases may be as high as 90 per cent. False positives of any magnitude would make a suicide prevention program prohibitive in terms of cost, particularly for a preventive program like in-patient treatment.

Another problem is that even among high risk groups, suicide is a rare event. Prediction of a rare event is extremely difficult.

Based on demographic and clinical data, researchers have developed at least a tentative taxonomu of predictors of self-destructive behavior.

One predictor relates to attitudes and values of particular ethnic groups. French has pointed out that Indians, as members of phenomenological or folk cultures, share positive and negative personal experiences with significant persons. Feeling shame in prison, but having no way to share it, the Indian is an increased risk for self-destructive behavior.

Johnson reports clinical data on Blacks, Latins, and whites in prison.[28] Blacks are under-represented in prison suicidal behavior while Latins are over-represented. His thesis is that susceptibility to destructive behavior in prisons may reflect differences in the degree of fit between pre-prison experiences or socialization and necessary survival behavior in jail. Ghetto experiences for the Black generally prove functional. For the Latin, there is dissonance between his family-centered dependence and the survival requirements of prisons. For some white inmates, problems of guilt and self-hatred after incarceration trigger the suicide crisis; for others, relatively sheltered life experiences create susceptibility to panic in the face of peer pressures involving assaultive behavior or homosexual overtures.

A second variable relates to pre-prison coping skills in dealing with major life changes. Incarceration, because of the suddenness of change, may lead to self-destructive behavior. In addition to being totally uncertain about his future in court, an inmate has decreased control over his life as well as severe limitations on ways of expressing dissatisfaction.[29]

Several researchers have noted that many prisoners commit suicide in the early phases of imprisonment. Esparz reported a French study in which of 86 prisoners who committed suicide, 20 were carried out in the first 24 hours of confinement and 40 succeeded in the first month of imprisonment.[30] According to Stengal, suicides are rare among long-term prisoners contrary to commonly held expectations.[31]

Wilkerson calls this initial jail crisis "traumatic reception dynamics."[32] First, the inmate can't actually believe he is going to jail. The pre-trial detainee may receive a legal message that he is not guilty, but he is still fingerprinted, photographed, stripped of personal property, and locked up. In the second phase, there is an intensive effort to get out of jail legally. When this fails, there is increasing loss of hope due to not getting bail, isolation from his family, infrequent visits from his attorney, and unremitting boredom. This third stage could lead to passivity, aggression, or suicide.

Inmate characteristics are a third variable which under the right circumstances predispose a person to destructive behavior. Stengal,[33] Danto,[34] and Maris[35] summarize major factors indicative of impending self-destructive behavior: (1) depression with guilt feelings, self-depreciation, and self-accusation; (2) previous suicide attempt; (3) suicidal preoccupation and talk; (4) perceived parental rejection or marital break-up; (5) alcohol and drug addiction; (6) occupational and financial difficulties; (7) psychopathic personality (in such individuals the tendency to acts of violence against others and violent self-destructive behavior often co-exist); (8) suffering from a neurosis or psychosis.

A fourth variable relates to jail characteristics which may precipitate suidical behavior: (1) isolation or segregation (isolation may not be sufficient to cause self-destructive behavior but may assume significance when coupled with depression or a history of mental illness); (2) social contagion. Fawcett stated that contagion is especially likely in a jail where inmates are relatively isolated from outside contacts;[36] (3) over-crowding with its resultant peer pressures may be extremely threatening to some inmates; (4) the prison staff may unconsciously sympathize and encourage a suicide plan in light of the inmate's history of anti-social behavior.[37] At present, our prediction tools are inaccurate. Suicide prevention in jails, if it is to occur, is likely to result from tertiary prevention. Prison administrators, psychologists, correctional workers, legislatures and courts are involved in these preventive efforts.

The role of the prison administrator in reducing self-destructive behavior should be to improve the general conditions in jails. Specific recommendations include: (1) Improvement of prison programs such as education and recreation. Even a minor release of tension for a brief period away from the cell can alleviate frustrations; (2) Reduction of peer pressures by establishing a screening system which separates the young or first-time offender from the recidivist; (3) Effecting minor architectural changes such as removal of bars and pipes in cells would reduce the possibility of hanging, the chief method of suicide in jails;[38] (4) Reviewing administrative decisions whereby "troublesome" inmates are shifted from jail to jail. Any move results in the inability of the self-destructive inmate to form "rescuer" ties with other inmates;[39] (5) Considering the use of trained inmate trustees to patrol the corridors at night or to talk with depressed inmates; (6) Increasing the involvement of volunteers in jail since they provide important linkages with community resources. Volunteers might be used to contact an inmate's family or to provide transportation so that a family member could visit an inmate; (7) Developing procedures for increased interaction of inmates with non-institutionalized persons (e.g., in drug or alcohol programs); (8) Reviewing administrative policies relating to mail and visitors. Withdrawal of these "privileges" can be unusually significant for the self-destructive inmate; (9) Hiring correctional workers to reflect the ethnicity of the inmates. Self-destructive inmates may not feel so isolated and alienated if correctional workers of their own culture are available to discuss problems.

Because of the limited number of jail psychologists, the role of the prison psychologist must focus on providing training for correctional officers, trustee inmates, para-professionals, and community volunteer workers instead of clinical work with inmates. In crisis intervention centers, the largest amount of professional staff time is devoted to training activities. Service demands are met by trained non-professional workers and volunteers.[40] Psychologists can also develop orientation programs for prisoners to help new inmates understand prison discipline and expectations.[41]

Since many suicides are likely to occur very early in the inmate's imprisonment, the correctional worker will need to make an immediate assessment about problem behavior. Generally, he has to make these decisions with limited information regarding the inmate.

Wick suggests that the correctional officer with training in suicide prevention will be alert to suicidal symptoms of inmates, especially where there is more than one symptom or they are exaggerated:[42] (1) loss of appetite; (2) difficulty sleeping; (3) lethargic; (4) extremely tense, restless or agitated; (5) shuns fellow inmates.

After the potential suicide is tentatively identified, there is a temptation to turn the problem over to medical or psychiatric workers. Since this is generally not possible nor practical, the need for crisis intervention by the correctional officer is crucial.

Psychiatrists repeatedly warn crisis workers that a suicidal gesture* or any act of self-damage inflicted deliberately which looks like a suicide attempt ought to be treated seriously. Chronic suiciders do kill themselves.[43]

Effective communication between personnel who deliver the inmate from the court and jail personnel is important so that disturbed behavior is reported.[44] One drawback to this approach is the problem of false positive identification. Persons who are not self-destructive are singled out for differential "treatment" (usually isolation) and that label could follow the inmate for life.[45]

Inmates suffering from alcohol or drug addiction are particularly vulnerable. Medical attention is often inadequate in jails and the correctional officer needs to be vigilant in his observation of addicted inmates since severe depression is common. The correctional officer's failure to dispense prescribed drugs to an inmate could also trigger self-destructive behavior.

One recommendation of the New York City Board of Corrections reported by Wick was that a system should be developed so that information on disturbed inmates is passed from one jail shift to another.[46]

Attitudes of correctional officers toward suicidal inmates are often negative and this may result in isolation or segregation of that inmate. This practice should be discontinued. Isolation or segregation may actually trigger suicidal behavior, particularly at night.

The training of correctional officers should include awareness of their own feelings about death.[47] The trained correctional officer could permit an inmate the chance to air negative or destructive feelings. In Pasadena, California,

---

*Suicidal gestures are sometimes considered as manipulative, rather than self-destructive.

trainees in a Suicide Prevention Center were told to listen and then as questions such as: Why do you want to kill yourself? How will that help? Have you thought of something else to solve your problem other than to kill yourself? Death is forever.[48]

Legislatures and courts are also involved in tertiary suicide prevention. Their role may have great significance in affecting public attitudes about jail conditions and inequality in the criminal justice system.

Pre-trial detainees remain in jail because they can't make bail. Bail reform in the last 10 years has been expanded to include a bail program wherein 10% of the bond is paid into court with the return of all but one percent if the defendant is present at trial. Some prisoners are released on their own recognizance, based on a point system which reflects community ties. In addition, many commmunities have taken advantage of enabling legislation to provide release under supervision. Increased use of bail or release procedures will reduce jail over-crowding and relieve many of the tensions which could lead to destructive behavior. According to Roberts, liberalization of bail laws in Canada contributed to a decline in jail self-injury rates.[49]

Alternatives to 24-hour confinement through programs such as work release for those in jails as well as prisons are becoming more frequent. The inmate is released from jail to work and returns to the institution at night. This program could alleviate family and financial problems of the inmate and reduce guilt and depression.

A promising approach to reducing jail crises are the numerous 8th Amendment Court cases based on jail conditions which do not meet constitutional standards. Recently, a Federal Court issued a sweeping order requiring major improvement in Rhode Island's correctional systems. The Court specifically found that pre-trial detainees are subject to conditions worse than convicted offenders. The Court ordered that pre-trial detainees be housed separately from convicted prisoners within three months. Health care delivery systems were to be brought into compliance with minimum standards of the American Public Health Association and other bodies.[50]

This is the last in a series of cases throughout the country in which physical conditions, policies and management practices in jails and prisons have been scrutinized. In all cases, the facilities were old, poorly designed, ill-equipped, inadequately maintained, and over-utilized. Violence, brutality, lack of medical care, unsanitary conditions, inadequate plumbing, lack of ventilation and the absense of other necessities of life characterized these correctional facilities.[51]

The American Bar Association conducted a survey to determine whether judicial court orders mandating improvements in jails and prisons were being implemented. It was found that the conditions of correctional confinement as well as the administration and management of the institutions were improved. Equally important was the increasing public awareness of the problems of administering and funding constitutional jails and prisons.

These cases also showed that changes in other parts of the criminal justice system affected jails. In Jefferson Parish Prison (a jail), judges relaxed the criteria for selection of persons released on their own recognizance. The district attorney's office implemented a pre-processing program with authority to dismiss cases or issue citations instead of booking an offender.[52] Both of these procedures reduced the institutionalized population without adversely affecting social control.

National standards are being promulgated to effect all parts of the criminal justice system. Legislatures are passing statewide jail standards. Equally important are standards such as 5.10 of the National Advisory Commission which details judicial visits to institutions. During his first year of tenure a judge would visit all correctional facilities within his jurisdiction and converse with staff and committed offenders. According to the standards, judicial visits would be repeated annually. Legislative and court intervention in prison management should assure that the incarcerated offender will not remain in degrading or dehumanizing conditions. It would be expected that improving jail conditions will reduce self-destructive behavior.

Durkheim contends that reduction of social isolation and integration of the individual within a group were the most important tasks for suicide prophylaxis.[53] To reduce anomie, the pre-trial detainee must be rapidly reintegrated with his family and community. Until that reintegration can be accomplished, suicide prevention in jails will require administrators and correctional workers who recognize the crisis-prone inmate and provide services to alleviate the boredom, hopelessness, and depression of all inmates.

There is a vocal minority who urge the abolition of the prison system as dehumanizing to the keeper and the kept. However, while prisons and jails exist, administrators, psychologists, correctional workers, legislatures, and courts have an obligation to ameliorate the conditions which lead to jail crises.

Primary prevention of jail crises is not likely at this time. Problems of social, political, and economic change remain unresolved. Secondary prevention or prediction of suicidal behavior will require more sophisticated research tools. Involvement of the community, public officials, legislatures, and courts

in correctional reform will increase the chance that tertiary prevention by
front-line workers in jail will result in a reduction of self-destructive
behavior.

REFERENCES

1. Leonard, J. *Local Jails*. Washington, D.C.: U.S. Government Printing Office (2700-00178), 1973.

2. Carter, R. et al, "Local Adult Correctional Institutions and Jails," *Correctional Institutions*. Philadelphia: J.B. Lippincott, 1972.

3. Lemert, E. *Social Pathology*. New York: McGraw-Hill, 1951.

4. Jamieson, D. "Jails," *Criminal Justice Issues,* Vol. 3, No. 9 (May), 1977.

5. Mitford, J. *Kind and Usual Punishment*. New York: Vintage Books, 1974.

6. Francis, T. "Jails," *Criminal Justice Issues,* Vol. 3, No. 9 (May), 1977.

7. Goldfarb, R. *Jails*. New York: Anchor Books, 1975, pg. 3.

8. Marx, K. and F. Engles, *The Communist Manifesto* (edited by F. Randall). New York: Washington Square Press, 1967.

9. Durkheim, E. *Suicide* (edited by G. Simpson). New York: Free Press, 1967.

10. Freud, S. *Civilization and its Discontents* (edited by J. Strachey). New York: W.W. Norton and Company, 1962.

11. Merton, R. *Social Theory and Social Structure*. New York: Free Press, 1968.

12. Fromm, E. "Alienation under Capitalism," *Man Alone,* (edited by E & M Josephson). New York: Dell Publishing Company, 1962.

13. Palmer, S. *Deviance and Conformity,* New Haven: College and University Press, 1970.

14. Palmer, S. *The Psychology of Murder*. New York: Thomas Y. Crowell Company, 1962.

15. Goffman, E. *Stigma*. Englewood Cliffs, New Jersey: Prentice-Hall, 1963.

16. Gibbs, J. *Suicide*. New York: Harper and Row, 1968.

17. Shneidman, E. and N. Farberow. *Clues to Suicide*. New York: McGraw-Hill, 1957.

18. Humphrey, J. et al., "The Process of Suicide," *Diseases of the Nervous System*, Vol. 35 (June).

19. USET, "Native American Stress-Assessment Scale." Nashville: United Southeastern Tribes, Inc., 1975.

20. NIMH, *Suicide, Homicide and Alcoholism*. Rockville, Maryland: (National Institute of Mental Health DREW #ADM 74-42). U.S. Government Printing Office, 1973.

21. Freud, 1962.

22. Piers, G and M. Singer, *Shame and Guilt*. New York: W.W. Norton and Company, 1971.

23. Esparz, R. Attempted and Committed Suicide in County Jails. In B.L. Danto (Ed.) *Jail House Blues*. Orchard Lake, Michigan: Epic Publications, 1973, pp. 30-46.

24. Rieger, W. Suicide Attempts in a Federal Prison. *Arch. Gen. Psychiat.* 1971, 24, pp. 532-535.

25. Caplan, G. *Principles of Preventive Psychiatry*. New York: Basic Books, 1964.

26. Beck, A.T., Resnik, H.L. and Lettieri, D.J. *The Prediction of Suicide*. Bowie, Maryland: The Charles Press, 1974.

27. Ibid.

28. Johnson, R. *Culture and Crisis in Confinement*. Lexington, Mass.: Lexington Books, 1976.

29. Roberts, A.R. (Ed.) *Self-Destructive Behavior*. Springfield, Ill.: Charles C. Thomas, 1975.

30. Esparz, 1973.

31. Stengal, E. *Suicide and Attempted Suicide*. New York: Jason Aronson, 1974.

32. Wilkerson. Considerations of Suicidal Trauma in a Detention Facility. In B.L. Danto (Ed.) *Jail House Blues*. Orchard Lake, Mich.: Epic Publications, 1973, pp. 119-126.

33. Stengal, 1974.

34. Danto, B.L. (Ed.) *Jail House Blues: Studies of Suicidal Behavior in Jail and Prison*. Orchard Lake, Mich.: Epic Publications, 1973.

35. Maris, R.W. The Sociology of Suicide Prevention. *Social Problems*. 1969, 17(1), pp. 13-49.

36. Fawcett, J. and Marrs, B. Suicide at the County Jail. In B.L. Danto (Ed.) *Jail House Blues*. Orchard Lake, Mich.: Epic Publications, 1973, pp. 83-106.

37. Danto, B.L. The Suicidal Inmate. *Police Chief*, 1971, 38, pp. 56-59.

38. Hilig, S.M. Suicide in Jail: A Preliminary Study in Los Angeles County, In B.L. Danto (Ed.) *Jail House Blues*. Orchard Lake, Mich.: Epic Publicattions, 1973, pp. 48-55.

39. Danto, 1971.

40. Farberow, N.L. Ten Years of Suicide Prevention--Past and Future. *Bulletin of Suicidology*, 1970, 6, pp. 6-11.

41. Wick, R. *Correctional Psychology: Theme and Problems in Correcting the Offender*. San Francisco: Canfield Press, 1974.

42. Wick, R. Suicide Prevention: A Brief for Corrections Officers. *Federal Probation*, 1972, pp. 29-31.

43. Danto, 1971.

44. Wick, 1974.

45. Ferrence, R.G., Jarvis, G.K., Johnson, F.G., Whitehead, P.C., The Self-Destructive Patient: Sociological and Medical Profiles and Implications for Prevention. In A.R. Roberts (Ed.) *Self-Destructive Behavior*. Springfield, Ill.: Charles C. Thomas, 1975, pp. 97-119.

46. Wick, 1974.

47. Danto, 1971.

48. Roberts, 1975.

49. Ibid.

50. Criminal Justice Newsletter, 8(18), September 12, 1977.

51. Harris, J.K. and D.P. Spiller. *After Decision: Implementation of Judicial Decrees in Correctional Settings*. Washington, D.C.: American Bar Association, 1976.

52. Ibid.

53. Durkheim, E. *Suicide*. New York: Free Press, 1951.

BEHAVIOR MODIFICATION AND CORRECTIONS:
AN ANALYSIS
Thomas M. Alonzo and Michael C. Braswell

INTRODUCTION

In recent years prison strikes, demonstrations, riots, and killings have continually focused public attention on the American correctional establishment.[1] This type of publicity coupled with spiraling recidivism rates has precipitated a growing disillusionment and criticism of correctional programs. Consequently, prison administrators, judges, federal and state legislators, correctional psychologists, and other concerned individuals have undertaken the task of designing and implementing innovative treatment programs which might bring about worthwhile and lasting correctional reform.

Currently, there are a number of correctional programs being designed to facilitate the rehabilitation of the incarcerated public offender.

> The best judgment that can currently be made about their effectiveness is that the majority of these approaches are effective for some people at some point in time under some conditions. None of them, however, are universally effective. At present we should neither accept any one approach as a panacea nor arbitrarily dismiss any technique that does not frankly go counter to known facts about behavior.[2]

Of the rehabilitation programs being implemented, however, it seems those with a behavioral approach often end up being the most controversial. As a result, corrections officials are caught in the middle of the "behavioral" dilemma. Some persons abhor the behavioral approach in controlling and treating offender behavior; they feel it is dehumanizing and unethical. Whereas, others cry out for a return to more stringent and punitive control of offenders. Where does the correctional administrator draw the line?

To place the behavioral approach in a current and appropriate correctional perspective, it might be helpful to examine the evolution of correctional philosophy.

THE DEVELOPMENT OF CORRECTIONAL PHILOSOPHY

The American correctional establishment first began during the early colonial period. Initially, correctional administrators advocated punishment as a means of eliminating deviant behavior. As a result, offenders were often publicly humiliated and incarcerated for long periods of time for relatively minor offenses.

Prisoners were seen as comprisong a homogeneous category of
people whose past behavior had been so reprehensible that individual differences were insignificant. The law of the time
was far behind the ancient code that specified an eye for an
eye since the seriousness of the crime was not considered.
During this period, the offender, by his act of offending, was
considered to have forfeited his membership in the community
and his claim to any social concern . . . confinement was the
sole purpose of prisons.[3]

The Quakers eventually initiated a movement of correctional reform and
were the predominant force behind the establishment of a new correctional
philosophy; a philosophy based on the view "that adequate meditation and
moral instruction would cause the offender to terminate his illegal behavior."[4]
Moreover, in order to reduce the chance of offenders contaminating one another,
the concept of strict separation was also advocated. It was during this
period that the famous Auburn and Pennsylvania systems came into existence.
In these two institutions no verbal contact was allowed between prisoners,
and heavy emphasis was placed on religious instruction. Obviously, this idea
failed; it seems that, due to the total social isolation, many of the offenders
were driven mad.

In 1870 the New York Reformatory for Men was opened and the correctional
movement entered the so-called reformatory era. The central notion behind
the establishment of this "progressive" institution, and others patterned
after it, was that of education - academic and vocational-technical. Its
founders were determined to curtail the rising post-Civil War crime wave, not
by punishing the offenders, but by reforming and rehabilitating them through
education.[5] Unfortunately, the optimistic hopes of these reformers were to be
short lived. By 1910 most correctional experts admitted the adult reformatory
idea had been labor in vain. "(Its failure) was due largely to an unrealistic
faith in the effectiveness of unselective education for all and other mass
treatment programs."[6]

As the reformatory era faded from the correctional limelight, the United
States was emerging into an industrial revolution. Within a brief span of time
the entire country became industrially oriented and the correctional system was
no exception. Consequently, for the next two decades a great deal of emphasis
was placed on the "industrial prison". By transforming the prisons into huge
industrial complexes and utilizing the inmates as the work force, penal authorities hoped to provide the offenders with the desire and training which might
facilitate their rehabilitation - an idea which was very similar to the underlying philosophy behind the reformatory era. However,

> For a variety of reasons, this approach was no panacea and when
> the depression struck this country with the associated lack of
> employment, laws were rapidly passed which greatly diminished
> the ability of our correctional institutions to maintain indus-
> try that was in competition with civilian industry.[7]

It was soon after this period, nearly forty years ago, that we first saw
the arrival of the behavioral sciences. For the first time a more professional
classification system began to appear and many of the theories from the Freudian
and other schools of psychology became quite prevalent with respect to causation
and cure of antisocial behavior. During this era the "treatment philosophy"
made its first significant entry into the field of corrections. Behavioral
scientists began arguing that deviant behavior was learned and not the result
of genetic factors; they felt, therefore, that modification was feasible.
Clearly, it was a time in which the American correctional system was about to
embark on a new, and hopefully, constructive, era.

Today, the American correctional system still faces many difficulties. Reports of increasing recidivism rates, prison riots, killings, and abusive inmate
treatment, have focused a great amount of negative public attention on correctional administration and the treatment efforts of our criminal justice system.
In retrospect, it seems unfortunate to note that many of the "treatment approaches"
developed by the behavioral sciences have never been appropriately implemented
in many viable areas of the correctional environment. "Even when so-called intensive programs have been tried, it has frequently been with the use of personnel with limited professional training, in an atmosphere which is suspicious
of, or even hostile to, new approaches."[8]

As noted earlier, however, the success or failure of varied types of treatment approaches which might be utilized in corrections (e.g., consultation,
human relations, self-actualization, morita therapy, etc.) is not of primary
interest in this paper. The behavioral model is the prime concern; therefore,
the ensuing discussion will be limited only to that approach and the effects it
may or may not have on the rehabilitation of inmates.

BEHAVIOR MODIFICATION IN THE CORRECTIONAL SYSTEM

Whenever the issue of behavior modification and control is raised, whether
in a correctional setting or any other environment, there are those persons who
immediately equate the process with a "Big Brother" world of 1984 or Stanley
Kubrick's "Clockwork Orange". However, a bad connotation does not always have
to be placed on the word "control". Barbara Bishop explains:

Control is not necessarily equated with tyranny. Tyranny refers to a dictatorial relationship in which one party intends to somehow increase his own welfare at the expense of another person. Control, however, need not take on this meaning. It is simply a functional relationship between two variables. The variables may be "tyrannical" such as variable one, the fire burns and variable two, the trees are therefore consumed; the variables may be self-governing, such as a desire for money and yet denying yourself the act of burglary.[9]

When addressing the same point, Parker and Meier state:

The goal for any behaviorally oriented intervention is self-control on the part of the client. Achieving this goal may initially require the distribution of incentives by another individual. Teaching a person adaptive behaviors which will lead to rewards in the natural environment and which will eventually become self-sustaining, seems far from the tyranny of "Big Brother".[10]

Consideration of these points should help dispel many of the derogatory contentions regarding "control", especially punitive, as behavior modification's primary *modus operandi*.

Behavioral technology can be very effective in creating personality and behavioral changes in incarcerated individuals. Such an approach can accomplish its objectives, not through the introduction of artificial variables, but by focusing on the very reinforcers and contingencies used within society. In addition, "this method allows the utilization of the individual's own motivation as a means of achieving desired behavior changes."[11] Of course, there is no one behavioral approach which is suited to all inmates. Just as offenders bring a variety of problems to the correctional professional, so the correctional professional must also bring a variety of intervention strategies to the helping process.[12]

CONTRACT COUNSELING

Several behavioral techniques have in recent years been designed and adapted for utilization in a correctional setting. One such program is contract counseling. Although the idea of contracting is very old, its application in counseling is relatively new. The following are some basic characteristics of contract counseling when applied in a correctional setting:

1. The correctional worker and offender establishing and maintaining a high level of communication and understanding that builds trust between them.

2. The correctional worker and offender agreeing on the existence of a problem and defining this area as completely possible.

3. The correctional worker and offender deciding on behaviors that are needed in order to correct the problem. This may involve the offender agreeing to perform certain behaviors singularly and this may involve both the offender and correctional worker agreeing to perform certain behaviors.

4. The correctional worker and offender agreeing on the method or methods of evaluating how well the contract has been fulfilled and what the reward will be.

5. The correctional worker and offender deciding upon the terminal dates for the completion of segments of the contracts or the contract as a whole.

6. The correctional worker and offender writing out the terms of the contract and both of them signing it. It may prove beneficial to have the terms typed out, the signatures witnessed by a notary, warden, or someone important to the offender. When this is done it is necessary to complete two contracts, one for the correctional worker and one for the offender.

7. The correctional worker and offender proceeding to fulfill the terms of the contract. The correctional worker acting as a resource person while providing encouragement and support to the offender.

8. The correctional worker and offender determining if the contract has been fulfilled. If not, the offender may be granted additional time, the contract may be renegotiated or he may simply fail to receive the reward he contracted for.[13]

Contract counseling not only provides structured reinforcement, but is also a system which can be used very easily by non or para professionals in the institutional treatment setting. Although most types of offender behavior can be handled through contingency contracting, it is most appropriate in a program designed to help inmates acquire certain specific skills.

THE TOKEN ECONOMY

Another behavioral technique which can be utilized in a correctional environment is the token economy system.[14] This system can be useful because it attempts to shift the responsibility for inmate behavior from the correctional personnel to the individual offender. More importantly, however, aversive or punitive control of inappropriate behavior is de-emphasized and attention is directed toward positive reinforcement of more appropriate, or desired, behavior.

The token economy system is based on the use of tokens to provide reinforcement. The person earns a specific number of tokens for desired behaviors and may lose tokens for inappropriate behaviors. The tokens are then exchanged for necessities and luxuries, such as food stuffs and tobacco. As Syllon and Azrin note, tokens have several valuable features:

1. The number of tokens can bear a simple quantitative relation to the amount of reinforcement.

2. The tokens are portable and can be in the subject's possession even when he is in a situation far removed from that in which the tokens were earned.

3. No maximum exists in the number of tokens a subject may possess, whereas dimensions such as intensity, as with volume of music, have practical maximum reinforcing value.

4. Tokens can be used directly to operate devices for the automatic delivery of reinforcers.

5. Tokens are durable and can be continuously present during the delay, in contrast, say, with a brief flash of light or sound.

6. The physical characteristics of the tokens can be easily standardized.

7. The tokens can be made fairly indestructible so they will not deteriorate during the delay.

8. The tokens can be made unique and unduplicable so that the personnel can be assured that they are received only in the authorized manner.[15]

In general, the token system teaches the offender that if he wants something, he must earn it by demonstrating the proper behavior.

MODELING

A third approach worth noting is that of "modeling". In this approach the offender's behavior is shaped through the use of a "role-model". The "role-model" (e.g., correctional worker, psychologist, counselor, etc.) assumes the role of "valued friend". The offender learns the desired behavior by modeling himself after the "role-model". It is important when utilizing this system, that the "role-model" be an empathetic, genuine, and responsible individual.[16]

CONCLUSION

Before effective behavioral approaches can be successfully implemented in the correctional realm, there must be better training for correctional staff, a greater utilization of professional expertise, and a substantial increase in state and federal funding for "responsible" treatment innovations. Far too often, individuals are quick to criticize innovative programs, pointing out that the programs do not seem to be significantly improving the situation. What they fail to realize, however, is the atmosphere in which many of these programs are implemented.

Furthermore, should effective behavioral programs in correctional institutions be our only or even primary concern? Herbert C. Quay thinks not. He states:

> The new behaviors and skills which the offender takes with him when he returns to society must somehow be maintained in that society. Currently, we assume that such maintenance will be facilitated by some form of aftercare. This aftercare is only rarely under the control of those responsible for his institutional correction. Equally rarely is aftercare anything more than a casual contact between agent and parolee with the content of the interaction generally about the wrong things. Until aftercare can become an integral part of the correctional process, oriented toward the same ends, the institution's responsibility essentially stops at the door of the correctional facility. Consequently, an evaluation of its efforts cannot be entirely based on success or failure in environmental circumstances over which institutional corrections has no control.[17]

In the final analysis, the so-called failure of behavioral programs is a great deal more than simply a failure resulting from the technique itself. It is human failure. Behavior modification offers the effective practitioner a means of improving and correcting the human situation - in and out of prison.

REFERENCES

1. David A. Ward, "Evaluative Research for Corrections", in *Prisoners in America*, ed. The American Assembly, Columbia University (Englewood Cliffs: Prentice-Hall, 1973), p. 184.

2. Herbert C. Quay, "What Corrections Can Correct and How", *Federal Probation* 37 (June 1973): 4.

3. Charles W. Dean, "Contemporary Trends in Correctional Rehabilitation," in *Introduction to Correctional Rehabilitation*, ed. Richard E. Hardy and John G. Cull (Springfield: Charles C. Thomas, 1973), p. 4.

4. William E. Amos, "The Philosophy of Corrections: Revisited", *Federal Probation*, 38 (March 1974): 45.

5. Jessica Mitford, *Kind and Usual Punishment: The Prison Business* (New York: Alfred A. Knopf, 1973), p. 34.

6. Dean, "Contemporary Trends", p. 5.

7. Amos, "Philosophy of Corrections", p. 43.

8. Charles L. Newman, *Sourcebook on Probation, Parole and Prisons*, 3rd ed. (Springfield: Charles C. Thomas, 1972), p. 209.

9. Barbara R. Bishop, "Self Control is Learned: External Control Precedes Internal Control", in *Behavior Therapy with Delinquents*, ed. Jerome S. Stumphauzer (Springfield: Charles C. Thomas, 1973), p. 54.

10. L. Craig Parker, Jr. and Robert D. Meir, Interpersonal Psychology for Law Enforcement and Corrections (St. Paul: West Publishing, 1975), p. 203.

11. Gerald H. Fisher, G. Robert Leslie, and Donald G. Martin, "The Role of Comprehensive Facilities in the Rehabilitation of the Public Offender", in *Introduction to Correctional Rehabilitation* ed. Richard E. Hardy and John G. Cull (Springfield: Charles C. Thomas, 1973), p. 202.

12. Richard D. Jones, "The Use of Contract Counseling in Corrections", in *Readings in Correctional Casework and Counseling*, ed. Edward E. Peoples (Pacific Palisades: Goodyear Publishing Co., Inc., 1975), p. 222.

13. Ibid., p. 223.

14. See Roy Gerard, "Institutional Innovations in Juvenile Correction", *Federal Probation* 34 (December 1970): 41; and D. Richard Laws, "The Failure of a Token Economy", *Federal Probation* 38 (September 1974): p. 33.

15. Teodora Ayllon and Nathan Azrin, *The Token Economy: A Motivational System for Therapy and Rehabilitation* (New York: Appleton, Century, and Crofts, 1968), p. 77.

16. Fisher, Leslie and Martin, "The Role of Comprehensive Facilities", pp. 203-204.

17. Quay, "What Corrections Can Correct", pp. 4-5.

REFLECTIONS ON EDUCATION IN THE PENITENTIARY
Kenneth W. Evans

The development of academic education in the correctional institutions of the United States has occurred for basically two reasons. First, the line between education and indoctrination is thin indeed, and consequently there have been those who have advocated correctional education as a means of social control since the advent of the penitentiary system. Second, since the opening of Philadelphia's Walnut Street Jail in the fading years of the eighteenth century there has been a far-sighted but politically impotent group of Americans who have argued that the pursuit of self-preservation obligates the state to provide the inmate realistic opportunities that aid his adjustment to free society upon release.

America's first penitentiary housed a school. Apparently the Walnut Street Jail's board of governors felt that education was one of the few methods of making beneficial use of the abundance of leisure time generated by the philosophy of the separate system. Accordingly, in 1798 shop work was complemented by a modest school of letters which offered reading, writing, and arithmetic. Though primitive in its curriculum, the school boasted books, desks, and lecturers. Pennsylvania thus gave birth to American prison education.[1]

Despite fundamental disagreement with the philosophy of the separate system, in 1801 New York began providing elementary education to *meritorious* convicts during the winter months. This "carrot on the stick" approach, however, had no real significance in the rapidly developing philosophy of the silent system. It appears that "education" was merely seen as a lesser evil than total inactivity. No state appropriations were forthcoming, and instruction was provided by the "better educated" prisoners. Thus began the notorious American penal tradition of thrifty educational administration: the blind led the blind.[2]

In 1825 it occurred to the religious zealot Louis Dwight that penal institutions represented fertile ground for the resurrection of fallen souls. Seeking to tap a captive market, Dwight took the lead in establishing the Boston Prison Discipline Society. Backed by a large group of Baptist and Congregational ministers, the Society put forth the idea that the salvation of inmates was best achieved with the aid of Sabbath schools and revivals consistent, of course, with the silent system's emphasis on the development of industrious habits in congregate workshops.[3] Such a view of affairs meshed nicely with the rapidly developing bourgeois ethic of the early Victorian years, and during the first half of the nineteenth century Sabbath schools became customary features in many northern penitentiaries during the winter months. Inmates were swamped by donations of Bibles and other literature which, quite significantly, formed the nucleus from which prison libraries would later develop.[4]

While Dwight and his followers were primarily concerned with religious instruction for inmates, the Sabbath schools provided the basis for continued progress in prison education. By learning to read the scriptures under the direction of the prison chaplain, inmates were better prepared to make a satisfactory adjustment to society upon release from prison.[5]

In 1840, the first prison library was opened at Sing Sing by Warden Seymour and Governor Seward. New York was also the first state to make annual appropriations for the improvement of prison libraries. Soon other states followed New York's example. Unfortunately, these early libraries were filled with pious religious books donated by ministers, which provided little more than relief from the boredom of prison life.[6]

In 1844, the eastern Penitentiary of Pennsylvania hired a full-time secular school teacher, established a library, and permitted lights in the inmates' cells until 9 p.m. for those inmates seeking education.[7]

These early developments set an important precedent in prison education, since prior to their occurance very few prisons taught even the three R's, and education consisted only of the chaplain teaching through the door of the inmate's cell in a poorly lit corridor.[8]

Orlando F. Lewis presents the situation in the following manner:

> The evening period was the only available time for instruction, and the picture is vivid . . . of the chaplain standing in a semi-dark corridor, before the door of the cell, with a dingy lantern hanging to the grated bars, and teaching to the wretched convicts in darkness beyond the grated door the rudiments of reading or of numbers.[9]

In 1846, a Sunday School was established at Maryland State Penitentiary, under the leadership of Warden William Johnson. This school operated only on Sunday afternoons, using the prison's custodial officers as teachers to instruct illiterate males in reading and writing.[10]

The growth of public education outside the prisons and the establishment of circulating libraries during the mid-1800's had an important impact on prison education. New awareness of the need for education prompted the passage of a law by the New York legislature in 1847 that required the employment of two full-time instructors at the state's two prisons (Auburn and Sing Sing). However, these teachers were very limited in the amount of teaching they could actually do, since they had to pass from cell to cell just as the chaplains had done before.

Due to their heavy load of pupils, their visits to the cells of inmates were so far apart that the value of their instruction is questionable.[11]

By 1865, instructors in New York and Pennsylvania, and chaplains in Connecticut and New Hampshire delivered all of their instruction to inmates in their cells. Only in the state of Ohio were regular classes conducted with inmates in a classroom. Education in all other prisons continued to be given in the Sabbath schools.[12]

In 1867, the Massachusetts state legislature was convinced by Warden Gideon Haynes to provide one thousand dollars for the purchase of textbooks to be used in the instruction of illiterate inmates. A regular schedule of classes that met twice a week was also established at the Massachusetts state prison.[13]

Little or no educational activity was occurring in Southern prisons. After the Civil War, Southern prisoners were exploited under the lease system, which in effect partially replaced the lost slave labor force. Little attention was given to the education of convicts, and the religious and educational ideals that developed in the North were absent in the South until the end of the nineteenth century.[14]

A second phase of American prison education occurred between the years of 1870 and 1929. The first meeting of the American Prison Association in Cincinnati in 1870 signaled the opening of this era. The association adopted a Declaration of Principles which became a starting point for changes in correctional systems. The thirty-three guiding principles adopted included emphasis on academic learning and improved vocational training.[15]

During the 1870's, the Detroit House of Correction had probably the most progressive example of prison education. Zebulon Brockway, superintendent at Detroit, had innovative ideas and a realization of the need for penal reform. He wrote, in 1865, the following:

> I feel . . . that there are very gross defects in the prison system of the land, and that, as a whole, it does not accomplish its design; and that the time has come for reconstruction. There are doubtless, in operation in the prisons of this country, religious and moral agencies, physical and hygienic regulations, and a system of employment for prisoners which, if combined in the management of one institution, would produce a model prison indeed. To find them, combine them and apply them is, in my mind, the great desideratum . . . . In my own quiet corner here, I am at work at this and trust that by the next year the practical operation of our system of labor and partial gradation of prisoners will add at least a mite to the progress of prison reform . . . . This is an age of demonstration, and the practicality of the movement proposed must be demonstrated at every step to secure its adoption.[16]

Brockway was particularly aware of the importance of education for inmates, and offered the following description of the program to be implemented at Detroit:

> Education was not introduced to relieve the monotony of imprisonment, but to discipline the mind and fit it to receive and to involve in the life, the thoughts and principles that constitute their possessors good citizens. Attendance upon the school is made obligatory, and the general schools are two and one-half hours each two evenings every week, and are for recitations chiefly. The writing school is also held on two evenings each week for both men and women . . . all prisoners who attend school are supplied with a light in their cell for study, and all draw books from the library. Every Saturday, at five o'clock, all the prisoners in the institution . . . assemble in the chapel to listen to a lecture. This is the crowning feature of our educational effort.[17]

The Detroit House of Correction was the exception to the general conditions that prevailed at most prisons. Education was still carried on by chaplains at the cell door in many prisons, since most prison administrators did not share Brockway's progressive views. They believed that prison education would merely result in more clever burglars, forgers, and other types of felons.[18]

The International Penal and Penitentiary Congress of 1872 joined Brockway in pointing out the need for reform and improved prison schools. This led to the development of an era in the late nineteenth and early twentieth centuries in which reformation and rehabilitation became the announced goal of prisons. Following the Congress, more educational programs were established in prisons and the prison's purpose gradually changed. Whereas punishment had once been the prominent feature, as in the whipping posts and the gallows, humanitarian reform became an equally important mode of correcting the inmate.[19]

Zebulon Brockway's presentation of a paper to the New York Prison Association in 1868 resulted in the establishment of the first reformatory (the Elmira Reformatory) in 1876. Brockway left Detroit to become the first warden at Elmira, and he tried to implement the following humanitarian measures for the inmates there:

1. A modified Auburn-system structure with some cells like those in the Eastern Penitentiary.
2. Uniform, but not degrading clothing (stripes).
3. A liberal dietary.
4. Gymnasium and modern appliances.
5. Manual training for about one-third of the population.
6. Instruction in trades at one time numbering thirty-six.
7. Military training with band.
8. School of letters with classes from kindergarten level through high school, and special classes in college subjects.
9. Library with reading room available to appreciative prisoners.

10. Weekly institutional paper.
11. Entertainments in the auditorium such as middle cultural people of a community would enjoy.
12. Religious opportunities optional.
13. Emotional occasions for expression of artistic tastes.
14. Use of indeterminate sentence to induce improved behavior, dependent on the initiative of the inmates.
15. Reliance upon education rather than punishment or precept.[20]

The Elmira Reformatory was located near Elmira College, and Brockway found it advantageous to work with specialists from the college campus. Beginning in 1878, some inmates were chosen to serve as teachers of elementary classes which met six nights a week. Dr. D.R. Ford of the Elmira Women's College was employed to conduct classes in physical geography and natural science. The results were so positive that Dr. Ford was employed full-time to coordinate and expand the educational program of the reformatory in 1879. Six public school principals and three lawyers were secured as instructors. In 1883, Brockway brought in Professor N.A. Wells from Syracuse University to conduct classes in industrial art for inmates that proved uninterested in academic study.[21]

Within twenty-five years of the establishment of Elmira, reformatories using the educational program developed by Brockway were constructed in twelve other states. Enthusiasm about the reformatory program ran high; and many predicted that it would sweep the country, but the movement began a sharp decline after 1900.[22]

However, even after its decline, the reformatory movement left a lasting effect upon prison education in America. It had a relatively friendly constructive aim, and it placed much emphasis upon education. The prisons that followed Elmira tended to emphasize the positive educational programs developed and implemented by Brodkway. Many of his reformatory methods remain today, though individualization has come to be the newer emphasis.[23]

Taft summarized the principles of prison education that evolved in American penal institutions as a result of the influence from the reformatory movement as follows:

> The education of adult prisoners has characteristics somewhat different from education of children or of adult men and women on the outside. (1) Prison education, to be successful, must be based upon a knowledge of the prison population. Their achievement and capacity must be measured. Interests and plans for the future must be known, and the possibility of developing new interests estimated. (2) Prison or reformatory education must be individualized, and an organization permitting the individual to progress at his own speed has an important place in prison education. (3) . . . prison education should be adultized. Even though the training may be of first grade, its vocabulary and method must be adapted to the life of the adult.

(4) Education to reform must be sought. Hence, compulsion has little, if any, place in prison education. Indirect compulsion, through making educational achievement pre-requisite to other goals, including release, is sometimes justified. (5) Finally, prison education must be socialized. If genuinely "reformed", the self-centered exploiter who entered the prison emerges a man who takes satisfaction in useful work and cooperation, and feels uncomfortable if his associates suffer.[24]

Prison libraries began to develop around 1860. The library had the potential to be of great value to the inmate. During a tour in 1865, Wines and Dwight found libraries in all the prisons of the North. However, most of the books on their shelves had been contributed by charitable individuals, and were usually discarded religious books of little interest or value. Some of the states, realizing the poor state of their prison libraries, began making annual appropriations of $25 to $200 to purchase desirable books and magazines. In 1877, the New York Prison Association compiled a listing of one thousand titled to guide chaplains in building a better library selection. This listing was never utilized, however, and libraries remained poorly stocked. Also, adequate accounts were not kept on money allocated for libraries. Thus, very little of this money reached the prison libraries due to petty graft by prison officials, or it being diverted to other uses at the prison due to demands for thrift in prison operation.[25]

The year of 1929 is recognized by some criminologists as the opening of the modern era of prison education. During this era, education has been recognized and developed as an essential element in criminal correctional treatment.[26]

A survey, completed by Austin H. MacCormich in 1929, revealed that there were no schools in thirteen out of the sixty prisons studied; and, that none of these prisons made provisions for suitable vocational education. MacCormich stated that their educational work had been a failure due to a lack of clear goals, poor teaching, failure to individualize programs and adherance to public school methods. But the chief reason for this was that of a lack of funds.[27]

Thus, the period beginning in 1929 to the present, has been guided by two ideas: (1) the belief that education is essential in modern programs of correctional treatment; and (2) the premise that prison education should be of the type and quality found in effective adult education programs in free society.[28]

In 1933, the Englehardt Commission was established in New York State to study the effectiveness of education in the adult correctional institutions of that state. The Commission's findings and report acted as a stimulus to criminologists to devise more effective educational systems. It recommended that prison education be based on guidance. Guiding the inmate to the attainment of

well-defined ends, such as the acquisition of vocational skills and a changed
social attitude reflected in a willingness and ability to practice cooperative
living upon release from prison, should be the basis for all prison education.[29]

In 1933 and 1934, sixty percent of the inmate population of Federal prisons were enrolled in some kind of educational program. New emphasis was placed
on individual study in the cell, correspondence, and individualized instruction.
One major problem faced by all prison education programs in the 1930's was that
of finding well-trained civilian instructors for academic and vocational education.[30]

In 1935, *The Proceedings of the 65th Annual Congress of Correction of the
American Prison Association* set new objectives for prison education that included the following: (1) teaching every inmate to read and write, (2) helping
each individual develop a variety of interests, (3) developing an attitude of
social responsibility by the inmate toward himself and society, (4) the development of individual thinking and problem-solving abilities, and (5) the development of mental ability and mechanical skills enabling the inmate to earn a
living upon release.[31]

By the year 1940, the state governments had begun to realize the importance
of juvenile education; thus, twenty institutions out of a total of 165 in existence in the country were subject to standards set by their State Departments of
Education.[32]

Following World War II, the Federal Bureau of Prisons has taken the lead
in providing education for its inmates in forty-three institutions. The Bureau
has found that areas in which most inmates are severely deficient are education
and work skills. Consequently, it has established three basic objectives to
help inmates improve their knowledge and skills. These are:

1. Every inmate leaving the federal prison system will be able
    to read at the sixth grade level, at least.

2. Every inmate capable of doing so will earn a high school
    diploma or equivalency certificate by the time released.

3. Every inmate who does not have a work skill will have been
    given training that will qualify him for post-release em-
    ployment in a relevant, career-oriented occupation.[33]

All federal prison general education programs have been designed to meet the needs
of three types of inmates: (1) those who score below the fifth grade level on
standardized achievement tests, and are thus considered functionally illiterate;
(2) those who score between the fifth and eighth grade level and want to upgrade
their educational level; and (3) those at the secondary level who wish to complete

high school or earn college credit.[34]

During the 1950's, some of the criminological theories developed in the preceeding decades began to be applied in the planning and development of prison education programs.[35] Many state institutions placed new emphasis on education programs, but the expansion of programs was not carried out due to a lack of funds.[36]

Many innovative programs have been implemented in prison education since the late 1950's, and highlights of these will be discussed briefly below.

In 1962, over 24,000 inmates were enrolled in literacy classes in the federal prisons of the United States. It was estimated that the mean reading level of male inmates was at the fifth grade level. At the Maryland State Penitentiary in 1965, 70% of the inmates were adult functional illiterates, 98% had not completed high school, and only .001% had a bachelor's degree. Studies showed that 47% of the inmates would return to prison. Therefore, there is a need for an expansion of penal education since studies have revealed that inmates who are high school graduates are seldom recidivists.[37]

A study conducted at the Ohio State Reformatory on the teaching of illiterates to read showed that these adults could improve their reading skills. A population of 153 inmates were given literacy instruction and the incremental grade achievement was 1.25 with twenty weeks of instruction.[38]

An innovative program of penal education has been initiated at the Nassau County Jail on Long Island, New York for young offenders that has made it unique in the prevention of recidivism. The program involves the building of the inmate's self-respect by offering him the chance to complete high school, and by the building of a positive self-image. Nineteen remedial reading teachers come into the jail several times a week and work with the inmates on a one-to-one student-teacher ratio. If an inmate is released before he completes his schooling, a follow-up worker continues the educational process. A work-release program is also an important part of the program. It allows the inmate to acquire a job and begin work while still serving his sentence. This makes for an easy transition to free society when the inmate is released, since he usually will continue to hold the same job.[39]

The Bartow Road Prison in Florida has also devised a program to allow inmates to complete high school through the adult education program of the Polk County School District. The program was initiated due to inmates being unable to get jobs upon release due to their lack of a high school diploma, and the alarming rate of recidivism among those released. The prison school meets every Monday and Thursday night for three hours each night in the mess hall of the prison camp. Students are grouped around tables according to the courses they are taking. One teacher, textbooks and audiovisual equipment from the public school system are used extensively in the training. The credits earned at the school are honored by the Florida Department of Public Instruction, and a regular high school diploma is issued after the completion of the prescribed number of credits.[40]

The Pace Institute, located within the walls of the Cook County Jail in Chicago, was founded in 1967 as a private philanthropic organization. It provides basic education in reading, writing, arithmetic, science, constitutional governmental, communication skills, with expert instruction in each area. Such instruction allows the 175 youthful inmates who go through the institute each year, the opportunity to enter a trade school, high school, college or secure employment at their level of competence.[41]

In 1967, the Texas Department of Corrections began a cooperative effort with Lee College, a state supported junior college in Baytown, Texas, to bring the noninstitutional educator into the prison atmosphere to offer instruction in grades one through twelve. The program was funded by the Federal Vocational Rehabilitation Program, the Texas Department of Corrections Education Fund, and the state appropriation to Lee College. The program was so successful that it was expanded to include eight different units of the Texas Department of Corrections; and, in 1970, it received permission from the Southern Association of Colleges and Schools to grant credit through the junior college level. This allowed an inmate to earn a junior college degree regardless of his prior educational deficiencies.[42]

Today, Lee College boasts the largest correctional education program in existence in the United States. It now has 42 sections of academic work and 28 sections of technical-vocational work offered to a total of 920 students. The program has had tremendous success and preliminary reports showed a reduction of the recidivism rate from 50% in 1965, to 15% in 1970 in the Texas Department of Corrections.[43]

A similar program, called NewGate, was developed in 1967 at the Oregon State Prison by Thomas E. Gaddis, the author of *Birdman of Alcatraz*. This program provides educational enrichment classes to inmates to prepare them for college entrance upon their release from the prison. The program was so successful in its first year that the Office of Economic Opportunity funded the project's expansion in 1968. One feature makes the NewGate project unique . . . that is its post-release components. Efforts are made within the prison to prepare the inmate to move to the outside to freedom and college upon his release. Before the inmate is released, he is briefed on university policies, housing has been arranged and scholarships or work-study grants available. On the day of release, and for several weeks thereafter, the counselor who aided the inmate in his preparation inside the prison works closely with him to aid him in the transition to freedom. When the recidivism rates were checked for individuals in the program, it was found that those inmates who participated in the program had a recidivism rate of 20% as compared to a rate of 40 to 50% for those released and not participating in the program.[44]

In 1959, the National Institute of Mental Health gave a grant to Dr. John McKee, a psychologist and director of the Rehabilitation Research Foundation, to finance a research project in the reduction of recidivism at Draper Correctional Center in Alabama. The inmates selected for the program were given programmed instruction, under which they were allowed to proceed at their own individual pace in educational classes. The inmates were given instruction in academic and vocational areas, and spent eight hours a day in the program. A high school equivalency certificate was issued to inmates who successfully completed the course work and tests. A study of the recidivism rate for prisoners who completed the program ran about 30%, as compared to 65 to 70% for those who did not participate in the program.[45]

This program has been continued and expanded to further develop the concept of programmed instruction as a rehabilitative tool to prevent recidivism by prison inmates.[46]

One possible direction for future prison education efforts has been outlined by the American Association of Junior Colleges. The Association has suggested that its member colleges become actively involved in prison education. According to Adams and Connolly, the junior college is well suited to conduct prison education programs because:

> Most public institutions are "open-door" so admission problems
> are few. Their offerings range broadly, from purely vocational
> to the primarily intellecutal and esthetic. The occupational
> curriculums are varied and can accomodate a wide array of stu-
> dent needs, interests, and abilities. The colleges are rela-
> tively experienced in meeting the special requirements of dis-
> advantaged persons. They are . . . readily accessible to most
> of the nation's correctional facilities. Finally, community
> services and adult education are both major functions of the
> community college, and a cooperative prison educational pro-
> gram falls into either of these categories.[47]

The majority of American penal institutions have inadequate provisions for inmate education.[48] Roberts states that for an effective program to be implemented, six principles must be a part of that program. They are as follows:

1. Educational activity must be meaningful to the learner.
2. Correctional education must be offered in short, attainable and measurable segments.
3. There must be reinforcement of learning.
4. There must be balance in the total correctional program in which education is but a part . . . a meaningful part.
5. The institutional educational program must be an accredited one, perhaps even provided by the state educational agency.
6. Above all, there must be a substantial interpersonal relationship established between the teacher and student.[49]

Today, many penal institutions have educational programs that are not doing the job of rehabilitating the prisoner they should. Some reasons for this are their failure to develop proper instructional materials, proper subject matter and teaching methods that suit the student body of the institution. The curriculum is too often transplanted from other school settings into the prison without proper adaptation to the situational needs.[50]

Solutions to these problems will come about only with an understanding of the nature of the prison population, the further education of the staff, employment of more full-time staff members, and more classrooms.[51]

Thus, the period from the early 1960's to the present has seen the development of more effective and innovative educational programs in American prisons. Programmed instruction on an individual basis, innovations in academic and social correctional education, and innovations in vocational training have been developed and implemented to a large extent in most prisons around the country. These programs have also received more adequate funding than prison education programs of the past. Criminologists hope that these present-day programs will continue to be modified, new ones developed, and that these will receive adequate funding so that the rehabilitation of a larger percentage of inmates will become a reality.[52]

Today, as in the past, the criminologist realizes that the education of the inmate is one of the most important tasks to be performed by the prison system. The system of penal education still has many imperfections, but it continues to be the best means available to achieve the rehabilitation of the incarcerated criminal so that he will be able to cope and productively participate in a free society upon release.

REFERENCES

1. Harry E. Barnes and Negley K. Teeters, *New Horizons in Criminology* (3rd ed., Englewood Cliffs, New Jersey: Prentice-Hall, 1959), p. 482.

2. Albert R. Roberts, *Sourcebook on Prison Education* (Springfield, Illinois: Charles C. Thomas, 1971), p. 3.

3. Blake McKelvey, *American Prisons* (Chicago: University of Chicago Press, 1936), pp. 9-10.

4. *Ibid.*, p. 12.

5. Roberts, *Sourcebook*, p. 4.

6. McKelvey, *American Prisons*, p. 42.

7. Donald R. Taft, *Criminology*, (New York: MacMillan Company, 1952), p. 480.

8. Roberts, *Sourcebook*, p. 5.

9. Orlando F. Lewis. *The Development of American Prisons and Prison Customs, 1776-1895.* (Albany Prison Association of New York, 1922), p. 51.

10. Roberts, *Sourcebook*, p. 5.

11. McKelvey, *American Prisons*, p. 41.

12. *Ibid.*, pp. 41-42.

13. Roberts, *Sourcebook*, p. 5.

14. McKelvey, *American Prisons*, pp. 180-182.

15. Donald R. Taft, *Criminology.* (New York: MacMillan Company, 1952), p. 481.

16. McKelvey, *American Prisons*, p. 52.

17. Roberts, *Sourcebook*, p. 7.

18. *Ibid.*

19. Albert R. Roberts, *Readings in Prison Education*, (Springfield, Illinois: Charles C. Thomas, Publisher, 1973), p. 6.

20. Taft, *Criminology*, pp. 481-482.

21. McKelvey, *American Prisons*, p. 110.

22. Robert G. Caldwell, *Criminology* (New York: The Ronald Press Company, 1965), p. 516.

23. Taft, *Criminology*, p. 482.

24. *Ibid.*, pp. 482-483.

25. McKelvey, *American Prisons*, pp. 85-86.

26. Roberts, *Sourcebook*, pp. 9-10.

27. *Ibid.*, p. 10.

28. *Ibid.*

29. W.M. Wallack, G.M. Kendall and H.L. Briggs, *Education Within Prison Walls* (New York: Columbia University Press, 1939), p. 9.

30. Roberts, *Sourcebook*, p. 13.

31. *Ibid.*, p. 15.

32. Edwin H. Suterland and Donald R. Cressey, *Principles of Criminology* (New York: Lippincott, 1960), p. 533.

33. Harry E. Allen and Clifford E. Simonsen, *Corrections in America* (Beverly Hills, California: Collier Macmillan Publisher, 1975), pp. 458-459.

34. Roberts, *Sourcebook*, p. 17.

35. *Ibid.*, p. 19.

36. *Ibid.*, p. 22.

37. Richard W. Cortright, "Inmate Illiteracy", *Journal of Reading*, VIII (January, 1965), p. 164.

38. *Ibid.*, pp. 164-165.

39. Eleanor Roth, "Learning Behind Bars:, *Phi Delta Kappan*, LI (April, 1970), pp. 440-442.

40. Robert E. Potter and Peter B. Wright, Jr. "School in a Prison", *Clearing House*, XXXIII (February, 1959), pp. 365-367.

41. Allen and Simonsen, *Corrections*, p. 434.

42. James P. McWilliams, "Rehabilitation versus Recidivism", *Junior College Journal* XLI (March, 1971), pp. 88-90.

43. *Ibid.*, p. 90.

44. Ray A. Allen, "Inmates Go to College", *Personnel and Guidance Journal*, LIII (October, 1974), pp. 146-149.

45. Roberts, *Readings in Prison Education*, pp. 180-183.

46. *Ibid.*, pp. 194-195.

47. Stuart Adams and John J. Connolly, "Role of Junior Colleges in the Prison Community", *Junior College Journal*, XL (March, 1971), p. 94.

48. Roberts, *Sourcebook*, p. 28.

49. Roberts, *Readings in Prison Education*, pp. 78-82.

50. Ute Auld, "What a Prison Education Program Faces", *Education Digest*, XXXI (March, 1966), p. 25.

51. *Ibid.*

52. Roberts, *Sourcebook*, pp. 23-25.

THE FUTURE OF PRISONS
Norman A. Carlson

The future of imprisonment in the United States will be largely determined by the outcome of three critical issues now facing the criminal justice system.

The first is the current debate over the mission or objective of prisons and what they can reasonably be expected to do in terms of controlling crime. The second issue is the population explosion now taking place in jails and prisons throughout the country. The third is the impact of recent court decisions on the administration of corrections institutions.

The entire criminal justice system is the subject of debate today because of rapidly rising crime rates. FBI reports show that crime rose 18% last year over 1973, and the rate increased by an additional 13% in the first half of 1975. Despite increasing sums invested by federal, state and local legislatures in fighting crime, despite current annual spending of $810 million by the Law Enforcement Assistance Administration, the average citizen feels less safe than ever walking the streets of his neighborhood.

As a result, law enforcement authorities are being blamed for failure to solve more crimes and to apprehend more offenders; the courts, probation, and parole are being criticized for imposing excessive sentences; they accuse law enforcement officials of violating the constitutional rights of suspects; and they claim imprisonment is a failure because it is inherently brutal and degrading and because prisons allegedly breed crime. Public concern over crime and the shortcomings of the criminal justice system has touched off a debate which, insofar as it concerns corrections, focuses on the objectives of incarceration.

Historically, offenders have been committed to institutions for three reasons--retribution, deterrence and rehabilitation. Retribution was society's only response to crime from earliest recorded history until well into the 18th century. The traditional view was stated by German philosopher Immanuel Kant (1724-1804) in his classic work, *The Science of Right:*

"Juridical punishment can never be administered merely as a means for promoting another good either with regard to the criminal himself or to civil society, but must in all cases be imposed only because the individual on whom it is inflicted has committed a crime . . .."

This harsh view collided with the Utilitarian philosophy that emerged from the intellectual ferment of the Age of Enlightenment which swept across Europe during the latter part of the 18th century. The Utilitarian philosophy espoused public policies which created the greatest good for the greatest number,

and taught that man was guided by the principles of pain and pleasure. As a
reasoning creature (this, of course, was well before the days of Freud) he
would do what gave him pleasure and refrain from doing what produced pain. This
philosophy held that criminal justice should stress deterrence rather than retribution. One of its earliest spokesmen was an Intalian reformer, Cesare
Beccaria, whose 1764 essay, "On Crimes and Punishments," maintained that society's
purpose in punishing offenders "can only be to prevent the criminal from af-
flicting new injuries on its citizens and to deter others from similar acts."

But whatever the philosophical base--retribution or deterrence--society
continued to punish offenders in traditional ways--by mutilation, public humiliation, banishment, slavery, and death.

Prisons came into use as a humanitarian reform late in the 18th century
when the Quakers created a penitentiary in Pennsylvania as a reaction against
the cruel punishments that were in widespread use up to that time. They hoped
to reform offenders by confining them to private cells where they could read
the Bible, meditate on their transgressions, and become "penitent" (hence the
word, penitentiary). The failure of this system to achieve its goals did not
result in its abandonment. Society could not face the prospect of going back
to floggings, brandings, mutilations, and hangings characteristic of the past.
Efforts were made to improve the system and rehabilitation was added to the
concepts of retribution and deterrence as society's responses to crime.

Because of its association with humaneness, rehabilitation has grown in
importance over the years. During the 19th century, it led to the introduction
of such innovations as parole, probation, and the indeterminate sentence. During
the past several years, rehabilitation has come to dominate the criminal justice
dialogue almost to the exclusive of retribution and deterrence. The 1966 Manual
of Correctional Standards published by the American Correctional Association
stated this modern view in succinct, unequivocal terms:

"Punishment as retribution belongs to a penal philosophy that is archaic
and discredited by history . . . Penologists in the United States today are generally agreed that the prison serves most effectively for the protection of society against crime when its major emphasis is on rehabilitation. They accepted
this as a fact that no longer needs to be debated.

The demand that prisons abandon any thought of retribution and devote themselves entirely to rehabilitation became almost overwhelming after the Attica
tragedy in September, 1971, which claimed the lives of 40 correctional officers
and inmates. Few were willing to listen to the cautionary warnings coming from
those most intimately involved in the day-to-day administration of correctional

programs. As the National Conference on Corrections in December, 1971, at
Williamsburg, Virginia, was informed by a summary of workshop reports:

". . . The point was repeatedly made that correctional staffs lacked con-
fidence in their own ability to produce the rehabilitative effects which society
expects of them."

The truth is, correctional administrators would be glad to rehabilitate
all offenders--if they only knew how. Society's illusion that they can is a
result of the language that has surrounded corrections in recent years. Psychiatrists, psychologists, caseworkers, and a number of other professionals have
joined prison staffs and brought along their own terminology. Medical concepts
such as diagnosis, observation, therapy, and treatment were introduced. Gradually a medical model was created that implied offenders were sick, that we
could diagnose their ailments as we do with people who are physically or mentally ill, and then prescribe a "treatment" program which would bring about a
cure.

As a result of such a "treatment" program--which included a variety of education, training, and counseling programs--the released offender would be returned to society as a law-abiding citizen. "It would be a good trick if we
could do it . . . but we cannot," Norval Morris, dean of the University of
Chicago Law School, wrote in his recent book, *The Future of Imprisonment*.

The case against the current overemphasis on rehabilitation was highlighted
by a study of 231 rehabilitation projects (conducted here and abroad between
1945 and 1967) by Dr. Robert Martinson, professor of sociology at the City College,
City University of New York. Summarizing his findings in the Spring 1974 issue
of *Public Interest* magazine, Dr. Martinson reported: "With few and isolated
exceptions, the rehabilitative effects that have been reported so far have had
no appreciable effect on recidivism."

Finding a reasonable mission for prisons and corrections is complicated by
the population explosion now occurring in institutions throughout the country.
Figures compiled by the Law Enforcement Assistance Administration indicate that
the number of offenders in state prisons increased from 174,000 at the end of
1972 to 196,000 by the end of 1974. A recent study by Dr. John J. Flanagan of
the University of Wisconsin indicates that this population increase will probably continue until 1985 (perhaps until the end of the century) before beginning
to level off. These projections were reported in the November-December, 1975
issue of the *American Journal of Corrections*, and the following reasons were
given:

The population at risk is increasing. People most likely to commit crime are in the 20-30 age range and this group, according to Census Bureau figures, will reach its peak in 1985, when it will be roughly 50% higher than it was in 1970. The 20-30 age group in inner-city neighborhoods, which produce a disproportionately high number of criminal offenders, will continue to grow until the end of the century.

The percentage of convicted offenders who can be diverted from institutions is limited. Probation rates in some states, for example, are above 70% (in the federal system the rate is 54%) and cannot be expected to go much higher.

Public attitudes are hardening, which may lead to mandatory sentencing policies and longer sentences and time served for offenders.

Continuing inflation and high unemployment will create social stresses that will tend to keep crime rates high.

There already is evidence to support these positions. Crime is unquestionably on the increase. President Ford called for mandatory sentences for certain types of federal offenders in his June 19, 1975 Crime Message. Sen. Edward Kennedy introduced a bill November 10, 1975, providing mandatory sentences for certain violent offenses and for trafficking in heroin. Reports flowing into the Bureau of Prisons during the last half of 1975 indicate that at least half the states are experiencing sudden and dramatic upsurges in jail and prison populations.

The third major issue, the growing involvement by the courts in the administration of institutions, may in the long run have the greatest impact of all. For many years, the judiciary maintained a hands-off attitude towards prisons and jails and refused consideration of inmate claims; for example, in Ruffin v. Commonwealth, (62 Va. 790, 796 (1871)), an inmate was designated as a "slave of the state." As recently as 1948, the Supreme Court in Price v. Johnson, (334 U.S. 266, 285 (1948)), ruled that:

"Lawful incarceration brings about the necessary withdrawal or limitation of many privileges and rights, a tradition justified by the considerations underlying our penal system."

On the basis of this reasoning, most courts would dismiss inmate complaints summarily. As a consequence, their dockets were kept free of inmate litigation and the prisons remained virtually free from any external scrutiny.

This situation has changed drastically in the past 15 years. During the 1960's the courts (primarily federal courts) began to hear inmate complaints as part of a wider revolution which included judicial review of the rights of all persons accused of crime.

Inmates brought suits charging - and in many cases they were upheld by the courts - that their constitutional rights were violated by the treatment they received. The most widely-used vehicle for inmates challenging the authority of prison administrators was the Civil Rights Act of 1871 (42 U.S.C. 1983) which provides:

"Every person who, under color of any statute, ordinance, regulation, custom, or usage of any State or Territory, subjects, or causes to be subject, any citizen of the United States or other person within the jurisdiction thereof to the deprivation of any rights, privileges, or immunities secured by the Constitution and laws shall be liable to the party injured in an action at law, suit in equity, or other proper proceeding for redress."

By use of the courts, inmates have obtained access to courts and counsel, freer exercise of religion, more liberal correspondence and visitation rules, protection from cruel and unusual punishment, petition for redress of grievances, group injunctive relief, and protection of their safety and lives.

In one notable case, Holt v. Sarver, (309 F. Supp. 362 (E.D. Ark. 1970)) the entire Arkansas penal system was declared unconstitutional and in violation of the cruel and unusual punishment prohibition of the Eighth Amendment because of conditions in that state's prisons. The landmark case of Wolff v. McDonnel, (94 S. Ct., 2963 (1974)) assured inmates a large measure of due process in prison disciplinary proceedings including advance notice, a written statement of the evidence, the right to call witnesses and to present documentary evidence, the aid of a counsel substitute in complex cases, and an impartial disciplinary board.

"Perhaps the most significant change in the past few years is the discarding of the notion that there is a separate 'law of corrections,' largely made up of the 'hands off' doctrine," according to a summary publication, *Emerging Rights of the Confined*, published by the South Carolina Department of Corrections in 1972.

Despite immediate concerns presented by the shift in correctional philosophy, by overcrowding and by court intervention, in the long run the eventual outcome seems certain to improve corrections and prisons in this country. What will slowly emerge is a more humane system, one that provides for better housing and treatment of offenders, and which is more sensitive to the demands of the public and the courts.

In terms of philosophy, there will be less emphasis on rehabilitation and a more realistic, honest approach to the problems of corrections. The medical model will be discarded. Medical language will be dropped and programs will be described in more accurate terms. Education, vocational training, and similar activities will be called education and vocational training, not "treatment" programs. Inmates will no longer be coerced, openly or subtly, to take part in these programs. Corrections will recognize that rehabilitation can occur only if it is voluntary. A more balanced system will be the ultimate result, one that recognizes that retribution, deterrence, and rehabilitation all have parts to play in our criminal justice system today.

The combined effect of overcrowding and court protection of inmate rights will lead to enlarged community-based programs; the construction of new institutions; the elevation of correctional standards particularly in terms of quality and training of personnel; and to intensified research and evaluation of correctional activities.

In the short run, population pressures on existing institutions will be relieved by placing more offenders in such community-based programs as probation, parole, and halfway houses. Caution must be exercised, however, to insure that offenders do not use and manipulate these programs as a license to engage in further criminal behavior. There will be greater development of victim restitution and pre-trial diversion programs such as are now being used in Georgia and other states. Parole will survive its present tribulations and will not be eliminated, as some are now advocating. The indeterminate sentence, now under heavy criticism because it tends to keep offenders in suspense over release dates, will be dropped.

In the long run, however, more correctional institutions will have to be built. Crime and the prison population are both climbing rapidly and community-based programs alone cannot handle the increased flow. As the University of Wisconsin study shows, probation and other alternative programs will soon be exhausted and there will be an increase in both prison populations and alternative programs. Nor can alternatives completely replace prisons. If parole, probation, and other alternatives are expected to work, offenders must know that a violation will lead to the ultimate sanction, which is imprisonment. Without the sanction of imprisonment, most alternative programs would not succeed.

Even if prison populations were not increasing, new institutions would have to be built. Half the maximum security institutions in this country were constructed prior to 1900. They resemble fortresses with row on row of iron cages housing eight and ten men to a cell and are totally obsolete. They must be replaced by new, more humane institutions of no more than 500 inmates, located near urban centers whose medical, educational, and other facilities can be tapped.

The courts may force the construction of these new institutions. In a lecture delivered November 4, 1975, at the University of Alabama, Federal Judge

Frank M. Johnson, Jr., commented on recent federal court decisions, including one of his own, that prison systems in four states were unconstitutional under the Eighth Amendment.

"At present, constitutional litigation frequently arises because the state has attempted to provide public services which are so inadequately funded that they have forced some citizens to live in inhumane and hazardous conditions. While it is distinctly the province of the legislature - and not the judiciary (state or federal) - to budget state funds, the state must, in providing services, do so in a manner that comports with minimum constitutional standards. This is particularly true . . . where the state's mentally ill, retarded, and criminally-convicted citizens are involuntarily confined in institutions where conditions justly have been described as barbaric and shocking."

Prison standards will be raised further by creation of a system of accreditation, much like those now governing hospitals and schools. The American Correctional Association will soon promulgate accreditation standards for every aspect of corrections ranging from living space for inmates, to qualifications for correctional officers and other personnel, to nutritional requirements. These standards will not be based on theory. They are being compiled on the basis of day-by-day experience of correctional institutions attempting to meet the requirements of the courts and of humanity in the treatment of incarcerated offenders. These standards will be published in 1976 and will enable correctional administrators to articulate needs with greater precision when they appear with funding requests before legislative bodies.

Meanwhile, research cannot be neglected. The Juvenile Justice and Delinquency Act, enacted into law in September, 1974, created the National Institute of Corrections. The Institute's mission will be to improve correctional practices by funding such activities as staff training for federal, state, and local correctional agencies, research and evaluation, clearinghouse and information services, policy formulation and implementation, and technical assistance. Research is vital to the future of corrections. Until the behavioral sciences can provide these basic insights, there can be little hope for large-scale rehabilitation of offenders.